Pike & Shotte™

Written By:

Steve Morgan

Based on the Black Powder game by:

Rick Priestley and Jervis Johnson

Photography:

Barry Hilton, Warwick Kinrade, Mark Owen, Alan Perry,
Michael Perry, Paul Sawyer, THS club and Wargames Illustrated

Cover and Interior Artwork:

Peter Dennis

Design and Layout:

Mark Owen and Paul Sawyer

Editing:

Andy Wheale and Duncan Macfarlane

Cartography:

Sven Lugar

Thanks To:

Richard Caldwell, Andrew Chesney, Alan Davies, Nick Eyre,
Andy Fox, Robert Giglio, Kristen Hager, Bernhard Hennen,
Barry Hilton, Adrian Howe, David Marshall, Daryl Nichols,
Peter Rossetti, Ania Rutkowska, Konrad Sosinski, Bob Talbot,
Neil Tew, Tim Vincent, Wargames Illustrated, Andy Wheale,
Darek Wyrozebski and Steve Yates.

Special Thanks To:

John Stallard, for all his support, experience
and use of his extensive collections

ISBN: 978-0-9563581-6-5

www.warlordgames.com

CONTENTS

FOREWORD

I feel a good place to start with this book is an explanation of its aims. My hope is that people with an interest in the era of Pike & Shotte, whether fully developed or newly nurtured, will flick through the pages and emerge on the other side entertained, intrigued, even inspired to put some miniatures on a table to play a game with friends. If it achieves all three then that would be a grand thing indeed.

The book in your hands is based on Rick Priestley's *Black Powder*; the rules mechanics are the same and hopefully also the tone of the book. *Pike & Shotte* aims to be 'foremost an entertainment', as Rick would eloquently put it.

This book began life as a supplement to *Black Powder*, but it quickly became apparent that too much would be missed if it was not treated as a stand-alone rule set. It has also overrun by rather a long time, a fact I was constantly reminded of in the Warlord Games offices. The thing is, this is a period that I am very passionate about and I wanted it to be right. The delays have caused a few more grey hairs and much gnashing of teeth, but we got there in the end.

The old adage *'If it ain't broke, don't fix it'* seems to be appropriate, with much of what made the rules tick in *Black Powder* staying in this set. However, there are many facets of warfare during the period 1500 to 1700 that really deserve their own specific rules to get a feel for the period on the gaming table.

Now there are many trains of thought on exactly where the era of 'Pike & Shotte' sits in terms of timeframe. For the sake of this volume we will be looking at 1500 to 1700, and focussing on Europe. Now I understand that there are those of you reading this aghast that I have not included the Turkish campaigns of the early 16th century. Also, many history buffs will be aware that pikes were still being used by the Swedish in the Great Northern War as late as the second decade of the 18th Century. My reasoning is quite simple; these fall outside my area of both knowledge and interest, and it seems only fair to those wars that they be covered in future by someone who can bring both to bear.

Some of you may disagree with my rules interpretations for 'hedgehog' formations against cavalry, or even how Dragoons would operate on a 17th century battlefield. If that's the case, please feel free to make changes in your games to ensure you get the most use and fun out of this book. I promise not to send the 'Rules Police' to your door in the small hours!

So, whether you fancy yourself in the role of Wallenstein, Cromwell or even a Mercenary Captain leading his Landsknechts to war, prepare your troops and get ready for battle.

Dedicated to my children, Siân and Liam Morgan.

THE AGE OF PIKE & SHOTTE
1500-1700

Bloodshed and Divergence

The 16th and 17th centuries were 200 years of near constant European conflict. Although this book will concentrate on five major wars, they were set against a backdrop of huge upheaval, smaller campaigns, dynastic changes and human advances on many levels.*

The Renaissance, which had begun in Italy, had spread to the rest of Europe by the turn of the 16th century. It has been said that this was a watershed between the medieval and modern worlds, a time of new political, social, religious and cultural movements. The cohesion of a united Catholic Christendom was shattered by the Reformation as national identities began to emerge; often under the pressure of the expanding Ottoman Empire.

Spain and Portugal were at the forefront of carving new empires in the New World, setting up global trade links and taking their civilisation to new, and often horribly exploited, subjects. As stories of cities made of gold quickly came back to the Old World other powers wanted a share of the spoils. All that gold had to be used for something – new armies to gain supremacy of Europe seemed a good place to start...

The Reformation

Religion has often been the catalyst to mobilise the masses and to start a 'good' war. The Protestant Reformation, led by Martin Luther and John Calvin, saw many people move away from the established teachings of the Catholic Church.

City walls are stormed during the English Civil Wars.

* For the more discerning reader, bottled beer was first produced in London in 1568 – a great advance!

1500 - Portuguese navigator Pedro Álvares Cabral discovers Brazil and claims the land for Portugal.

*Imperial
Harquebusiers*

The epicentre of this move was in the German States and it gradually spread across Europe. The Hapsburg Empire was hit first, with many of its provinces and states demanding freedom of religion, causing the Empire to begin to fragment. Not to be outdone, the Papacy encouraged the Counter-Reformation to get things back to the 'good old days'.

Seeing the Hapsburgs' troubles, especially as they were additionally occupied by the Ottoman menace on their south-eastern borders, other dynastic powers moved to gain advantage, with France and Spain at the fore. The Protestant faith spread from Germany through Switzerland and into France, where the Protestant Huguenots were soon to be in for a rough ride. England too was soon to quit the Catholic Church by creating a Protestant Church – though England's conversion had more to do with Henry VIII's inability to 'keep it in his oversized codpiece' than any messages from on high. What all these changes did mean, unfortunately, was that European conflicts in the 17th century were blighted by religious persecution and other unpleasantness that were more in keeping with the barbarism of previous times.

Technology

This was the period of the 'Scientific Revolution' which laid the foundations for modern knowledge. Physics, astronomy, medicine and chemistry were all to advance in leaps and bounds. Luminaries such as Copernicus, Galileo, Newton and Pascal were the leading lights; sometimes facing the wrath of the Catholic Church which was becoming very annoyed by the erosion of its power and its well established ideology.

*"He who wages war
fishes with a golden net."*

16th/17th century saying

1501 - Michelangelo returns to his native Florence to begin work on the statue of David.

Such advances were not restricted to the social wellbeing of the ever increasing population; there were some very useful lessons to be learnt in the art of warfare. New and ingenious ways of killing the enemy in ever increasing numbers were soon developed. Gunpowder firearms and artillery were becoming more readily available and reliable, and the dominance of medieval style armies of knights and archers was replaced by well drilled troops and firepower. This was the background to the era of Pike & Shotte, but no wars could be won without the fighting soldiers; men who laid down their lives in their thousands for country, king or religion. These men are covered in more detail in the following pages - what they wore, how and who they fought, and what they fought with.

What was Pike & Shotte Warfare?

The term 'Pike and Shotte' warfare has been coined to encapsulate a period when battlefield tactics changed to enable the close combat troops of the time (in many cases armed with pikes) to work closely together with the 'shotte' or musket-armed troops.

Throughout the Middle Ages bow and crossbow armed troops were commonplace, but considerable practice was needed to use these weapons with skill. The introduction of early black powder weapons meant that new units of recruits could be formed rapidly, being easy to train and cheap to equip. These factors meant that by the beginning of the 16th century the use of bows and crossbows was very much on the decline.

The Spanish 'Tercio' system of blocks of pike supported by units of arqubus proved to be hugely successful against the more traditional French/Swiss armies in the Italian Wars and a blueprint was set down that was to last, with a few alterations, for 200 years. We will cover the tercio and other formations later in the book on page 29, but it seems sensible to illustrate the basics here to ease us into things.

The classic battle configuration of the period consisted of a chequer board formation of foot regiments. A standard infantry regiment would have a core of pikemen in the centre, along with the colours and other command elements. On the wings would be 'sleeves' of musketeers or arquebusiers who could pour fire on the enemy before the pike closed in for the assault. Several such regiments would form a battalia with pike and shotte working in unison.

Most of the 'horse', or cavalry, would be placed on the wings of the army or as a reserve, their first priority being to drive the opposing horse from the field. Supremacy achieved, the victorious cavalry could sweep into the flanks of enemy infantry already engaged in combat, which would often prove decisive.

Dragoons were effectively mounted infantry, trained to fight on foot but with the ability to move rapidly on their horses. They would be used to take key battlefield objectives at the beginning of a battle, often positions that could be fortified or enable enfilading fire on enemy advances. If that position became untenable they could redeploy and reinforce areas where the fighting was in the balance.

Artillery was used throughout the pike and shotte era. Although advances in artillery development and tactics were made, guns remained generally unreliable. It is almost certain that the artillery's impact on morale was rather higher than its ability to cause heavy casualties.

The Rise and Fall of the Pike

The use of the pike was certainly not new at the turn of the 16th century. The Macedonian phalanx, introduced nearly two thousand years before by Alexander the Great's father, Phillip II, was probably the earliest introduction of 'pike blocks' on the battlefield. The limitations of these formations, especially if unsupported, were exploited by the might of Rome, and pikes fell out of fashion until medieval times.

In the 14th century the pike was seen as a cheap and easy way to equip the masses, and if used well was devastating to heavily armed mounted troops, as evidenced by the use of 'schiltrons' by the Scots at Bannockburn in 1314. However, the limitations of lack of manoeuvrability and vulnerability to missile attack were still there. These limitations were overcome by the Swiss armies of the 15th century, whose aggressive use of pike armed combat columns swept all before them in the Burgundian Wars 1474-1477. This was due to extensive training that could allow the pike block to be used as an offensive hammer to bludgeon through the enemy lines, as well as a defensive formation against cavalry. At this time, the well trained block of pikemen dominated the battlefields of Europe.

This brings us to the beginnings of the Pike and Shotte era that will be covered in the following pages. The Battle of

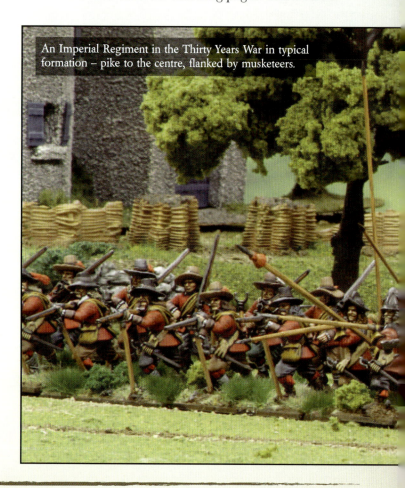

An Imperial Regiment in the Thirty Years War in typical formation – pike to the centre, flanked by musketeers.

1502 - Christopher Columbus leaves Cadiz on his fourth and final voyage.

Biocca in 1522, a bloody affair in the Italian Wars, was a turning point. This was the first battle that saw a balance of the combat power of the pike arm, coupled with the shooting power of firearms adapted by the Spanish. Well positioned arquebusiers devastated the advancing Swiss columns as they closed and the invincibility of the Swiss pike blocks was gone forever.

New formations were seen on the battlefield, the' tercios', consisting of 'the shot' flanking the pikes, raining fire on the enemy before the pikemen engaged in hand-to-hand combat. The pikemen in return could offer a safe haven for the shot should cavalry threaten, as no horse would close with that 'hedgehog' of metal points. If armies laid out their tercios in a mutually supporting manner with cavalry protecting the wings, real tactical flexibility could be attained.

By the mid 17th century great advances in firearm technology were being made. The arquebus and matchlock musket were being replaced by the firelock, a far more reliable weapon, especially in inclement weather. This led to a higher ratio of firearms to pike, and this was accelerated by the invention of the bayonet, as the 'shot' could now defend themselves with a wall of steel.

By the Dutch Wars and Wars of the Grand Alliance at the end of the 17th century, the pike's days were numbered. Pikemen were often relegated to the sidelines as firepower alone could break the enemy, and at worst they became mere targets, having to take awful punishment from a distance.

Some forces, notably the Swedish, did persevere with the notion of 'Pike & Shotte' beyond 1700. The Swedes in fact won some outstanding victories in the Great Northern War with courageous charges of pike, but by the first decade of the 18th century the undisputed master of the battlefield was the musket armed infantryman.

Fighting Men of the Pike & Shotte Era

The average fighting men of the period had little knowledge or understanding of who they fought or why. Many were hastily gathered into local levies, while some hired themselves out as mercenaries, fighting for whoever paid the most. National standing armies were a rarity at the turn of the 16th century and were not introduced by most countries until the end of the 17th century.

Troops were often raised by wealthy landowners who were sworn to follow a cause or faction, and these men were responsible for the equipping of their men and their training. Uniforms were uncommon. In fact many countries – the Spanish especially – actively resisted the introduction of them. Civilian wear was common on the battlefield throughout the period, although uniforms and cohesive styles of regimental flags were slowly introduced throughout the 17th century.

No self-respecting general would enter a battle without elements of Horse (Cavalry), Foot (Infantry) and Ordnance (Artillery). Following is a summary of the basic elements of all three. A more detailed look into specific troop types by conflict and army will be taken in the relevant sections throughout the book.

1503 - Naples is captured by the Spanish.

THE FOOT

Pike

Organised into a large block of men in ranks and files, pikemen were kings of the battlefield at the start of this period. Used aggressively a block of charging pikemen was an awesome weapon. A fully formed pike unit with regimental colours flying was a fiercesome sight to behold, and it was the pikemen that generally held the honour of carrying the colours as they were invariably the best fighters. Their defensive duties were primarily to keep the enemy cavalry at bay, as only a desperate cavalry commander would order a charge into a 'hedgehogged' block of pikes.

The pike itself was a wooden pole varying in length between twelve and twenty-five feet, tipped with a metal blade (though by the mid 1600s eighteen feet was the usual length). A drilled block would present a wall of metal points to any enemy. The men themselves often had armour of breast and back plates, and a morion helmet. Tassets, or thigh guards, were sometimes issued to better equipped companies. During most of the 16th and up until the latter half of the 17th century it was the pike arm of an army that bore the brunt of the fighting, and attracted the fittest and most able of men.

Many pikemen also carried a short sword into battle, commonly called a 'tuck'. These weapons were generally treated poorly on campaign finding most use in foraging. This generally meant that they were of little use in the heat of battle should the wall of pikes be breached and individual combat be joined.

Other Close Combat Weapons

Other pole arms were certainly used throughout the period by a number of armies. The bill (or billhook) was common in the English armies throughout the 16th century. With a shorter haft it was less effective than the pike against cavalry; but for infantry close combat on broken ground it could generate awesome killing power (as inflicted on the Scots at Flodden in 1513). At the same time billhooks were also used extensively by Italian and French armies, while the Spanish and Welsh preferred the glaive.

The halberd was used extensively at the beginning of our period and was used in close support of the pike. As defensive duties were given over more to the pike, and the attacking power of the 'shotte' developed, the halberd started to fall from favour. By the beginning of the 17th century the halberd was reduced to being used more as a symbol of office for NCOs, while the similar partizans were more commonly found in the hands of officers, having been

Newcastle's Whitecoats,
English Civil Wars

1504 - The Battle of Wenzensbach, Frundsberg's first victory as a commander of Landsknechts.

replaced completely in most armies by the pike for the common foot soldier.

The standard broadsword was used as a primary weapon in a few armies, and these tended to be those of Eastern Europe. In Western Europe the Spanish were the exception, and commonly went to war with a good number of men armed with sword and shield.

The famous Irish Gallowglass made great use of the double handed axe, as did the Scots right through the 16th century. Double handed swords appeared throughout the period, right from the Doppelsoldners of the Landsknecht regiments in the early 16th century to the famous claymores of the Scottish Highlanders.

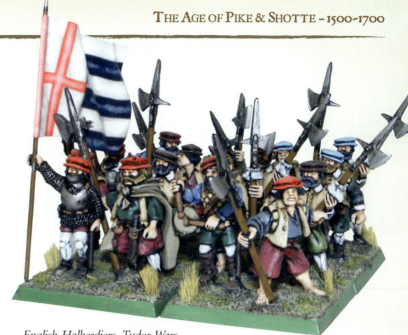

English Halberdiers, Tudor Wars

Landsknecht Doppelsoldners, Italian Wars.

Imperial Swordsmen, Thirty Years War

Highland Clansmen

1504 - Pedro Reinel's Atlantic chart is the earliest known nautical chart with a scale of latitudes.

Shotte

The 200 years from 1500 to 1700 saw vast strides in both the technology and the tactics of the 'shotte'. Handguns had been introduced into warfare in the 15th century and advances in design throughout that century meant that 'true' matchlocks were common by the beginning of the 16th century.

Bandolier and rest of a humble musketeer, 17th century (Stallard Collection)

A unit of commanded shot, English Civil Wars

The term 'matchlock' was derived from the action of firing the piece, rather than any specifics on weight or bore, so was used to describe a whole range of handguns. 'Match' referred to the matchcord, a length of saltpetre treated smouldering rope. This was held in place by an 'S'-shaped lever called a serpent, and lowered to a priming pan via the trigger action. 'Lock' came from the trigger mechanism which was similar in shape to the locks found on chests and doors of the time.

By the beginning of the 16th century these handguns had become known as arquebuses and were beginning to be used in large numbers, initially by the Spanish. In conjunction with a defensible position the arquebus destroyed the aura of invincibility that the Swiss pikemen had enjoyed. A similar weapon, the caliver, was also developed at this time with a slightly larger bore.

Although armies still employed the bow and crossbows, the new handguns had the advantage of being relatively cheap to manufacture and, more importantly, needed far less training to use. However, the simple bow still had a couple of key advantages; the rate of fire was higher than the new arquebus and the bow could be used in wet weather without the problem of keeping a match cord lit.

At the beginning of the 16th century the first muskets were introduced, and again the Spanish were at the forefront of developing the battlefield roles for these new weapons. Muskets had originally been developed as much heavier guns, used mostly on fortified walls; but the Spanish introduced a lighter model that could be fired using a forked musket rest. Although more powerful than the arquebus these muskets used in the field were still very heavy and unwieldy, so much so that many of the fittest men were being drafted into the musket units rather than the pike simply because of the strength needed to use them.

It was not until the 1630's that the problem was addressed to any real satisfaction, both in shortening the barrel and altering the design to make them lighter, so they could be used properly without rests (although rests continued to be used widely).

By the English Civil War other issues were being addressed. The matchlock musketeer needed to carry an awful lot of equipment, not least the yards of matchcord and different flasks for priming and barrel powder. The introduction of 'bandoliers' meant that enough powder for each charge could be carried separately, which meant ammunition could then be rationed more efficiently.

The introduction of the 'flintlock' was a further evolution of the shotte. In the early 16th century these weapons (also called firelocks or doglocks) were used by mounted troops in pistol or carbine form, as a man on horseback had his hands full already without the added problems caused by smouldering match!

The flintlock mechanism gave a number of advantages over a matchlock. It used no matchcord, which was a huge logistics development as a marching army had to transport tons of the stuff around. It was far more reliable in wet conditions and less likely to misfire, and a far better weapon for night advances as there were no 'glow-worms' of lit match burning in the dark. It was more expensive to manufacture than the matchlock and certainly more prone to damage. Yet the advantages far outweighed these considerations to the extent that by the end of the English Civil War, flintlock manufacture surpassed that of the matchlock. Guarding the powder reserves was also a far less dangerous prospect than with a lit matchcord!

The final development in our period for the shotte was the introduction of the bayonet. Until now the musket units had to be protected from enemy horse by supporting pike.

1505 - Archangel Cathedral in Moscow begun

The bayonet allowed the musket to be turned, temporarily, into a short pike, thus making pike blocks all but obsolete. First introduced in the second half of the 17th century, the first bayonets were simple belt knives jammed into the muzzle of the musket. These were known as 'plug' bayonets and had the major disadvantage of not allowing the gun to be fired when fixed. Later, the 'ring' bayonet was introduced briefly which was (unsurprisingly) attached to the musket by a two ring connector. In the 1670s the French introduced the socket bayonet, and this was quickly adopted by all the European armies and remained pretty much unchanged for over 250 years.

In addition to providing continuous fire, the musketeers or 'shotte' were now able to act as effective shock troops as well as being able to defend themselves adequately against cavalry. Of the main western armies only the Swedish retained its pikemen into the 18th century.

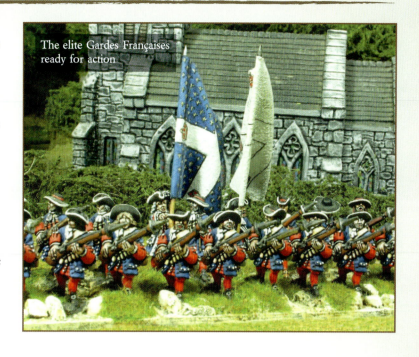

The elite Gardes Françaises ready for action

"Those which are ordained for their guard to be firelocks or to have snaphances for the avoiding of the danger that might happen by the coal of the match."

Benefit of firelocks guarding the artillery train

*Firelock carbine 1620-1660
(Stallard Collection)*

Scots Covenanters man the walls during the English Civil Wars.

1506 - The Papal Swiss Guard are created, to protect the Pope and Vatican.

THE HORSE

The role of the Horse, like that of the Foot, changed a great deal during the Pike & Shotte era. This section will concentrate on the main cavalry types used by most armies across Europe: Lancers, Cuirassiers/Pistoliers, Harquebusiers, Carabineers and Dragoons. A number of other types of cavalry were used by a number of armies throughout the 16th and 17th centuries. These included horse archers, Spanish Genitors, and Cossacks, which will be covered in specific detail throughout the book.

Lancers

For the first part of the 16th century fully armoured lance-armed cavalry were dominant on the battlefields of Europe. These men were a throwback to the medieval knight, spectacular in their Italian or Maximillian style armour and mounted on barded horses. Most commonly known as Gendarmes , they were used as shock troops to drive away opposition cavalry and were deadly against all infantry apart from well ordered pike troops. They would charge home at the gallop, line abreast, and punch holes clean through the enemy. Hardly surprising when the armour alone for man and beast often topped 100 lbs (45 kgs)!

This armour came at a cost, not only in manoeuvrability but fiscally, and so the ranks were generally drawn from aristocratic families. Interspersed with the Gendarmes were lighter armoured lancers, often retainers of their better fortified superiors, to run down the fleeing enemy. With the invention of the pistol, many lancers added a brace to their arsenal.

As the inability to combat pike blocks effectively, coupled with the widespread use of musket armed men on the battlefield became apparent, the heyday of the lancers passed. By the beginning of the 17th century armour had been cut down to a three-quarter length (finishing at the knees) and horse barding had disappeared almost completely. The heavily armoured lancer had almost passed into obscurity by the Thirty Years War.

Lancers in the 17th century tended to be lightly armoured men mounted on small but sturdy steeds; common in Eastern Europe, but also epitomised by the Scots Lancers of the English Civil Wars.

A special note should be made of the Polish Winged Hussars, one of the most iconic of all the fighting men of this period. They were used to devastating effect against the Swedes, Russians and Turks (and pretty much anyone else who got in their way), in both the 16th and 17th centuries.

Pistoliers & Cuirassiers

The other common form of heavy cavalry on the Pike & Shotte battlefield was the Pistolier, later known as the Cuirassier. The invention of the pistol, coupled with a need for heavy cavalry to combat pike armed regiments, led to

Cuirassiers were an awe-inspiring sight on the field of battle...

1507 - Leonardo da Vinci completes the Mona Lisa.

Royalist Cavalry

pistolier regiments replacing lancers in the second half of the 16th century.

Fortified by three-quarter or half armour, and carrying a brace of pistols and a sword, units of Cuirassiers would normally form in close order and ride to within pistol shot of the enemy. The front rank would fire and then retreat to the rear to reload, allowing the next rank to fire. Formed six ranks deep, this tactic of 'caracoling' was developed to disorder the enemy unit to the point where a charge was possible. Although history has not looked favourably on the caracole, it was successfully executed for many years by the German Reiters, although it was not an effective tactic when faced by cavalry who charged in at the gallop.

By the Thirty Years War a far more common tactic for Cuirassiers was to charge in, discharge their pistols and fall on the enemy with the sword at the trot; this tactic being successful enough to warrant large numbers of Cuirassier regiments to be raised.

The Cuirassier regiments of the English Civil War were a different animal, preferring to caracole. This, arguably, made them far less effective than their European counterparts. Many suits of armour were stockpiled at the beginning of the war, but very few records of full Cuirassier regiments exist in Britain. In fact only a handful of regiments, including Essex's Lifeguard and Haselrigg's 'Lobsters' (both for Parliament) are recorded as such, although there were bound to be a lucky few in many regiments who grabbed some more complete armour for themselves!

Harquebusiers & Carabineers

The development of firearms to be employed on horseback led to completely new types of cavalry. Mounted arquebusiers were seen for the first time in the 1490s, and by the mid 1500s were common on most European battlefields. By this time they were a versatile force, trained to act as true cavalry and also skirmish on foot.

At the turn of the 17th century these regiments, along with those originally armed with a carbine, had converted themselves into heavier cavalry armed with pistols and swords. For the most part they had abandoned the weapons for which they had been named, and had established themselves as the 'standard' horse regiments in most armies.

Protected by back and breast armour or the ubiquitous buff coat, these regiments were easier and cheaper to raise than Cuirassiers while packing a punch that meant they could be used aggressively. During the English Civil War these units were used far more vigorously by the Royalist commander Prince Rupert than their Parliamentarian counterparts, to the extent that the war was turned in the Royalist favour until Cromwell's 'Ironsides' effectively countered them.

Dragoons Artois of Louis XIV's French army

Dragoons

The first mention of 'dragoons' dates from the early 1600s, although some claim they were not fully utilised until the 1620s in Germany (the French will disagree). The name is derived from the French *dragon* which was a short but large bored flintlock firearm, slung from a leather belt which would not impede riding.

Although dragoons are listed in the cavalry arm of the forces, their original role was that of mounted infantry. They were organised in companies, not troops; had a drummer not a trumpeter; and the officers were ranked as infantry. They were also armed in the same way as the infantry with a mix of pike and shot in the ranks. The use of pike armed dragoons seems not to have made it to the English Civil War, but for some time was common in Europe.

The dragoons' roles were many and varied and they were relatively cheap to equip and keep. They were given the poorest quality horses. These troops could be used to control large areas of the countryside through raiding ambushing and foraging; whilst they could easily dismount and hold key positions. Although rarely used in assaults, their constant usefulness to commanders has made some historians speculate that dragoons, despite being the "maids of all work", were often tough and experienced troopers.

Swedish cavalry clash with Cossacks in Eastern Europe.

1509 - Henry VIII is crowned king of England, and will reign for 38 years.

THE ORDNANCE

Advances in the infantry and cavalry throughout the period were matched by steady developments in gunpowder artillery (also known as the ordnance). Originating in China, a few early artillery pieces had made their way to Europe by the 13th century. It wasn't until the protracted sieges of the Hundred Years War that there was a real need for artillery pieces, and by the 15th century most armies had adopted some ordnance.

Bombards were simple smooth tubes placed on a static base that were muzzle loaded with iron, lead, stones or even lumps of scrap. They were used extensively by the Turks in a series of sieges to great effect.

Mortars were also developed, again almost exclusively in sieges, being little more than an iron bowl loaded with shot. These were not particularly accurate, but scared people on the receiving end silly.

By the end of the 15th century a base with wheels and an axle made the 'cannon' mobile and therefore far more useful on the battlefield. Their usefulness in battle was limited as the development of muskets meant that the artillery's poor reliability and rate of fire led to the guns being often overrun. They did however offer a good psychological weapon, and often terrified inexperienced soldiers facing them for the first time. It is worth remembering that until the arrival of cannon the loudest noises a person might encounter in life would come from tree felling and cathedral bells.

In the 1620s the cartridge was invented, which combined the shot and powder together for the first time. This helped with the speed of reloading artillery pieces. In the Thirty Years War it was the Swedish king, Gustavus Adolphus, who made real strides in the tactical use of artillery on the battlefield. He advocated the use of lighter, more mobile guns that could be moved in battle to support the main assault. He felt so strongly about this 'combination of arms' that he banned artillery pieces bigger than 12 pounders in his armies on campaign. His victory at Breitenfeld in 1631 against a numerically superior force was in part due to the combining of infantry, cavalry and artillery tactics; his formula was to form a template for future great commanders.

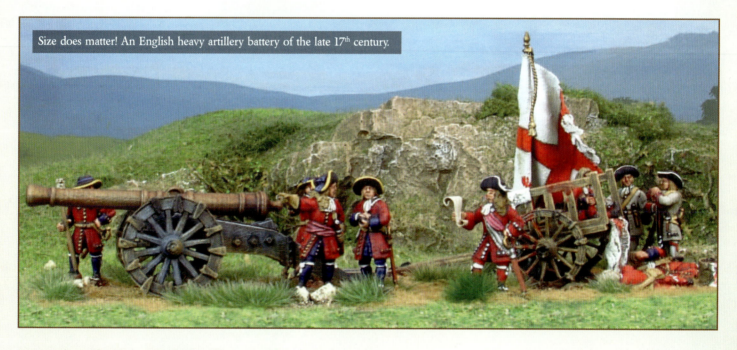

Size does matter! An English heavy artillery battery of the late 17th century.

WHAT NEXT?

Hopefully you have now got a feel for the period and a rough idea of the sort of troops at your disposal for your all conquering army, their strengths and weaknesses, and how they fought.

The next part of the book covers how the rules fit together. Later sections delve into specific conflicts of the 16th and 17th centuries in more depth; starting with a brief (ish) background dealing with the key characters and some specific troop types. There is also a scenario and army lists in each section and some guides to uniforms and flags to round things off. Most importantly there are lots of pictures of wonderful miniatures, hopefully offering up inspiration to get painting yourself and making the choice of 'What army should I get?' a little easier.

1510 - Peter Henlein makes the first pocket watch.

The Pike & Shotte Game

This book recreates the warfare of the 16th and 17th centuries using armies of tabletop model soldiers to represent the forces of the time. Our armies of miniatures will strive to carry all before them on the gaming table, just as their real life counterparts attempted to defeat their enemies centuries ago.

We, the players, take on the roles of the commanders and generals whose task is to lead our forces to victory through tactical guile, strength of arms and a little bit of luck!

Many of the rules in this book are the same as those in *Black Powder*, although it has been necessary to discard, amend and create new rules to more accurately reflect the conflicts of our period. Also included are a number of battles that have been played amongst a group of friends and very helpful gaming clubs which will hopefully inspire the reader. I appreciate that many players will have used other sets of Pike and Shotte rules before and have their own ideas on how games should play out. For those already immersed in the history of the period and veterans of many a campaign, I hope you find this book

both entertaining and credible. The aim of this rules set is to produce a friendly style of game best suited for an evening of battlefield carnage with like-minded individuals over a mulled wine or three. For those of you who are looking at 16th and 17th century warfare for the first time, hopefully this will provide the springboard you need to get started.

How the Rules are Constructed

The rules of our game can be readily adjusted to suit different sized battles, different numbers of players, and differing levels of complexity. This reflects the game's development, having evolved amongst a core of players, but also having to accommodate friends and visitors who were not familiar with the method of play. The heart of the rules concern command, movement and combat. The basic values and ratings assigned to the armies facilitate these core mechanics – they define how troops move, how effectively they fight in different situations, and how they react to casualties suffered. In addition, the specific qualities

A great-looking Thirty Years War game in full swing.

1512 - The Battle of Ravenna. The French defeat the Spanish under Raymond of Cardona.

Gonzaga's Imperial regiment faces down the Swedish assault at the Battle of Breitenfeld.

of troops, technologies and fighting traditions are represented by special rules that we apply according to our tastes and the type of game being played. These additional rules have been largely improvised through play-testing, and they can be readily extended or changed as the occasion demands. Often they were devised as part of a specific scenario and not necessarily used regularly. We leave it up to the players themselves to decide how much of this kind of detail to apply. Our aim is to provide an adaptable framework, plus a suggested 'kit' of extra rules that can be altered or expanded at will. To illustrate how this works we have included examples of quite different games that demonstrate the rules as applied to specific battles and eras.

What is Needed to Play

We mostly play games with groups of players on each side, but games can be just as enjoyable when fought between just two opposing players. Whatever your preference, you will need at least one opponent to fight, and both sides will require a model army to command. It will be necessary to find a good-sized table and hopefully some model terrain such as buildings and trees.

Players will also need a number of ordinary six sided dice – a dozen should just about do, but the more the better. A tape measure marked in inches will be needed to determine distances for movement and ranges for shooting. It is preferable to have several such tape measures, especially if two or more players are taking part on each side

Although it is not a strict requirement, where possible we play with the benefit of a neutral third party, or umpire, whose job is to interpret the rules where necessary, impose his own should he feel the need, and otherwise help out to ensure the game proceeds at a pace. We find games far more entertaining when fought in this way and heartily recommend it.

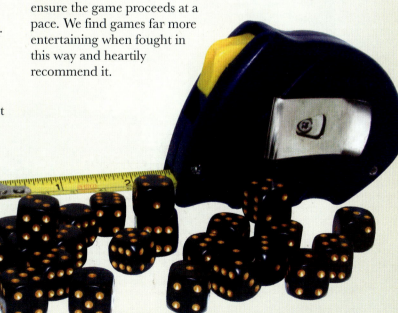

THE ARMY

Before it is possible to play a game of Pike & Shotte it will be necessary to muster an army in miniature. Many people reading this will already have hordes of figures (some might even be painted) or even complete armies ready for the battlefield. For those delving into this period for the first time, the choices available are immense, unsurprising when we are looking at about 200 years of history. For now we will confine ourselves to matters that affect all armies equally.

If you are about to collect a Pike & Shotte army for the first time, I would recommend finding an opponent to play against. If you already know somebody who has their own Pike & Shotte army, then you might want to collect a force specifically to oppose them. Some players like to collect both sides of a conflict if they have a keen interest in a particular period. This can be a definite bonus with many wars of this period (especially the English Civil Wars) where opposing sides would look very similar. With judicial swapping of the unit colours, units can be used on either side. Suddenly that Royalist King's Guard regiment magically transforms into Parliamentarian red coats!

Either way, be aware that most players prefer to play games between armies that actually fought each other in history. Our own preference is to play within a historical setting and all the games described in this book are of that kind. There are those, however, who want to fight battles between forces that never met, often separated by many years. Although these games may be frowned upon by the purists the occasional 'what if' scenario can be great fun and can certainly be accommodated by these rules.

Models

The game can be played with models of any size or scale, but for the most part we have settled upon models that are 28-30mm tall to illustrate this book. This is the most popular size amongst serious collectors of model armies because the individual pieces are sufficiently large and detailed to reward careful painting. However, there are other sizes available, all of which have their advocates and all of which can be used to play our game should you wish to do so. Our choice is for models of the size stated, but players who prefer to collect 6mm, 10mm, 15mm, 1/72 '20mm' or 40mm models – to list the most popular alternatives – may wish to refer to the appendix on page 204 for more about using these scales.

The majority of collectors purchase models as metal castings or plastic kits, which they proceed to assemble and paint before mounting the finished pieces onto bases for ease of handling. For those that do not wish to go to all this

A PIKE & SHOTTE ARMY IN BATTLE ORDER

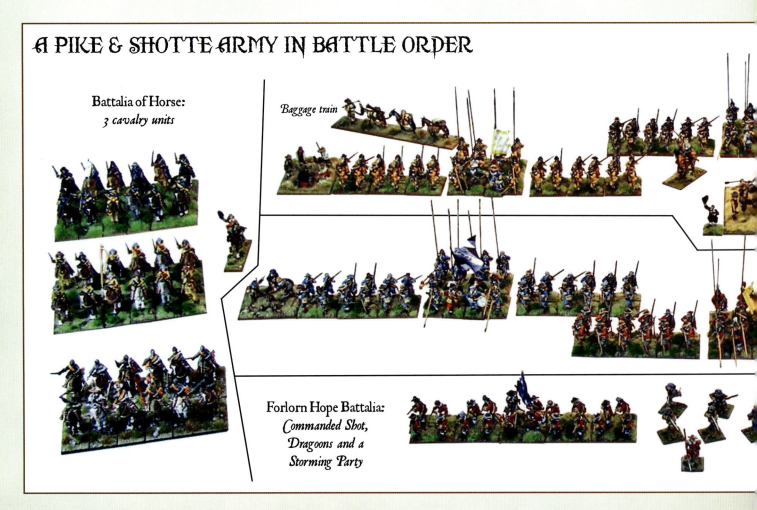

Battalia of Horse:
3 cavalry units

Baggage train

Forlorn Hope Battalia:
Commanded Shot, Dragoons and a Storming Party

1513 - The Battle of Flodden, the English smash the Scots.

effort, it is possible to buy models that have already been painted. Some wargamers will gladly pay a professional artist to paint their collections for them; though they will need deep pockets, for such skills are not purchased cheaply. Models painted to the highest artistic standards are always in demand amongst serious collectors of whom there are a growing number. At the other end of the scale there are some gamers to whom building the army takes second place to the game itself, and they are happy to make use of unpainted models, being content to let their imagination alone colour the spectacle before them. The majority of players prefer to build collections of models they have painted themselves, finding the construction and painting of

miniatures as much fun as actual wargaming. There is undeniably something satisfying about completing each new regiment and adding it to the growing army.

Organising the Models

Whatever army the player chooses to collect, be it a Swiss army of the Italian Wars, Scots Covenanters of the English Civil Wars, or perhaps Thirty Years War Swedes, it will be necessary to organise the troops into bodies of men which we shall henceforth refer to as units. These units are in turn formed into larger groups called battalia. A number of battalia make up our army.

"Your advance upon an Enemy, in what posture soever he be, should be with the constant, firm and steady pace; the Musketeers (whether they be on the Flanks or interlin'd with either the Horse or the Pikes) firing all the while; but when you come within Pistol-shot, you should double your pace, till your Pikes closely serr'd together, charge these, whether Horse or Foot, whom you find before them. It is true, the business very oft comes not to push of Pike, but it hath and may come oft to it, and then Pikemen are very serviceable."

Sir James Turner on an infantry advance. Mid 17th century

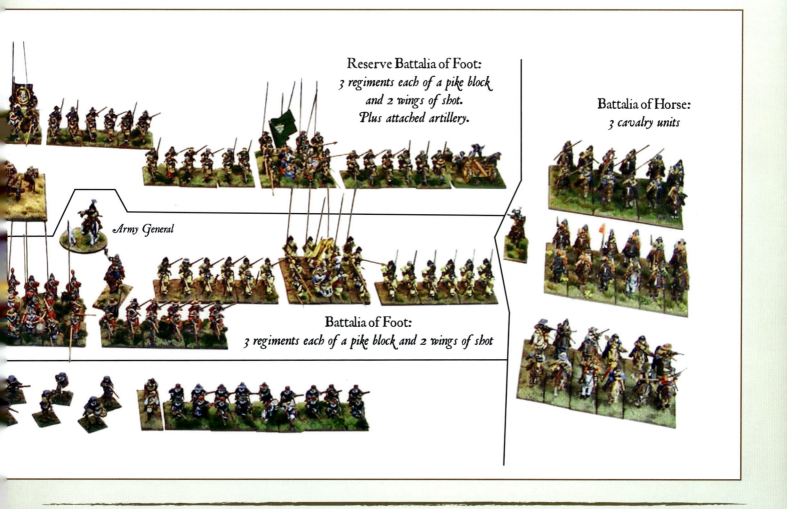

Reserve Battalia of Foot:
3 regiments each of a pike block and 2 wings of shot. Plus attached artillery.

Battalia of Horse:
3 cavalry units

Army General

Battalia of Foot:
3 regiments each of a pike block and 2 wings of shot

The Unit

Each unit represents a typical body of fighting troops of its day, for example, an Imperialist pike block or a detachment of New Model Army musketeers. The word unit is admittedly a very generic term; but it has the advantage that it allows us to devise rules in an even-handed manner without distinguishing between the varied military terms used in the different armies. . During the game itself we would encourage commanders to use the actual names – ''Forward Prince Rupert's Regiment of Foot''- sounding far better than – ''Forward that Foot unit''.

Battalias and Battalia Commanders

The armies' various units must be properly organised into battalias and each battalia assigned a senior officer model – or battalia commander – to lead it. A typical battalia may contain a handful of units (three being a practical minimum) up to maybe a dozen. There is no limit, but the more units a battalia contains, the harder it will be for its commander to control the battalia's movements. It is up to each player to allocate his units into battalias in a manner that he believes will be effective and reflects historical practice.

The General

The entire army is led by a Commander-in-Chief (C-in-C) represented by a suitably impressive model. This character is more commonly referred to as the General and is not

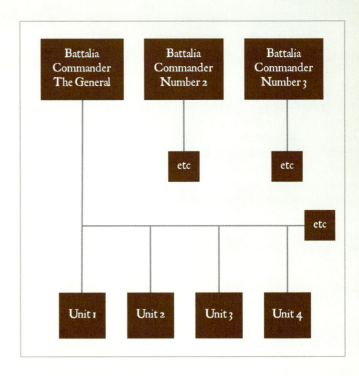

only the most important individual in the whole army but also the figure that represents the player in person.

The whole army therefore consists of the General plus a number of battalia, each consisting of a number of units led by the battalia commander.

Earl of Essex regiment of foot

1515 - The Battle of Marignano, a French victory in Italy over the Swiss League.

Troop Types

For purposes of describing our game we will divide our units of troops into easily recognisable and distinct types as follows.

The Foot – soldiers fighting on foot, commonly called the infantry, formed the bulk of most armies. Infantry units are further subdivided into Block, Battle Line, Warband Infantry and Skirmishers.

The Horse – mounted troops, or cavalry, formed a vital part of any Pike & Shotte army and some forces contained as many cavalry as infantry. Horse units are further subdivided into Lancers, Cuirassiers, Harquebusiers, Dragoons etc. and by type (Heavy Cavalry, Cavalry and Light Cavalry).

Ordnance – artillery had an important role to play in siege warfare and were taken to the field in most armies in varying numbers and with varying degrees of success. Artillery units have been subdivided into light artillery, medium artillery, heavy/siege artillery and mortars.

Wagons & Baggage – all armies required a huge amount of logistical support, which we represent with these units. We shall make do with one category – wagons and baggage, also referred to simply as baggage.

Within these standard troop types, units can be better armed or motivated; they can carry different weapons and may have different capabilities. The broad definitions given here are useful basic types that enable us to ascribe core abilities and rules to our troops.

Fighting Qualities

We attribute appropriate fighting qualities to each of our units by allocating game values that best reflect their abilities on the battlefield. These values determine how effectively each unit performs in different combat situations. By way of an example, the values for a unit of Imperialist Pikemen are shown below.

Unit	Type	Armament	Hand-To-Hand	Shooting	Morale	Stamina	Special
Imperialist Pikemen	Foot Block Infantry	Pike	6	-	4+	4	Hedgehog

Unit

As discussed above, a unit is the basic building block of all armies within these rules. A unit can either represent an independent fighting force or 'elements' of the same troop or regiment. These units can be pulled together in formations that best suit the army you are using within a battalia.

Type

We divide all units into broad types of which the most common are Foot, Horse and Artillery. These different types fight in different ways (for example warband or battle line) and have appropriate rules as explained throughout the book.

Armament

This indicates how the troops are principally armed. A key part of the Pike & Shotte period was how differently armed units combined to offer both hard hitting melee and destructive shooting formations.

Hand-to-Hand Combat

This value shows how proficient the unit is at close quarter fighting. The higher values represent better, more efficient, aggressive or otherwise superior troops. Lower values represent troops either more suited to shooting or poorly trained and equipped units. This is covered at length in the rules for fighting.

Shooting

This value shows how proficient the unit is at delivering ranged fire. The higher the number the more able the troops. Many units that specialise in hand-to-hand combat have a reduced shooting ability or no shooting ability at all. This is covered at length in the rules for shooting.

Morale

A unit's morale value indicates its ability to shrug off the debilitating effects of both shooting and close combat. The value is expressed as a minimum dice score required to withstand enemy attacks. A value of 3+ is therefore excellent, as a roll of 3, 4, 5 or 6 will succeed. A value of 4+ is good, 5+average, 6+ poor and a value of 0 indicates the unit is very fragile and no dice roll is permitted.

Stamina

A unit's stamina value shows how many casualties it can take before it is 'shaken', at which point it becomes vulnerable to collapse. Casualty markers are used to represent the reduction of stamina as a result of close combat fighting or shooting. A high stamina rating indicates sturdy troops who can take a lot of punishment before wavering. Once again, this is explained under the rules for shooting and fighting.

Special

Any special rules that apply to the unit will be listed here. Such rules may reflect tactical doctrine or other particular advantages or disadvantages.

The Unit's Leader

During the game we will have recourse to arrange formations, measure distances or calculate targets and this is done from the centre of the unit's front rank. Where practical it is a good idea to place the unit's 'leader' in this position to mark the middle of the unit's front edge, and it is helpful if this model is instantly recognisable.

Apart from the need for each unit to have a recognisable leader, it is left to the player to add colourful standards, officers, drummers to represent their chosen subject. Naturally we would recommend that units include such figures where they would have had them in reality, as this contributes greatly to the appearance of units in play (and also in the display cabinets when in "winter quarters").

The centre-front or 'leader' position – during play many measurements are made from the centre of the unit's front rank as shown here.

Size of Units

Units of troops are categorised into one of three arbitrary sizes: large, standard and small. We should emphasise that the majority of close fighting units in the army always conform to the standard size. Large units are employed only in the biggest games or where convention can be conveniently represented by double-sized formations. Such instances will be covered with each particular army list later in the book.

SIZE OF UNITS			
Unit Type	Standard Size	Large	Small
Pike/Infantry Block or Warband Units	12 to 25 models	26 to 40	8 to 11
Infantry Battle Line Units	8 to 20 models	21 to 30	6 or 7
Cavalry	6 to 12 models	13 to 20	4 or 5
Artillery	One gun and crew	–	–

UNIT FRONTAGES TABLE				
Type of Troops	Formation	Standard	Large	Small
2 deep foot	2 deep battle-line	80-200mm	200-300mm	80-120mm
3+ deep foot	3+ deep battle-line/block	80-200mm	100-300mm	80-120mm
Horse	2 deep battle-line	75-150mm	150-200mm	50-75mm
Artillery	1 deep battle-line	80-120mm	160mm-240mm	40mm

Casualty Markers

Fighting effectiveness declines during the heat of battle due to degradation of equipment, bodily fatigue, failing morale, and certainly if men or officers becoming casualties. We represent all these factors by means of casualty tokens or markers placed beside or behind the units. The maximum number of casualty markers a unit can take is referred to as its stamina, and appears on the 'fighting qualities' line for all units. This number assumes the unit is of a 'standard size', but it can be modified for larger or smaller formations of the same troop type. This is explained later in the game rules.

Any kind of markers can be employed to record casualties, such as actual models, card chits or plastic tokens. Players are welcome to use whatever method they feel most comfortable with, and can also resort to pen and paper to record casualties if that is their preference.

Command Ratings

Commanders have a far different role from their troops. In our game they are required to direct their forces rather than fight, and for the most part they do this by issuing orders to units under their command.

We shall therefore assign a value to all commanders to represent their effectiveness within the army's overall command structure. This value can vary from army to army, and from commander to commander, and is the 'Command Rating' which varies from 10 (the best) to 5 (the worst) as shown below. We recommend that players stick to a command level of 8 for all commanders until they have a fair grasp of the rules.

In the Pike & Shotte period the quality of the commanders and the troops varied widely within the same armies. Many forces were locally raised and trained, and improved over time as they gained experience. Other formations simply defied logic with their fighting abilities and downright stubbornness, the Irish Brigade regiments in the English Civil War being a prime example.

For these reasons the Command Ratings will be given for commanders by battalia type within an army, and this is the rating that will be used in the absence of a character of exceptional leadership qualities. In later sections of this book, as we cover specific conflicts and armies, we shall introduce key dramatis personae. Should you care to have Oliver Cromwell leading the cavalry wing of your Parliamentarian force it is right to expect him to be something more than a regular cavalry battalia commander. Such characters have special rules themselves and will be covered with each featured army. For now, let us assume that your battalia commanders are standard with no special rules.

A battalia commander will specialise in one of the main fighting arms of an army – Foot, Horse or Artillery – and for this reason most battalias will be comprised entirely of one of these types.

There are instances where a battalia consists of mix of unit types, for example three Foot and one Horse, and they will be classed as the type of unit that is dominant (in this case it would be classed as led by an infantry commander). If there is an equal split of units between infantry, artillery and cavalry the lowest command rating is chosen. This will be covered in more depth later in the book.

If the overall army general attaches himself to a battalia his command rating will be used in place of the battalia commander as long as he remains with that battalia.

Bases for Models

The models shown in this book have been mounted onto rectangular card, wooden, or plastic bases and suitably decorated. This makes the models easier to handle without knocking them over or damaging them, and also allows us to more easily arrange the units into neat blocks. It is not strictly necessary to mount the models onto bases in this way, but amongst collectors who intend to take their troops into battle it is the usual practice.

Some players like to mount every individual model onto its own small base. This has the advantage that it allows a unit to adopt any kind of formation simply by rearranging the models themselves. However, on the whole it is preferable to mount several infantry or cavalry models onto a larger multiple base as this makes it quicker and far easier to move an entire unit.

For those of you already aware of the perils of moving large amounts of pike-armed combatants from one gaming table to another the idea of basing entire units on one base is certainly appealing, and it certainly means you can go to town by adding small vignettes to your army that really add flavour.

For infantry we recommend (however you base your units) that each individual model takes up an area of 20x20mm. Individual cavalry models should cover 25x50mm each and artillery are based as required. Simply multiply these numbers up for multiple figures on a base.

Astute readers will notice that many of the troops shown in this book do not necessarily conform to these standards, but this makes no real practical difference within the rules as the flexibility in the 'standard' unit sizes allows for a variety of basing styles.

Command Rating	Description
10	**Military Genius.** A natural born leader who is worshipped by his men and adored by women. This individual is highly organised, courageous, with an instinctive feel for battle and sure to re-write the history books.
9	**Great.** An extremely capable, trustworthy, forthright, pious and popular commander.
8	**Good.** An able and confident leader, respected by his peers.
7	**Average.** An honest sort and a capable if uninspired leader.
6	**Poor.** An indecisive or reluctant commander, prone to dithering.
5	**Fool.** A feckless blustering imbecile, justly despised by his men, and a prime target for assassination at the first opportunity.
4 and less	**Unfit for Duty.** We shall not rate any of our commanders below 5 – these gentlemen will quickly have been assigned essential bean-counting roles down on the farm or a tragic munitions accident will have swiftly whisked them off to the hereafter.

1519 - Charles V is elected as Holy Roman Emperor, as well as being King of Spain.

Bases for Commanders

Our Commander-in-Chief and all the battalia commanders should be represented by individual models or, even better, a vignette with a number of figures. Ideally, these models need to be distinguished from the troops they command. We have not specified any set base dimensions for these models as we would hope that players will take the time to make these characters marvellous centre-pieces for their force.

Just as our units of a dozen or so models represent hundreds of men, so a commander model represents not only the great man himself, but also his entourage of staff, runners, guards and even pets.

INFANTRY

Infantry mounted on bases 20mm per man (40mm square per four miniatures)

CAVALRY

Cavalry mounted on bases 25mm per rider – this is the usual size

ARTILLERY

A cannon mounted on a 60mm wide base – whatever base is needed to fit the cannon and crew will be just fine.

COMMANDERS

Commanders can be based to suit – many players like to put their commanders on round bases to distinguish them from ordinary troops

1520 - Francis I and Henry VIII of England meet at 'the Field of the Cloth of Gold'.

Formations

Before our troops are ready to take part in a battle we must decide how to arrange them into fighting formations, so have a care, and look to your ranks and files. The following are all formations that are either used by all armies or often employed by specific but common troop types.

We sometimes refer to **formed** bodies of troops, by which we mean troops arranged in any formation aside from 'open order', where models are spaced apart with gaps between as explained later. This is a useful distinction to make as some rules only apply to formed units and other rules apply only to units in open order.

Infantry Block: This is a formation of close-ordered melee troops. They must be a minimum of three ranks deep and are often more than this. The most common unit of this type is the Pike Block. Pike blocks represent a real unit of maybe up to twenty ranks deep in many armies (some tercios had over twenty five ranks). The precise depth makes no difference in play but does allow for deeper formations to add flavour to your force. This formation is also used to represent a multitude of other weapons in addition to the pike used throughout the period, such as billhooks, spears and other pole arms, but we shall refer to all these as 'infantry block' formations for simplicity throughout the rules section of the book. These units should be roughly square in shape, with roughly equal numbers of ranks and files.

Battle Line: This is any formation that is two ranks deep (three occasionally) for infantry units. It is an ideal formation for shooting as it allows the unit to bring most men to bear on the target. Cavalry units in line formation can be in one or two ranks. This represents a real unit something like two to six men deep in the case of most infantry and perhaps two to four deep in the case of cavalry. It makes no difference in play, but deeper formations tended to be distinct for specific armies and troop types, and we provide the option for players whose collections reflect this.

Skirmish Order: Also known as open order, this is a loose formation that allows troops that can do so to skirmish and that also makes it possible to move through broken terrain. When a unit forms into skirmish order, the models are spaced apart from 1-2" so that they form a chain or loose mass. If you have based your models in multiples simply space the bases apart by a base width to indicate skirmish order.

1521 - War breaks out between France on one side, and England, the Empire and the Pope on the other.

Column: A column is a unit arranged for moving quickly and generally speaking for marching, but also for deploying into position. It is an extremely poor formation for fighting, and troops caught in combat by the enemy are not likely to fare well. An infantry column must be between two and five models wide and must have more ranks than files (i.e. the formation must be deeper than it is wide). All other columns must be one or two models wide and must have more ranks than files. Columns will often be marching along roads or tracks, or between buildings or around other troops, and must obviously be free to follow the necessary path.

Warband:
This is the default formation for most combative irregular troops such as Highland Clansmen or Militia. These units fight in a formation more akin to a mob than anything else and should form a rough square or oblong between three and six ranks deep.

Hedgehog: This is a defensive position rather like the formed Square of later periods. This formation occurs when infantry units best suited for shooting seek refuge in a pike unit of the same battalia, a particularly useful formation for defending against enemy cavalry. The converged units are formed with the (usually) musket armed unit(s) placed around or within the pike unit.

Changing Formation

Generally speaking, changing from one formation to another requires the specific instruction when the orders are given. We shall address the rules for giving orders and resultant moves in the following rules section. For now we will simply establish the procedures for changing from one formation to another.

- When changing formation from column to battle line, infantry block or warband or from any of these back to column, begin with the model or base in the centre-front or 'leader' position (see the Unit's Leader, page 23). Turn the model on the spot so that it faces the desired direction. Rearrange the rest of the unit around the leader so that the model or base is as near as possible in the centre-front position of the new formation. This manoeuvre takes the unit one move.

- In the case of a skirmish order formation the approximate 'middle' of the formation is used as the fixing point for changing formation. Place the leader model in the middle of the skirmish order formation and rearrange the unit into a new formation around him . To change from another formation to skirmish orders simply reverse the process. This takes troops without the skirmisher special rule one entire move (those troops forced into temporary skirmish order during the battle), but in the case of units with the skirmisher rule the change of formation into or from skirmish order can be followed by a normal move all counting as 'one move'. For example, a unit of infantry with the skirmisher special rule that is in column can form open order and move 6" in one move. See Moving Units page 38 for more about rates of movement.

Front, Flank and Rear

The areas to the front, sides and rear of a formation form its front, left flank, right flank, and rear quarters. This is a useful concept as it allows us to define how troops move, what they can see and react to as a body, how they shoot, and so on. This idea underpins many of the rules that follow so it's worth getting this nailed down straight away. These quarters, areas or zones are most readily demonstrated by means of the diagram below.

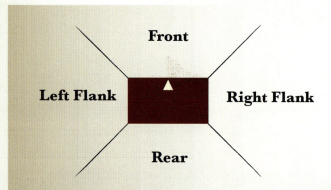

As you can, see the four quarters are determined by bisecting the corners of the outermost bases. In practice this need not be a precise matter and it is quite adequate to judge such things by eye.

Units in skirmish order are sufficiently dispersed for troops to face whichever direction they wish, and therefore have no flanks or rear as such. Units in skirmish order are treated as having one continuous front that extends all the way around their edge.

Units in a hedgehog formation still have four distinct quarters in the way illustrated above, but have no flanks or rear. Each face of the hedgehog is treated as a separate front.

Artillery

These units are a little different to infantry and cavalry units in that they comprise separate gun and crew. Each gun and crew is considered to be one unit (a battery). When artillery is deployed to shoot the crew are deployed around the gun and the 'front' of the deployed artillery unit is always worked out from the tip of the gun barrel.

Battalias

An army consists of a number of battalias. Each battalia consists of one commander plus a number of units. The most basic battalia will consist of a pike block with two support wings of musket to form the classic formation we have seen on many tabletops. These units can represent a convergence of a number of regiments into one fighting formation as was common in the period, or one large regiment split down into its pike and musket components.

We make no limit on the number of units in a battalia, and they can contain a mix of troop types. For example, a battalia could contain its commander, two pike units, four musket units, an artillery piece and a unit of dragoons; or any combination allowed that can be used to the best advantage. More units in a battalia will allow flexibility to adapt tactics and formations for those inclined to fight in the Swedish or Dutch style (as shown opposite), but just as importantly will look good on the table.

Units from the same battalia do not have to remain within any specified distance of each other during the game. However, if they are to be directed by means of a single order, battalias must form a loose body with no unit separated by more than 6". This is described in detail in the Command rules that follow. As a general rule, battalias operate more efficiently and can offer support to each other when forming a close group as described.

Commanders must remain within a move's distance of at least one unit under their command. The closer they are to the units in their battalia the easier it is for them to issue orders. Note that commanders can't normally be shot at or attacked in the game, so don't worry about their safety as they move.

Battalia Tactical Formations

Whichever army you choose to collect and game with, you may want to organise your troops in formations that emulate their historical counterparts. The advantage of having different units representing the pike/mêlée and shot/missile troops in your army is that it allows you the flexibility to do this.

Below are the tactical formations that were developed throughout the 16th and 17th centuries that you can reproduce with your units using the battalia rules. This is certainly not an exhaustive list as many variations were made to these tactics, but it will suffice for this work. Later in this book, we will explain the preferred formations of many of the armies covered during this period. This will be found in either their background or army list sections.

The Tercio

The tercio formation was a product of the Italian Wars, devised to meet the tactical needs of combining melee and missile troops and eliminating similar enemy formations. Originally a tercio could consist of more than 6,000 men, although by the mid 1500's this had been reduced to 3,000 – a mix of pike, sword and arquebus. On the field these tercios were usually formed in groups of three, hence the name, in a staggered formation to allow fields of fire to be improved.

Within a tercio the pike were grouped in massive numbers in the centre, with smaller units – or sleeves – of missile troops generally being placed at each corner of the pike, also many ranks deep.

Variants on the tercio were used throughout the period, although adaptations were continually being made through the Thirty Years War. Even in the English Civil War there was room for the reliable tercio.

The main advantages in battle are the hitting power of large pike units combined with solid rates of fire. What is lacking, and the main reason that new systems were adopted by more progressive armies, is flexibility.

The Dutch Brigade

The Dutch Brigade (or Dutch System) was named after Maurice of Nassau who used it to great effect at the battle of Nieuwpoort in 1600 against the Spanish tercios. The aim of this formation was to combine the main benefit of the tercio (combination of arms) with the flexibility of a Roman Legion.

The formation was broken down into smaller, shallower elements and formed into three battle lines. Each of these lines consisted of pike and musket armed units and together comprised one brigade – or 'battalia' in our terminology (as shown above). Not only did this allow far greater manoeuvrability than a Tercio, it also allowed far more firepower to be brought to bear at one time. Equally, the shallower units were also less susceptible to enemy fire, especially artillery fire.

The Dutch System was so popular throughout the Thirty Years War it became the default formation for many forces; it was also the standard formation for many armies in the English Civil War, especially amongst the Parliament and Covenanter forces.

The Swedish Brigade

The Swedish Brigade – or Swedish System – was developed in the armies of Gustavus Adolphus to meet his requirement for a greater concentration of firepower. It represented a major modification of the Dutch system, and made for far more linear formations. Pike blocks were smaller, and the number of ranks in musket units was reduced to maximise the number of men that could shoot at one time.

The army would be formed in only two battle lines, each consisting of a mix of brigades/battalias. For the infantry this would usually mean alternating units of pike and shot, while the horse would likewise be drawn up in two shallow lines.

The successes of the Swedish armies in the Thirty Years War meant that this formation soon began to appear in other armies. In the English Civil War Prince Rupert was a firm believer in the Swedish tactics, encouraging a swift engagement with the enemy united with massed firepower. The Swedish system had one major drawback, the need to have well trained troops to fully take advantage of its formations. Hastily raised troops in the English Civil Wars and the Thirty Years' War would be unable to grasp the complicated drills.

1522 - Rhodes falls to the Ottoman Empire after a protracted siege.

Game Rules

When looking at the rules we will make the assumption that games are played between two opponents, as this will make it easier to explain the various rules and procedures. That being said, the authors believe the best games are those played with a group of generals on each side, and with an umpire to adjudicate tricky decisions – and bring in the drinks! Each player rolls dice for his own Battalia, moves his own units, and attempts to stick to the grand strategy agreed before the game. With the Army General model resides the supreme command for that side – a role that can be passed between players as decided beforehand or prompted by events.

Preparing to Play

Before the game can begin it is necessary to set the scene of battle using whatever model terrain and miniature scenery best depicts our imagined landscape. This can represent the bleak moors of the north of England, a sleepy Bohemian village, or the mountainous landscape of northern Italy. An unadorned tabletop can deliver a perfectly satisfactory game, but for many the spectacle is every bit as important as the game itself. If you have spent many hours painting your assembled hosts, why not set them on a table that shows them at their best? We won't concern ourselves with such matters here, but we shall return to the theme of terrain and scenery later on.

Battles can begin in many different ways, depending on the scenario. A battle can begin with two armies lined up on opposing sides of the table (and many great historical clashes began in just such a way), the troops having marched out of camp and deployed to face each other. Other battles are known to have started with chance encounters between opposing troops, followed up by reinforcements, until whole armies became unexpectedly embroiled. That is to say nothing of ambushes, raids upon exposed baggage, foraging parties, or one side defending a hastily fortified position. These are all situations common enough in the history of warfare. But to begin with, let's assume our armies have simply marched from their respective encampments to face each other across the width of the playing area - and if possible they should be at least three feet apart.

With both forces fully deployed the battle is ready to begin.

Sequence of Play

The game proceeds in game turns. In each full turn both sides take an individual player turn – first one and then the other as shown below. We have dubbed our opposing armies 'blue' and 'red' for ease of reference. As you can see each full game turn comprises a blue player turn followed by a red player turn – after which the sequence just repeats itself blue, red, blue, red, blue, and so on until the game is fought to a conclusion. Note that during the hand-to-hand combat part of the game turn both sides fight regardless of which side's turn it is.

Blue

1. Blue Command – Blue moves his units starting with initiative moves.
2. Blue Ranged Attacks – Blue shoots with his units
3. Blue Hand-to-Hand Combat – both sides resolve any hand-to-hand fighting.

Red

1. Red Command – Red moves his units starting with initiative moves.
2. Red Ranged Attacks – Red shoots with his units
3. Red Hand-to-Hand Combat – both sides resolve any hand-to-hand fighting.

To begin the battle you will need to decide which side has the first turn – the 'blue' player in our sequence. Although it might seem that there is a great advantage in going first, in practice these things tend to even themselves out over the course of a game. Indeed, it is often beneficial to go second as it gives you a chance to take advantage of any partial or failed moves made by your opponent. Sometimes the game scenario will dictate who goes first – an ambush for example – but in most cases it is quite acceptable for both sides to roll a dice and the highest scorer decides whether to go first or second.

Measuring Distances

During the game the players will need to measure distances when issuing orders, moving units, shooting at the enemy

Landsknechts prepare for 'push of pike'.

1523 - Bonnivet leads a French army into Italy.

and in many other situations. Players are free to measure distances at any time they wish, whether it is their own turn or not. Generally speaking, distances between models are always measured from the edges of the bases on which the models are mounted rather than from the models themselves. There are a few exceptions to this convention. When a commander is giving orders the measure is taken from the commander model's head, and artillery measurements are always from the tip of the barrel of the gun. Exceptions such as these are noted in the rules.

Learning the Game Rules

It will be necessary to learn the basic rules of the game before committing your troops to their first battle, but this need not be too daunting a task. There is no need to memorise every rule before you play – but it is a good idea to read through the rules once to get a sense of how things progress. The best way to learn is to play a small game with a single Battalia on each side and then add more as you get the hang of things.

The following rules sections start with command, in which we describe how to give orders and move units on the tabletop. Then we deal with shooting, and then hand-to-hand combat. This running order seems the most logical as battles invariably begin with movement, progress to an exchange of shots as the armies close, and are finally decided with hand-to-hand combat.

An Important Principle

Battles with model soldiers are supposed to be enjoyable affairs: all questions of victory and defeat pale to nothing before this objective.

Our rules of play have been formulated for our own games, and our aim here is purely to explain, entertain and hopefully inspire other enthusiasts. We make no pretence that our game is superior to others and invite readers to adopt whatever portion of our game they happen to find pleasing. Different players find interest and satisfaction in different things, so there is plenty to be gained by amending any areas that you wish for your own games.

Command

In order to achieve victory in battle between well matched armies it will be necessary for a general to out-manoeuvre as well as out-fight the enemy.

In the command part of his turn the player gets a chance to move his army. Sometimes troops are allowed to move automatically, but in most situations they must be issued orders to do so. Orders are issued on behalf of the army's battalia commanders and occasionally by the army's general. To give an order the player first nominates a commander to issue the order; he then indicates which unit he wishes to move, and describes what he wants the unit to do before rolling the dice to determine if he is successful or not.

Orders

Giving orders is one of the most important parts of the game and also one of the most entertaining aspects of play. When framing orders participants are encouraged to get into the character of their commanders (though not too literally!) and to feel free to use the language of the day to add flavour to the game.

Units don't need orders to shoot or to fight when they find themselves in hand-to-hand combat – they do these things automatically. In most situations units do need orders to move in the Command part of the turn, although there are some situations where units are able to move without orders, which will be described later. There are also situations when units can or must move during other parts of the turn: for example, following hand-to-hand combat when defeated units are often obliged to give ground and victorious units have the opportunity to press forward or fall back.

Players should endeavour to state orders aloud, in good time, and in a straightforward, robust fashion without conditions or vagaries. Orders must always be stated before making the requisite test for success. For example "The King's Lifeguard pike will change formation from march column to a block, and advance to the pond." Failure to state an order before rolling the dice is considered a failed throw regardless of the dice roll and results in a blunder as described later. A gentleman falling foul of this rule should resolve to take such just punishment with a noble bearing, and any attempts to forego the consequences should be met with scorn.

The order must explain where a unit is to move and by which route where there is room for doubt. A unit must also be given a specific order if the player wishes it to change formation, to rearrange its ranks into a column for example. Most importantly, if you want a unit to move into hand-to-hand combat with an enemy then you must clearly and specifically state that you want the unit to charge, and indicate which enemy unit or units you intend the chargers to contact.

Units will always attempt to obey their orders in so far as they are able and in the most direct and straightforward way they can. If a unit's move proves inadequate to fulfil an order in its entirety, then the unit will follow its instructions to the best of its ability as far as it can. For example, if a unit is ordered to charge an enemy but has insufficient movement to do so, then it will move as far as it can towards the intended target before coming to a halt.

Command

Test for Success

To determine if a stated order is successfully announced and received, a test is taken as follows. Roll two dice, add the scores together to get a result from 2-12 and check the number against the commander's leadership rating as follows:

- If the score is greater than the commander's leadership rating then the test is failed and no order is issued. The unit cannot move unless it is entitled to a 'free move' in which case it makes one move (see Free Moves, page 36).

- If the score is **equal** to the commander's leadership rating or **one** less, the order is issued and acted upon in due course – the unit can make one move.

- If the score is **two** less than the commander's leadership rating, the order is speedily issued and acted upon immediately – the unit can make two moves.

- If the score is **three** less than the commander's leadership rating or lower the order is issued in anticipation of events and hurriedly obeyed – the unit can make three moves.

As you can see, a unit might not move at all or may have one, two or three moves to complete its order. Often a single move will enable only part of an order to be fulfilled; though sometimes it will be possible to complete an order in a single move even when more moves are available. Such things are matters to consider when formulating orders. Remember also that orders must be unconditional and cannot therefore be dependent on the results of the dice or the number of moves available.

Commanders, Units and Orders

A unit can only be issued **one** order each turn. If its order roll is passed then the unit obeys the order in so far as it can, but cannot then be issued any further orders. If the order roll is failed then the unit cannot be issued another order that turn.

A commander can only give orders to units belonging to his **own** designated battalia. Refer back to the section on Formations for a description of battalia (page 26).

The Commander-in-Chief does not usually command a battalia, but can give orders to *any* units in the army.

If a commander issues an order successfully then he can continue to issue further orders to other units in his battalia. He can issue any number of orders so long as he continues to do so successfully, and so long as his battalia has units able to receive them.

If a commander fails to issue a unit order then he cannot give any more orders that turn. This can sometimes result in some units moving and others staying where they are, or even for entire battalias to not move at all.

Each Battalia commander must finish giving **all** of his orders before another commander can begin to do so. It is not permitted for one commander to give an order, then a second commander to issue one, and then the first commander to go again. Where several players are playing on one side, it is usual for them all to issue orders and make moves at the same time as this is only sensible, but each player must finish giving orders from each of his own commanders one at a time.

If a double 6 is rolled when giving unit orders the order is failed and the result is a blunder. Blunders result in units moving out of control in some fashion and these are explained on page 35.

If a double six is rolled by the Commander-in-Chief when giving orders something has gone disastrously wrong! Not only does a blunder result but also no further orders may be issued by any commanders that turn. This means that Battalia commanders who have not yet issued orders will be unable to do so.

"...Great Brittaine is inferiour to no nation; and by the prowesse and valour of English and Scots, glorious victories have been obtained... General Norice in the Low Countries; of the worthily honoured Lord Grey in Ireland, of the never dying names of Drake, Furbisher, and Hawkins, of the right famous Earle of Essex, of the deservedly eternized Veres, of the invincible-spirited Greenfield, of the noble Cicill... Weigh your Enemies... Their success is but now of late, consider you the former times; stay and wonder at our incredible victories."

The rector of Batcombe, Somerset 1632

1525 - The Battle of Pavia, the Spanish arquebusiers shoot down the French Gendarmes.

Charge Orders

As we have discussed, it is necessary to give a specific order if you want troops to move into hand-to-hand combat against an enemy. This is the *charge* order. It is not necessary that the intended opponent be in sight of the charger when the order is given. Nor do we worry whether it is possible for a unit to mount its charge successfully at this point. The important thing is that the unit has been given a clear order to engage the enemy – charge!

Charge orders can be framed in as specific or general a manner as the players deem appropriate. For example, "Charge into the King's Lifeguard!" and "Advance to the ridge and charge any enemy that appear!" and "Charge the enemy to your front!" would all be perfectly good orders. In the last two examples given the player might also indicate which units he expected his troops to discover if only for the sake of clarity. Players should not give orders that are ambiguous, and where the umpire considers this to be the case he is encouraged to interpret such orders in as devious and disastrous a manner as possible. Units will always try and fulfill their orders in the most direct and straightforward way they can, so a unit simply instructed to 'Charge the enemy!' would naturally take the shortest route towards the closest enemy within sight up to its maximum move.

We will return to charges later on when we come to the rules for fighting hand-to-hand combat (page 58). There we will discuss how units interpret charge orders and attempt to fulfill them. We need not worry about such things for purposes of explaining how orders are issued and received.

Battalia Orders

So far we have assumed that an order is given to a single unit. This is a perfectly good and often useful way of issuing orders as it allows a commander to exercise precise control over the unit concerned. However, it is often more practical to issue the same order to a group of units at the same time. This is called a *Battalia order*.

A commander can issue the same order to any or all of the units in his battalia so long as all the units form a group and so long as none of the units in the group have already moved that turn. To qualify as a group, none of its units may be separated by more than 6" from another unit in the group when the order is given. Similarly, once the units have finished moving none can be more than 6" from other units in the same group. In short – the group has to remain together in a group as it moves. For example, "Lord Astley's Battalia of Foote will march directly forward in the same formation with all speed to secure the hill, Gerrard's regiment on the left, the King's Lifeguard in the centre and the Queen's Lifeguard on the right with the Saker gun."

It is important that the battalia order is essentially one order which all units can follow in broad terms: for example, all moving forward, all moving back, all moving to engage the enemy, or deploying into position as a body. This is why units are obliged to remain within 6" of each other. This 6" rule overrides any order issued. For example, imagine a mixed formation of infantry and cavalry are ordered to 'advance at maximum pace' with a Battalia order. The dashing cavalry would not be allowed to leave the plodding infantry behind but would be obliged to advance along with the infantry staying within 6" of them.

Where you wish units from the same battalia to do different things then it is necessary to give them separate orders. This allows battalias to be split apart where necessary. For example, if you needed a group of units to move more than 6" apart, perhaps one unit occupying a building whilst others foray towards the enemy. In this case, command dice would be rolled for the bulk of the units moving as a Battalia, while the unit tasked with taking the building would roll its own dice, as it has separate orders.

To issue a battalia order, the player indicates which units will receive the order and tests in the usual way. If successful *all* units are in receipt of the order and will attempt to carry it out. If he fails then *all* the units have failed to receive an order and will usually remain where they are. When a Battalia has several units, this can greatly speed up play while still allowing the player to direct separate units to do specific tasks.

For example: "Lord Haselrigge's two units of cuirassiers will advance in the same formation as a Battalia towards the windmill, while his dragoons will move across to the pond – dismount – and line the hedgerow." Lord Haselrigge has a command rating of 8. The cuirassiers roll one set of dice as they are acting under a Battalia order: rolling 7, their great horses can only plod forward one move. Meanwhile, the nimble dragoons roll 3, easily making their move and ensconcing themselves behind the dense briers of the hedgerow.

Command Modifiers

We assume orders are relayed by messengers who form part of every commander's staff or bodyguard – although there is no need for these individuals to be represented on the tabletop. Battlefield conditions can delay these orders, or in some cases units may already be positioned to efficiently carry them out.

Regardless of any modifiers that may apply, including bonuses afforded by any type of special rule, no commander ever has a command rating of better than 10 or worse than 5.

Distance

It can readily be imagined that messengers might be killed or captured, delayed, or distracted in some fashion. To represent this we apply a penalty to the commander's command rating if he is a long way from a unit he is trying to issue an order to. Note that skirmishers and units with the 'Marauder' ability are exempt from these penalties.

The player must measure from the commander model to the closest point of the unit being given an order. If a commander wishes to give a Battalia order to several units at once, measure to the unit that is farthest away. If the distance is more than 12" then deduct one from the commander's command rating for every full 12". For example: at 19" deduct one, at 38" deduct three, at 48" deduct four, and so on. Measurements are made from the commander's head, as this frees us to mount our models on bases of any size without conferring any advantage.

As already stated, no distance modifiers apply when orders are issued to skirmishers in skirmish order or units with the 'Marauder' ability. However, in the case of a Battalia order, distance modifiers apply if they would normally apply to any units included in the order. For example, a Battalia order to a unit of skirmishers and a unit of dragoons in skirmish order would attract no distance penalties; however, a Battalia order given to a unit of skirmishers in skirmish order and a unit of musketeers in a battle line formation would.

Enemy Close By

If there is an enemy unit within 6" of the unit you wish to give an order to then deduct one from the commander's command rating. When the enemy are this close, troops tend to be more concerned with the immediate threat and act instinctively rather than with any orders they may receive. Such instinctive actions are covered by 'Initiative Orders' later. If the commander is giving an order to several units at once, deduct one if there is an enemy unit within 6" of any of them (i.e., only ever deduct one in total).

March Column/Limbered Artillery

If a unit is in March Column or is Limbered Artillery add one to the command value of the battalia commander.
If the unit is also travelling along a road or track add two.
If the commander is giving a battalia order, the +2 bonus only applies if all the units in the battalia are either in March Column or Limbered Artillery travelling along a road or track.

Summary Table of Command Modifiers

Below is an 'at a glance' summary of the command modifiers. Of course, players who feel the need to add more detail are quite welcome to devise further modifiers should they wish to do so.

COMMAND MODIFIERS TABLE	
Modifier	**Situation**
-1	For every full 12" between the Commander and the unit he is issuing an order to.
-1	There are one or more enemy units within 6" of the unit receiving order
+1	Unit receiving the order is in March Column (or is Limbered Artillery) not on a road or track
+2	Unit receiving the order is in March Column (or is Limbered Artillery) on a road or track

Blunders

If a commander rolls a double 6 when giving an order this signifies that the unit has gone out of control in some fashion. We call this a **blunder**. A blunder means the order has failed, but it could also mean that the order has been misunderstood, spectacularly misinterpreted, or disobeyed in a surprising or fatal manner.

Players may choose to employ the blunder rule as described or not – we would not wish to impose it on the unwilling! We would suggest that anyone reading or playing for the first time ignores the rules for blunders until they have a good idea of how the game works. Indeed, players who abhor the lack of control that often results from blundered orders are entirely at liberty to ignore the following rule – no harm will be done!

The consequences are determined by making a test. Roll a dice and consult the blunder table below. The result is the unit's order for that turn and the affected unit must endeavour to obey as best it can. If a battalia has blundered the same result applies to all the units given the original order. A unit in skirmish order has no defined front, so for these purposes assume its front is the part of the unit closest to the enemy or the opposing player's table edge as seems most appropriate.

As mentioned before, should the army general roll a blunder something has gone disastrously wrong, not only is the blunder resolved in the same way as for any other commander, but also no more orders can be issued by other commanders in that turn.

Initiative Orders

Up to this point we have only dealt with orders issued by commanders. The initiative rule allows a unit to move just once without instruction from any commander.

Units that are within 6" of the enemy at the start of the Command part of their turn are allowed to use their initiative to move **instead** of receiving orders. This represents the leaders of these units taking matters into their own hands or acting according to some prearranged plan or signal. The important thing to remember is units that move using their initiative **cannot** also be given orders that turn – the two are mutually exclusive.

All units wishing to move using their initiative must do so **before** any orders are issued. Thus, during the Command part of his turn, a player always moves units using initiative first and then issues any orders for orther troops as required.

It does not matter whether a unit can theoretically see the enemy within 6" entitling it to an initiative move. For our purposes it is enough that there is an enemy within 6" for the unit to use its initiative. This rule can be overridden should you be playing an 'ambush' scenario and/or where troops are deliberately hidden until revealed through an attack or movement. All enemy units count for this purpose including artillery, baggage and civilians, but enemy commander models *do not* count. Commanders represent individuals or small groups whose presence otherwise goes unnoticed, and they are therefore ignored for purposes of triggering initiative.

Units using initiative are considered to be automatically in receipt of an order just like troops issued an order in the usual way, but they are limited to one move.

Note that units are not obliged to use initiative just because they are within 6" of the enemy. Units can always be issued orders instead. In the face of the enemy, whether it is better to take the certainty of a single initiative move, or roll for an order – potentially gaining one or two extra moves, but weighted against the prospect of ending up with none – is entirely at the discretion of the player.

Random Command Ratings

Within the army lists covered later the command levels of different types of battalia commander are set to reflect the strengths of each army. However, the overall command of an army was often 'hit and miss' to say the least. For this reason the commander's rating is random in the lists. This is derived by rolling a D6 and applying the result.

For example, a Thirty Years War Swedish army commander has a random command rating of 1-5=8, 6=9, so a D6 roll of a '4' would equate to a command rating of '8'.

Different armies have weightings to give a higher chance of better/worse ratings according to type.

Blunder Table

1 Rapid Retreat. The unit will attempt to make two full moves away from the closest enemy they can see. They may not charge other enemy who lie in their path – but must avoid them in so far as possible. If no enemy is in sight, they make full two moves towards their own rear or table edge as seems most appropriate.

2 Retreat. The unit will attempt to make one move away from the closest enemy they can see. They may not charge other enemy who lie in their path – but must avoid them as far as possible. If no enemy is in sight, they make a move towards their own rear or table edge as seems most appropriate.

3 Move left. The unit makes one full move to its left quarter. If an enemy unit presents itself, the unit can charge if the player wishes.

4 Move right. Thc unit makes one full move to its right quarter. If an enemy unit presents itself, the unit can charge if the player wishes.

5 Move Forward! The unit makes one full move to its front quarter. If an enemy unit presents itself, the unit can charge if the player wishes.

6 Charge! The unit will attempt to charge the closest enemy it can see. To find out how far the unit moves roll a dice:

    1-2: 1 move   **3-4**: 2 moves   **5-6**: 3 moves

If the unit cannot see any enemy then it must Move Forward one, two or three moves as described above.

1527 - Rome is sacked by mutinous Imperialist troops.

Gelb's Swedish regiment in action – musket move up in support of the pike.

Free Moves

As described in the preceding section, an initiative order is effectively a 'free move' because the unit always gets to move once if that option is chosen. But even if a unit fails its order roll, it may still be eligible for some other kinds of free move. The following free moves are exceptions to the normal ruling that units cannot move if an order is failed.

- A unit in *column* formation may move once if it fails its order.

- All *baggage, carriages, wagons* and such like will move once if they fail their order so long as they are on a road or track. In this instance wagons moving along a road are treated as if they are columns

  Some units have the special rule, *Superbly Drilled*. This entitles them to move once if an order is failed. See the section A Selection of Useful Rules on page 86 for more on this.

- *Shaken* units can move once if an order is failed or no order is given. However, such units are obliged to move directly away from the nearest enemy on a path that takes them no closer to other enemy units

Sometimes, several units will be included in the same order, some of which are able to make free moves as above, and some that are not. In these cases, units entitled to a free move can move once if the order is failed – other units cannot.

If an order is blundered all free moves are lost to units affected by the blunder. Resolve the result of the blunder in the usual way (see the Blunder rules).

The "Follow Me" Order

Every now and then a commander has to step up and take direct action (or just get stuck in). The basic notion is that the commander dispenses with the formality of issuing an order and instead gallops up to his men shouting "Follow me lads!" in a spirited fashion and then leads them off to glory.

A commander can attempt to give a follow me order to any unit from his battalia if it is within 12". In the case of the general, he can attempt to give a follow me order to any unit in the army, again as long as it is within 12".

Commanders can only give a follow me order to one unit – not to a group of units. The player nominates the commander, the unit and declares "Follow Me!"

A follow me order is given in the usual manner, make a dice test to determine if the order is given successfully.

If the result is a failure then the unit does not move, and the commander cannot move either. Maybe glory can wait a little longer.

If the result is a pass then the commander is moved to join the unit, and the unit together with the commander can be moved up to three moves in any manner the player wishes. It is not necessary for the player to state his intentions before moving, and the unit is free to charge or change formation if desired. The commander cannot move further that turn and he remains with the unit he has joined until he can move again in the following turn.

Note that some units have a free move as we have already explained. If a unit fails to receive a follow me order it will lose its free move too because it has no order to obey.

The Rally Order

This is in an important rule for all players when a unit falters in the face of casualties. A successful rally order enables a unit to remove one casualty marker and restore its fighting spirit. The rally order is similar to the follow me order in the way it works.

A commander can attempt to issue a 'rally' order to any unit from his own brigade if it is within 12" and has two or more casualties. The army general can attempt a rally order to any unit in the army so long as it is within 12" and has two or more casualties, and has not received a rally order this turn from its Battalia commander. A commander can only give a rally order to one unit – not a group of units. The player simply nominates the commander and the unit, and declares, 'Rally round me!'

Once a commander has issued a rally order he can give no further orders that turn whether successful or not. The rally order is always the last order a commander gives that turn.

A rally order is given in the usual manner; make a dice test to determine if the order is given successfully.

If the result is a failure then the unit does not move and the commander cannot move in that turn either.

If the order is successful then the commander is moved to join the unit and one casualty is removed from the unit's total. Neither the commander nor the unit can move further that turn – the commander remains with the unit that he has joined until he can move in the following turn. It is not possible to remove the last casualty from a unit in any circumstances. No matter how inspiring a commander, he can't completely dispel the effects of battle.

Note that some units have a free move as covered earlier; if a unit fails to receive a rally order it will also lose its free move as it has no order to obey – watch out for this!

Orders to Units in Combat

Units that are engaged in combat, whether fighting or supporting as described in the Hand-to-Hand Combat rules, cannot be given orders and cannot use their initiative. They must stay where they are whilst the combat continues. See the Hand-to-Hand Combat rules on page 58.

Orders to Off Table Units

There are two situations where units can be off the table but can still be given orders.

- If the units began the battle off table and are allowed to enter play during the game.

- When units are obliged to leave the table during the game for whatever reason.

Units that begin the game 'off table' are usually allowed to enter at a point designated by the umpire or the scenario, or agreed by the players before the game. Units that leave the table during play can re-enter at the same point they left the battle unless they are *shaken*, in which case they are gone for good and cannot return. In both cases a unit's first move will move it no more than 6" onto the table from the point of entry/re-entry, regardless of its formation or usual speed of movement.

Orders are given to units that are off table in the same way as to units already on the table, except that the distance between the commander and unit is always measured to the designated entry point on the table edge. If the commander is also off the table with his troops then he is assumed to be within 12" of his whole Battalia and no penalty is applied to his command rating for distance.

Where a Battalia or part of a Battalia is being ordered onto the battlefield all units are assumed to form a group, and a single order can therefore be given to all the units at once. Sometimes a battalia will be unable to deploy all of its units at the same time because it's impossible for them to fit in the space available: one example being a column of several units. In this case we simply place the lead unit on the table and declare that the rest of the units are deployed *following behind*. Those following behind can move straight onto the field at their full speed in subsequent turns so as to keep up with the rest of the battalia.

Disordered Units and Orders

There are various circumstances when a unit can become disordered during the game. This represents a temporary loss of formation and control. Disorder often follows from enemy shooting, from hand-to-hand fighting, and sometimes as a result of movement through other units or difficult terrain. Disordered units are always indicated with a suitable marker so their status is obvious to all. For more see Disorder on page 50.

Units that are disordered cannot be given orders in the Command part of the turn; however they can make one initiative move as per the rules in the *initiative moves* section although this move must be directly away from the unit that caused their disorder, or the closest enemy when disordered by other means.

Units otherwise entitled to a free move cannot make their free move if disordered.

Warbands & Compulsory Formation Changes

This rule only affects warbands – irregular militia and highlanders are notable examples of warband formations – and therefore won't apply to most armies. Warband units fight in a different way to usual units, their ability to move and change formation being limited in comparison.

If a warband leaves a road in column then it *must* reform into its default formation as its next move. The unit will do this regardless of the orders it is given and for this reason it is classed as a compulsory move. It is a good idea to bear this in mind when issuing orders!

A warband can be given an order to go into skirmish formation if it is the *only* way it can enter a particular type of terrain. This is the only situation where warbands can adopt skirmish formation. If such a unit leaves the area of terrain it automatically reforms into a warband as its next move.

Troops that Leave the Table

Units can leave the table in several circumstances, most commonly following a blunder or as a result of a *break test*. A unit is adjudged to have left the table once any models move over the edge of the tabletop or boundary of the playing area, or if a model would otherwise physically 'fall off the edge' having completed its move. Such units are removed at once, but can potentially return to the battle as already described opposite.

Note that a unit cannot return to the battlefield if it is *shaken* or if it belongs to a *broken Battalia*. Units become shaken once they have casualty markers equal to their *stamina* value as described later. Such units always retire from the battlefield for good once they have left the table. Battalias become broken once a proportion of their units are destroyed or deemed lost as described under Victory and Defeat (page 78).

Moving Units

A unit that successfully receives orders can potentially move up to three times in a single turn depending upon the result of the test when the orders were issued. The total distance a unit moves during the Command part of the turn therefore varies: for example, an infantry unit could potentially move 18", a standard cavalry unit 27".

The table below shows the standard move distances for units in inches. This is generally very straightforward: less mobile troops such as infantry and baggage move 6" at a time, faster troops such as cavalry and dragoons move 9", whilst light cavalry are allowed a move of 12".

Moving Units Table

Heavy and Siege Artillery, ...Immovable Hedgehog Formation

Manhandled medium artillery . . . . .3"

Infantry, Light artillery guns, ...6"
Limbered Artillery, Wagons, Baggage Train

Cavalry & Dragoons . . . . .9"

Light Cavalry . . . . .12"

Although the 16th and 17th centuries saw some major advances in the art of warfare, grand sweeping troop movements by highly mobile professional armies were still off in the far future. There are some notable exceptions to this rule, but the nature of Pike & Shotte lends itself to a more methodical approach to contact.

When a unit moves, the individual models or bases are free to move in any direction or orientation so long as the unit retains the same formation as a whole and no model moves further than the distance allowed (except where specifically permitted in the rules).

This enables a unit to wheel about, to reverse its facing, move to its right or left, move at an angle, go forwards or backwards, or make any comparable manoeuvre the player might wish. This rather free and easy method of moving is quite different to many sets of gaming rules and can take some getting used to – it is a 'no nonsense' method that gets the game moving at a good lick!

Proximity of Enemy

Our 'no nonsense' approach to the rules does have one caveat, and it's a major stipulation too. This is when movement is affected by the proximity of the enemy. This sounds like an obvious rule that most players will apply instinctively, but it's worth stating before we press on.

Once the enemy is within 12", the unit's ability to perform even the most basic manoeuvres is considered to be impaired – once close to the enemy, units must move roughly straight forward or straight back. There is to be no crazy crab shuffling of units sideways in the face of the enemy. In the course of warfare through the ages this would never happen (being more than a little bonkers) and we shall not permit our troops to do so either. We shall call this the *proximity* rule or 12" *rule*.

Once units are within 12" of any enemy units, all subsequent movement must be made entirely within their front or rear quarter. We have already covered front, rear and flank quarters – check back to page 28 if in doubt.

Moving Through Enemy Formations

Units are not allowed to move through opposing units, although they can move over opposing commanders freely. Commanders moved over in this way are obliged to move as described in the section on Commanders on page 84.

Moving Through Friendly Units

Units from the same side can move through each other where it is possible for the moving unit to completely clear the position of the unit(s) moved through. It does not matter whether it takes one, two or three moves to clear the position of friends, so long as their position is cleared once the unit has finished its movement. If it is not possible for a unit to clear a friend in this way then it may not move through.

Units cannot normally move through friends if they are engaged in hand-to-hand combat, but may do so if moving to join the engagement either as supports or by charging.

This interpenetration might sometimes represent literally moving through each other, but in practice it is a convention forced upon us out of the necessity to move one unit at a time. In reality the troops would be moving simultaneously, units wheeling and marching around each other with military precision.

Some unit types are very unwieldy, and can face penalties for moving through other units or having troops move through their formations unless precisely executed. Any heavy cavalry or pike armed infantry units that move through a unit suffering from *disorder*, have a disordered unit move through them, or have a friendly unit fall back through them due to a break test will themselves be subject to disorder on a dice roll of a 6.

1530 - The Knights of Malta are formed when the Knights Hospitaller are given Malta by Pope Clement VII.

Changing Formation

Formation changes must be stated when giving orders and it is necessary to do so even where a formation charge would be obligatory to fulfil an order. For example, a standard formed unit would have to form into skirmish order to enter a wood.

A formation change takes an entire move except in the case of skirmishers. In these cases a unit can change formation to or from skirmish order and then move counting this as a single move in all. However, these units are not allowed to change formation in this way and charge as a single move, their move must be a non-charge move. See Charge! on page 58 for more about charge moves.

A unit can only make one formation change in each command part of the turn. No matter how many moves a unit has, it can only make one formation change. For example, a musket unit with three moves could not adopt open order, move through a wood, and form a battle line all in the same turn.

Hedgehogs

Hedgehogs are essentially static defensive formations where non pike armed infantry units seek shelter in a pike block of the **same** battalia when threatened. Up to two units can converge with a pike unit and to do so they must be within 6" of that unit at the beginning of their move. A hedgehog cannot move and the only command it can be given is to change formation, that is to move the unit(s) seeking protection from the pike block element out of the formation. Units comprising a hedgehog cannot change to another formation and move further that turn. Regardless of the number of moves a hedgehog is allowed it can only change formation (release its protected units), and this it can only do if there are no enemy cavalry units within 6". Units successfully making a command roll to change formation to move out of a hedgehog formation move a maximum of 6" regardless of the margin of success.

Moving Limbered Artillery

There are a number of artillery pieces, classified as medium artillery that can be moved by horse limber and must be provided with separate horse drawn limbers to do so. These teams form part of the unit and are positioned behind and within 3" of the crew when the gun is deployed.

Limbered artillery take one whole move to either limber or to unlimber and deploy ready to fire. A limbered gun cannot move and fire in the same turn.

Any artillery piece that is classed as a Heavy or Siege Gun cannot be moved at all and is considered static for the purposes of this game.

Manhandling Artillery

Medium and Light artillery pieces can be manhandled by their crew if given an order to do so. If successful this enables any medium gun to make **one** move only regardless of the degree of success, i.e. 3". Light guns can move up to **two** moves i.e. 12"

As well as enabling the gun to be moved over short distances, manhandling also enables the crew to bring the gun to bear in a new direction should this be required.

Units Out of Formation

Any unit that has been formed into a line that is not straight – for example that has been formed behind the angle of a wall – must use a full move redressing its formation before it can move further. A proper battle line should be more or less straight, or gently curved if circumstances demand, but sometime the constraints of terrain make this impossible, in which case it can be bent around the obstruction with the provision that the unit must spend an additional move before it can move further.

In theory the same principle applies to other formations, but should be unlikely to occur with columns and never at all with units in skirmish order.

Moving Commanders

Each Battalia commander is allowed to move after he has completed issuing any orders he wishes and before the next Battalia commander begins to issue his. Commanders move automatically, so there is no need to issue them orders to move.

Apart from the "Follow Me" and rally orders covered earlier, a commander can join a unit simply by moving into contact with it with a declaration from the player that the model is joining that unit. Commanders who have already joined units do not normally move with them in the Command part of the turn (the obvious exception being the follow me order). However, commanders who have joined units do move with them in the shooting and combat parts of the turn where appropriate; for example, if a unit is obliged to *retire* as a result of enemy shooting.

Commanders are treated a little differently from units. As we shall see later, commanders are ignored when it comes to shooting, and in many other respects they are simply ignored by other units. Should commander models get in the way of units of troops from either side then they should be moved aside by their player as convenient, up to a full move if necessary. If commander models are obliged to move because of the movement of an enemy unit then they must join a friendly unit immediately – if unable to do so (out of a single commander move distance) the commander is deemed to have been killed or captured and is removed from play. A commander who has already joined a unit cannot be forced to move aside in this way – he is assumed to be part of the unit and can be arranged amongst its ranks.

Commander Move Distances	
Commanders on Foot .18"	
Commanders on Horseback . . . . .27"	

TERRAIN

To complete the rules for movement we must consider how terrain can affect the speed of troops or otherwise impede their progress. This is all fairly intuitive stuff. Troops moving through woods move more slowly than troops moving over open ground, watercourses of a substantial size present obstacles that must be crossed, and so on. The rules that follow have been devised to be both practical and flexible without being unnecessarily complicated. If you are reading through the rules for the first time no harm will be done if you skip this section – you can always come back to it later.

Woods

By woods we mean areas designated as being reasonably dense woodland or forest and covering an area that justifies representation on the tabletop. The boundaries of our miniature wood will need to be shown in some fashion. A usual method is to have the edges of the wood represented by borders of trees, with individual trees within the area to represent the tangled undergrowth within. In this way, models can still move inside the wood, but line of sight is limited and movement penalties clearly shown.

It is usual to assume that woodland can't be seen through or into by our troops, apart from those positioned along the edges who can see out and who can likewise be seen. We often allow for troops to lie in hiding at the edge of woods, in which case they remain unseen until they move or until the enemy approach within a specified distance, but such matters are up to the players or umpire to determine as part of the game scenario.

Infantry and cavalry in skirmish order, and commanders or other models representing individuals can move through woods. Other troops cannot move through woods at all. Troops able to move through woods do so at half pace (rounding up where necessary).

Players are at liberty to run roads or tracks through woods if they wish – in which case movement via road is treated as completely accessible if preferred. Make sure this is clear at the start of the game.

Rough Ground

This covers all manner of broken or difficult ground including scrub, marshes, heavily ploughed soil, steep or rocky slopes, areas of tumbled down buildings or ruins, and any other comparable terrain. Such areas need to be plainly identified, perhaps by arranging appropriate scenic features to mark a boundary – such as rocks, piles of rubble or patches of brambles.

Apart from infantry in skirmish order, cavalry in skirmish order, and commanders and other individuals, units moving over rough ground are restricted to a maximum of one move. A unit moving into rough ground completes its move and moves no further that turn, whilst a unit already in rough ground is limited to a maximum of one move. Cavalry and infantry in skirmish order can make up to three moves as usual.

As with woods, players are free to have roads or tracks cutting through rough ground if required, in which case movement will again be as normal.

Sir Hugh Mackay's regiment hold back the French.

Scots Lancers

Obstacles

By 'obstacle' we mean any linear barrier that might reasonably be assumed to slow down a unit's progress but which is not actually impassible. A battlefield might include any number of fences, ditches, boundary walls, streams, narrow rivers and such-like, and on the whole we simply treat these as decorative or use them to delineate the boundaries of rough ground, settlements or fortifications.

On occasions we will want to attach some significance to a dried up stream or riverbed, wall, or some such feature, in which case we have found the following rules useful.

Infantry in skirmish order, cavalry in skirmish order, and commanders or other individuals can cross linear obstacles without penalty to their movement.

All other units can cross an obstacle by giving up 3" of movement to do so. If a unit does not have 3" of movement remaining then it will halt in front of the obstacle without attempting to cross.

Pike block units can have real issues with obstacles; it was never easy getting an eighteen foot pole over a wall, never mind a whole regiment attempting to do so and stay in

formation. Any pike block unit that crosses an obstacle will become disordered on a roll of a 6. See the section on Disorder on page 50.

Alternative Rules for Obstacles

The rules in place for obstacles have been designed to allow the game to flow quickly without linear barriers interfering with progress across the battlefield too much. If you want such obstacles to more accurately effect the impact they would have on troops of our period you can use the following rules, although it will slow your games down more than somewhat.

When crossing obstacles, moving across rough ground or through woods, the following troops must roll to see if they become disordered:

• Pike armed troops become disordered on a 5 or 6

• Other block infantry become disordered on a 6

• All Horse units apart from Light Horse and Dragoons become disordered on a 6

If a unit wishes to charge an enemy behind an obstacle then the chargers must be close enough that they can reach their enemy with 3" distance to spare in order to cross the obstacle. If unable to do so the unit cannot charge – although it can move up to the obstacle ready to charge in its following turn. In situations like this it is best to leave a slight gap so no confusion arises over whether the units are engaged in combat.

Artillery, wagons and other wheeled vehicles are not permitted to cross obstacles other than at gates, fords, and other places of access.

Rivers

If a river is of such width that it can be crossed by infantry in a single move, then it is best treated as a linear obstacle. Otherwise rivers can be assumed to be either completely impassable, or fordable along their whole length, or crossable only at designated fording or bridging points.

Where a river is fordable it is necessary to represent the fording point and to decide whether the ford can be crossed by a unit in battle line formation or whether it will be necessary to form column. On the whole we find it best to assume fords are wide enough to allow a unit to cross without restricting its formation.

Any unit can cross a river at a bridge. The width of the bridge will naturally restrict the formation of the unit to a column – though for gaming purposes it is often easier to simply assume a unit can cross in any formation so long as

the front centre/leader model moves over the bridge itself. We leave this up to the players to arrange as convenient.

Buildings

It is usual to represent farmsteads, hamlets and even larger settlements such as villages by means of either a single large model building, or by a rough rectangular group of smaller buildings and yards covering a similar area. The total area must be sufficient to allow one infantry unit to be placed inside with a little room to spare, up to a maximum size of about 12x12". The size can be reduced or increased if you wish, to use units that are substantially smaller or larger than those described in our game. Larger settlements and fortifications can be represented by several such 'building blocks' placed together or next to each other, or designated as able to hold two, three or more units and modelled as correspondingly bigger.

At the start of the game it is a good idea to make sure the extent of all buildings is understood, as such areas are likely to play a major role in the game. The edges of a settlement can be partially defined by walls, barricades or similar barriers. In this case, it is important to state at the start of the game which features just mark the boundaries of the settlement and which are linear obstacles for the purpose of the game.

Only infantry and dismounted dragoons can enter or assault buildings, though artillery pieces can be included as part of a building's defences if set up at the start of the game. Aside

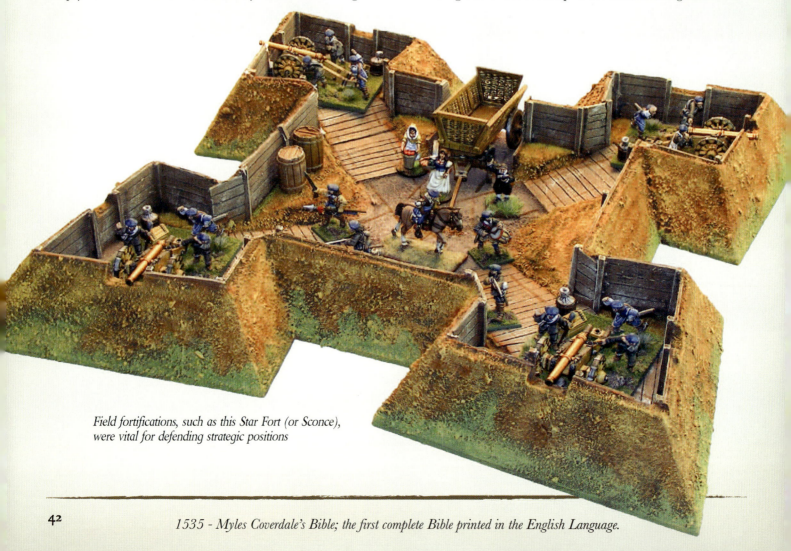

Field fortifications, such as this Star Fort (or Sconce), were vital for defending strategic positions

1535 - Myles Coverdale's Bible; the first complete Bible printed in the English Language.

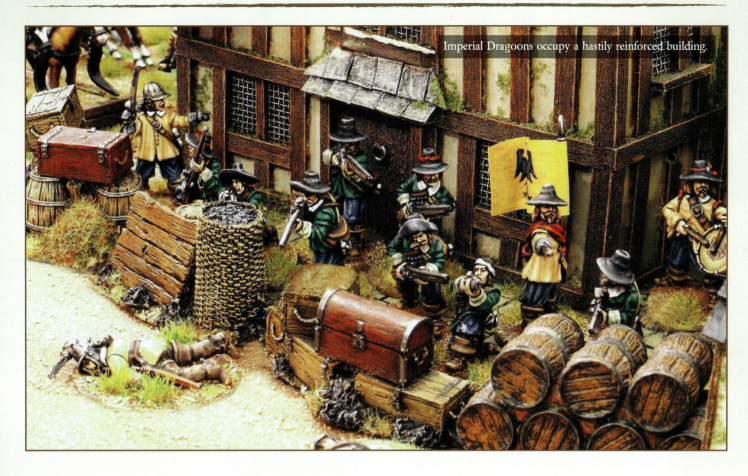

Imperial Dragoons occupy a hastily reinforced building.

from light artillery, artillery deployed in this way cannot be moved during the game. A single building block can hold a unit of infantry and up to one artillery unit with crew. We assume troops take up a position around the perimeter, fortifying the houses and outbuildings and so forth. For this reason troops occupying a building don't have a specific formation and artillery pieces can be mixed amongst troops to cover more than one direction if required.

To enter an unoccupied building a unit must move into touch with the perimeter and then expend one full move to move inside. Once a unit moves into a building its movement automatically ends for the player turn. A unit cannot move into a building and then continue moving, to emerge out of the other side. If a unit reaches the perimeter but does not have a move remaining then it cannot enter. Once the unit moves inside the models are arranged within the designated area as the player wishes. It doesn't matter that the unit has no formation or that the models become separated. The models simply serve to indicate the building is occupied. Don't worry if there isn't quite room for all the models, rather than risk damage by cramming figures together just leave some off the table

To leave a building one move is required. Begin by declaring the unit is leaving the building, and then measure a normal move from the edge of the building and place the unit's leader model on that spot. The rest of the unit is then arranged into a suitable formation around its leader. A unit leaving a building in this way can make up to three moves if issued orders, but the first move is always to leave the building and reform in the manner described. This first move **can** be a charge if enemy are within reach.

Note: units with pikes may move through buildings but cannot occupy them (the building counts as an obstacle).

We shall return to rules for fighting in and around buildings in the section on *Hand-to-Hand Combat*, page 58.

Impassable Terrain

Before the start of the game, players can agree to treat any terrain features as impassable. A scenario's background might sometimes specify that some terrain is impenetrable. Features that are typically represented in this way are very steep gullies or ravines, cliffs, and open water – unless you plan on staging an amphibious operation! Buildings can also be treated in this way if they are essentially decorative and you don't want troops to occupy them during a game. Perhaps they are filled with the local populace, cowering from the fighting that has suddenly broken out and engulfed their small town!

Embellishing the Tabletop

As you can see from the accompanying photographs, we do very much enjoy creating a scene for our warriors to fight over. A scatter of lone trees, winding tracks, low hedges, growing crops, farmyard carts, grazing cattle, locals going about their business – all help to create a sense of occasion. There is no need for such decorative features to hinder the movement of troops in any way. (Indeed, we do not consider it unreasonable for the odd tree, farmyard animal or curious spectator to wander a few inches as necessitated by military manoeuvres).

1536 - Francis I occupies the Duchy of Milan. Charles V invades northern Italy with 50,000 men.

43

Shooting

In the Pike & Shotte rules we are looking at two centuries of history where many advances in warfare were taking place, especially in the area of firepower. It is necessary to make provision for weapons as diverse as bows and arrows, early handguns and muskets as well as a plethora of artillery designs. Fortunately for us these technological differences, although considerable, are largely ones of degree rather than kind and therefore can be covered in a satisfactory manner for the sake of these rules.

What is Ranged Fire?

Throughout the 16th and 17th centuries, shooting took place over relatively short distances. The chances of hitting anything over 100 yards away was remote, although that certainly didn't stop troops from trying. By the end of the Pike & Shotte period, despite the many advances, this was still very much the case.

In our game, ranged fire represents all shooting at distances in the order of 10 yards or greater. Shots fired at closer distances are considered to be part of hand-to-hand fighting. For example, cavalry armed with pistols – which was most – whose tactics involved trotting up to the enemy, releasing volleys of fire as they approached, have a ranged attack capability, whilst Cavalry who closed rapidly on the enemy and released their shots immediately before impact have these attacks added to their combat capability instead.

When to Shoot

Units armed with ranged weapons with a shooting value can shoot in the Shooting portion of their side's turn. This is equally true of infantry, artillery and cavalry units, although dragoons are covered separately in the section on dragoon special rules on page 83. Units already engaged in hand-to-hand combat are not allowed to shoot – they are far too busy attempting to keep all their limbs in the appropriate place.

Some units that are charged in the enemy's turn are able to unleash defensive fire as their opponents close into hand-to-hand fighting. This is dealt with under the rules for Closing Fire on page 52.

Visibility

Before we proceed further it is necessary to introduce an important and fairly basic concept: namely a unit can only shoot at something it can see. So what do we mean by 'see' as our model warriors are but dumb metal or plastic and unhelpfully uncommunicative on such matters?

In principle, when we talk about what a unit can 'see', we mean something that a body of troops could clearly identify and take appropriate action against in real life. Whether individuals can actually see other individuals is not important in this sense. If a hill or wood lies between the attackers and their target then the target cannot be seen because the hill or

A musket unit with attached artillery piece defends an orchard.

wood is in the way. Where the enemy is obscured by topography, by buildings, or by the formations of other units, then it is not possible to see in the sense described. These matters do require some judgement within the rules, and players can hopefully be sanguine about such things.

For convenience of play a unit's ability to 'see' is always judged from the centre-front or leader model position. The unit sees what the leader sees, and if the leader cannot see the unit cannot see either. This gives another reason for giving our troops distinctive looking leaders.

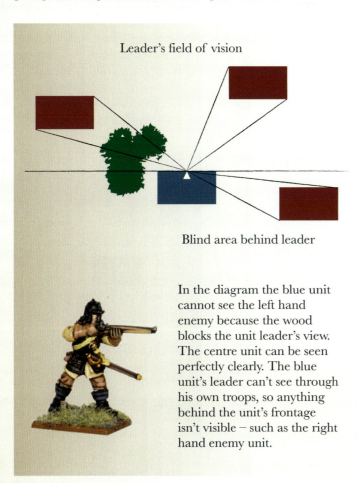

Leader's field of vision

Blind area behind leader

In the diagram the blue unit cannot see the left hand enemy because the wood blocks the unit leader's view. The centre unit can be seen perfectly clearly. The blue unit's leader can't see through his own troops, so anything behind the unit's frontage isn't visible – such as the right hand enemy unit.

At his stage it's worth pointing out that models representing the army's commanders and general can't be targeted by ranged attacks, and are simply ignored when it comes to deciding what a unit can see and any resultant shooting. Just imagine they are not there. Commanders represent a small number of mobile individuals who would largely go unnoticed amongst the hurly-burly of battle.

Note that aside from artillery (which will be considered in due course) units are not permitted to see through or over the heads of other formations even where some models might be on slopes or occupying ramparts overlooking others. This applies even if the intervening troops are in skirmish order and therefore have gaps within their formation. Any units in the way block line of sight.

Range

Below is a summary of the maximum tabletop ranges in inches for ranged weapons. Artillery will be covered in more depth later, but the ranges of main artillery types are included for comparative purposes.

RANGE	
Pistols and thrown weapons	6"
Arquebus, Carbines & Shortbows	12"
Muskets, Firelocks, Bows & Crossbows	18"
Light Artillery	24"
Medium Artillery	36"
Heavy & Siege Artillery	48"

Note that ranges have been fixed in convenient steps relative to each other, to the size of the tabletop, and to the movement capabilities of troops. Ranges don't accurately reflect actual ranges of different weapons – which would be far more extreme in reality. The ranges given have been found to provide the most satisfactory results for the purposes of these rules.

Measure Distance

The distance to the target is measured from the unit's centre-front or leader model to the closest visible part of the target unit. It doesn't matter whether other parts of the unit are in range or not, distance is always measured from the base edge of the leader model to the nearest base edge in the target unit. If the target is found to be within range then the whole unit is adjudged to be within range and can shoot.

Measuring range – measure from the leader model of the shooting unit to the closest model in the target – always measure distances base edge to base edge.

Units in skirmish order measure the range from the closest model to the closest part of the target. See Shooting and Skirmishers page 51.

Pick a Target

Generally speaking a unit always shoots at a single target. A typical target would be an enemy infantry, cavalry or artillery unit. As already noted, individual commander models can't be shot at and are always ignored when it comes to shooting. This doesn't mean they can't be harmed though – the perils of commanders are discussed in more detail later on.

Enemy units already engaged in hand-to-hand combat can't be targeted either. We assume that such troops become intermingled in melee making it impossible to pick out friend from foe. Such units are ignored when it comes to working out ranged attacks, excepting that they can in some cases block line-of-sight to other targets.

A unit can only shoot at a target to its front quarter. This can most easily be demonstrated by means of a diagram. Note that the range is measured from the leader model; the area covered by a unit's fire has the shape shown with a slightly longer range to the unit's centre.

A unit can engage an enemy to its front quarter and within range.

The uppermost blue and red units are fighting hand-to-hand combat and are considered 'intermixed' – the lower blue unit cannot therefore shoot at the red unit even though it is within sight and within range.

A unit is not entirely free to shoot at any old enemy unit that happens to lie to its front and within range. Where possible – with a few notable exceptions covered soon – a unit must shoot at the closest enemy unit in preference to a more distant one where several potential targets present themselves. If two units are equally close, the player can choose which to shoot at.

Here we have two enemy units within range and within sight – the blue unit must fire upon the closest.

Units that are Not Clear Targets

As already stated, troops must normally shoot at the closest enemy unit to their front that they can see. That said, there are a few exceptions. These exceptions cover situations where the enemy unit is 'not a clear target'. If the closest visible enemy does not present a clear target then it can be ignored in favour of the next closest unit that does present a clear target. It is harder to hit an enemy unit if it is not a clear target – more on that shortly.

The following units do not present clear targets:

- Units in skirmish formation
- All deployed artillery pieces
- Units that are only partly within the shooter's front quarter as shown
- Units that are only partly in sight as shown
- Units occupying buildings as shown
- Units that can only be seen through narrow gaps as shown

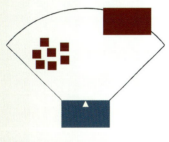

Here the closest target is a skirmishing unit which can therefore be ignored in favour of the more distant infantry unit. Skirmishers are not clear targets and can therefore be ignored in this way. Remember that a unit's leader cannot see right through a skirmishing unit's formation – the target must be clearly visible as in this example.

Often a target can only be seen through a gap between friendly units, terrain, units in combat, or enemy units that are being overlooked. It is silly to allow a unit with a frontage of, for example, 8" to shoot through a 1" gap, but where do we draw the line? Rather than relying on complicated graphs and charts, the following rule will cover such situations with the minimum of fuss. A gap of this kind must be at least 3" wide to shoot through. In addition, if the gap is not at least as wide as the shooting unit, then the target is not a clear target.

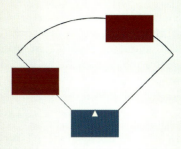

In this situation the closest enemy is partly outside the shooter's field of fire. If less than half the unit is within the shooter's front quarter it is not a clear target and can be ignored. The more distant unit is entirely to the unit's front quarter and can therefore be shot at – the fact that part of the unit is out of range does not matter – range is always measured to the closest part of a target.

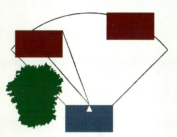

In this situation the closest enemy is partly behind a wood. If less than half the target is visible, the unit is not a clear target and can be ignored. In the example the target is not a clear target and can be ignored in favour of the more distant but fully visible target.

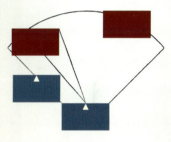

In this situation the closest enemy is partly behind a friendly unit and less than half is visible as a result. The target is therefore not a clear target and can be ignored in favour of the more distant but fully visible target.

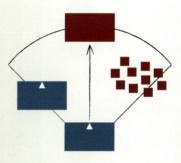

In this situation the blue unit can see its preferred target but must fire though a gap between a friend and an ignored enemy skirmisher. The gap must be at least 3" wide to shoot through. If the gap is less wide than the unit's own frontage, the enemy is not a clear target. Note that in this example the more distant target can't be shot at if it isn't a clear target because enemy skirmishers can only be ignored in favour of a clear target. This is an example of how skirmishers can be used to draw the fire of enemy units whilst more vulnerable formations advance behind them.

Shoot

Dice are rolled to work out the effects of a unit's shooting. The number of dice rolled equals the unit's shooting value with the following additions/subtractions.

UNIT SIZE MODIFIERS FOR SHOOTING	
Shooting Value	**Unit Size Modifiers**
+1 Dice	**Large Unit.** The attackers are a large unit.
-1 Dice	**Small Unit.** The attackers are a small unit.

Different formations that units are formed in will also impact their shooting value.

FORMATION MODIFIERS FOR SHOOTING	
Shooting Value	**Formation Modifiers**
None	**Column.** Units in column cannot make ranged attacks.
1 Dice	**Hedgehog.** Units with a shooting value that are in a hedgehog are limited to only one dice per unit.
1/face	**Buildings.** Units occupying buildings are limited to a maximum of one dice from any face up to their shooting value in total - see the rules for buildings.

Roll the appropriate amount of dice. Any dice scoring 4 or more indicate that the shooters have inflicted a hit on their target. So, three dice scoring 1, 5 and 6 = 2 hits; 4, 5 and 6 = 3 hits; 1, 3 and 3 = 0 hits.

In addition, if any dice score a 6, the target automatically becomes 'disordered'. Rules for disorder are covered later – for now it is worth noting that disordered units suffer penalties when moving, shooting, fighting and taking Break Tests.

In some situations it becomes easier or harder to hit. These situations are represented by adding or subtracting to the dice rolls as noted below. For example, if shooters are disordered they suffer from a -1 penalty and therefore require 5s or 6s to score a hit rather than 4s. Regardless of these modifiers, a 6 is always a hit and causes disorder, a 1 always misses. There is no such thing as an automatic hit or miss.

Morale Saves

Every unit has a Morale value as part of its fighting qualities. This value is a measure of a unit's ability to stand firm in the face of shooting or hand-to-hand fighting. It is both a measure of our troops' resolve as well as their physical protection. Standard values vary from 4+ (good), to 5+ (average), 6+ (poor) and 0 (heaven help us!).

To take a morale save a player rolls one dice for each hit inflicted on his unit. So, if a unit has suffered three hits the player rolls three dice, and so on. If a dice scores equal to or better than the unit's morale value then that hit is disregarded or 'saved'. Dice scoring less than the unit's morale value indicate that the hit is not saved and a casualty is inflicted. For this reason we commonly refer to morale checks as 'morale saves' or just as 'saves', i.e. the test is made to see if you can save your unit from taking casualties.

Casualties inflicted on a unit must be recorded, usually by means of a marker placed beside or behind the unit itself. See Casualties opposite.

For example: a unit has a morale save of 5+ and suffers three hits from enemy musket fire. Three dice are roiled scoring 4, 5 and 6. The roll of a 4 is a fail and the rolls of 5 and 6 are both successes, and as a result two hits are saved and one casualty inflicted.

There are some situations where we allow a modifier to the unit's morale save as noted on the table below. These modifiers allow for a greater chance of saving for units that have adopted defensive positions, but reduce the chance of saving for units that are in column and unprepared for combat. Artillery at the time may have been inaccurate but struck fear into the hearts of even the steeliest of veterans, and a single hit could cause havoc in the ranks. For this reason they have a significant effect on morale. Modifiers

'TO-HIT' MODIFIERS FOR SHOOTING	
Dice Roll	**Situation**
-1	**Attackers are shaken and/or disordered.** The shooters are either shaken, disordered, or both. These states are explained in due course and affect units in a number of ways.
-1	**Target is Not Clear, Skirmishing, or Artillery.** This applies if the target is not a clear target as already explained. This includes units in skirmish order and all fully deployed artillery pieces. Do not apply this penalty more than once, e.g. a half-visible skirmish unit is still -1 'to hit' and not -2.
+1	**Close Range/ Closing Fire.** If shooters are armed with firearms or artillery and the range to the target is 6" or less then the shot is considered to be at close range and it is easier to score hits. Closing fire is always given at close range and is covered later. This bonus is never added to the close range modifier, and is therefore never +2.

1541 - The Ottoman Turks seize the city of Buda, Hungary.

MORALE SAVE MODIFIERS

Dice Roll	Situation
+1	**Cover.** The unit is within woodland, behind hedgerows, low walls or barricades, or in other situations where it is felt it should rightly benefit from the physical protection and reassurance of cover. Add +1 to the morale value of such troops.
+2	**Buildings and Fortifications.** If a unit is occupying a building or is sheltering behind fortifications it benefits further from their cover. Add +2 to the morale value of such troops.
-1	**Column.** If a unit is shot at whilst in column it is unprepared for fighting and will quickly fall into disarray, to represent this deduct -1 from the score of each dice rolled.
-2	**Hit by Light or Medium Artillery.** If a unit is hit by light or medium artillery then deduct -2 from its morale value to represent both the penetrating power and demoralising effect of artillery fire. It really is rather scary stuff.
-3	**Hit by Heavy or Siege Artillery.** If a unit is hit by heavy or siege artillery then deduct -3 from its morale value to represent both the penetrating power and demoralising effect of artillery fire. Did we mention how scary artillery is?

are applied to the dice score rolled, but note that no penalty can reduce a save to worse than 6 if it started out as 6 or better, and no bonus can improve a save to better than 2+. In other words, a roll of 1 is a failed save regardless, and troops that start off with a save always save on at least a 6. Troops that have no morale save still benefit from positive modifiers: for example, with a +1 bonus a morale value of 0 becomes 6, with a +2 it becomes 5+, and so on.

If a unit is only partly within cover, consider what proportion of the unit is occupying cover relative to the shooter. If half or more of the target is behind cover then treat the whole unit as behind cover and apply the +1 modifier to all morale saves. If less than half the unit is behind cover then no bonus is permitted. When the issue is in doubt we normally err on the side of the player throwing the dice when it comes to making these calls, but players can adopt whatever convention they prefer when deciding such things.

Casualties

Casualties represent men killed or wounded as well as other factors that affect a unit's ability to fight, such as exhaustion, expenditure of munitions and loss of nerve. Casualties can be recorded in any fashion the players wish, but our preferred method is to use markers. For each casualty taken place a casualty marker beside or behind the unit. Models of dead or dying combatants make the most pleasing markers. We sometimes resort to using tokens as more practical where many casualties have been suffered. Card or plastic chits or similar tokens will do at a push, although our own preference is to avoid anything so mechanical. The advantage of using markers, rather than simply noting down how many casualties a unit has taken, is that its status is visually obvious to both players – which we consider to be an important element of play!

Shaken Units

When a unit has taken casualties equal to its stamina level it is *shaken*. In most cases a unit's stamina rating is 3, meaning that when a unit has taken three casualties it is shaken; although units will have higher or lower stamina values depending on their size and type. A unit can suffer more casualties than its stamina value, but these casualties are only recorded for the purposes of calculating Break Tests as explained later. For example, a unit that has suffered six casualties from enemy shooting is more likely to break and flee than a unit that has only suffered four casualties. Once these tests have been taken, all casualties in excess of the unit's stamina value are immediately discarded. Only casualty markers equal to the unit's stamina value are retained to indicate the unit remains shaken.

For example, a unit of Highlanders has already suffered one casualty from earlier shooting and is unfortunate to suffer a further two casualties from musket fire and then two more casualties from artillery. The unit has now suffered five casualties in total – four more casualty markers are therefore placed by the unit to go with the previous one for a total of five. As the unit has a stamina value of 3 it is shaken and because it has suffered further casualties a Break Test is required (as explained in the section on Break Tests and Shaken Units). Once this test has been taken, assuming the unit decides not to flee the battlefield, all casualties in excess of the unit's stamina are discarded – leaving three casualty markers in place to show that the unit is shaken.

Shaken units suffer various penalties and may even break and flee from the battle altogether in some situations. These various penalties are included throughout the rules, but are also summarised together with the rules for Break Tests on page 74.

1542 - The Battle of Solway Moss. In what was in reality a large skirmish, the English defeat the Scots.

49

Disorder

Disorder can occur as a result of shooting, close combat, or sometimes a test for moving through friendly units or terrain. Although this section concentrates on disorder from shooting, the effects felt by a disordered unit are the same for all causes.

If a shooter rolls one or more 6s when rolling for hits, the target automatically becomes *disordered*. Note that shooting can disorder a unit even if it passes all its morale saves and no actual casualties are caused.

Disordered units should be clearly indicated with a suitable marker, we generally use cotton wool which serves this purpose perfectly, but any marker readily distinguishable from a casualty token will do just fine.

A unit that becomes disordered remains so until the *end* of its following turn unless it is engaged in hand-to-hand combat; in which case the unit remains disordered until the end of the turn when it is no longer fighting.

When a unit is disordered, the following restrictions apply:

- A disordered unit cannot be given an order or be included in a battalia order. Note that a commander cannot give the unit a "Follow Me" or rally order. A commander who has joined a disordered unit can give other units orders as normal and can leave the disordered unit if he wishes.

- A disordered unit can act on initiative as already described in the section on command, but is limited to only being able to make this initiative directly away from the unit that disordered it. This represents the unit temporarily falling back under fire to regroup and reform.

- A disordered unit suffers a -1 dice roll penalty for shooting and combat as noted in the modifiers for each. This means it will normally be requiring a roll of 5+ to score a hit rather than 4+.

- A disordered unit suffers a -1 penalty on break tests as described in the Break Tests rules section. This means it is much more likely to break and flee from combat or following heavy casualties from shooting.

- A disordered cavalry unit cannot respond to a charge with a countercharge, evade, or turn-to-face move as described in the section on hand-to-hand combat.

As you can see, a disordered unit is unable to move in the Command part of its own turn – unless falling back under initiative – and it will shoot and fight with reduced effectiveness during the Shooting and Combat parts of the turn.

Take care to note that units fighting hand-to-hand combat *cannot* recover from disorder whilst they remain engaged. This means that such units continue to suffer the debilitating effects of disorder from turn to turn so long as the combat lasts.

There are two notable circumstances where a unit can overcome disorder before the command phase, effectively not suffering the penalties described above. These exceptions to disordered units are:

- 'Elite' special rule – as explained fully in the 'Selection of Useful Rules' page 87. Elite troops can overcome disorder on a successful dice roll at the start of the Command phase.

- Large Units. Any unit that is designated as being 'large' can elect to take a casualty marker rather than suffer from disorder; just as if they had failed a morale save. This represents the mass of troops relentlessly pressing on, back ranks pushing the hesitant front ranks forward. Units can never use this rule when shaken, nor can they elect to take a casualty that will make the unit reach its stamina level, thus making it shaken. Note, this rule can only be used by large units to overcome disorder from Shooting, not from disorder caused by other factors.

Further Rules for Shooting

Up to this point we have covered the basic process of shooting, including how to resolve hits, resolve casualties, and apply disorder where appropriate. As we have seen, units that have suffered casualties equal to their stamina become 'shaken', and shaken units that suffer further casualties are required to take a 'break test' that can cause them to break and run (this is covered in the separate section on *Break Tests*).

All the shooting rules from this point cover specific situations, formations, or different weaponry such as artillery. These mostly take the form of exceptions or additions to the rules already described.

Shooting at Hedgehog Formations

This represents the shooting unit firing upon a converged formation of more than one unit; the protective pike block and one or two units seeking protection. All hits on a hedgehog formation are allocated amongst the composite units by the defending player; this represents troops seeking shelter behind their comrades when they start to waver. In effect the player has the opportunity to spread the casualties across the formation, which can prove a very useful, if somewhat short term, defence.

The defending player cannot elect to allocate hits on shaken units unless all units within the formation are shaken; such units would naturally want to get out of harm's way.

Should any unit within a hedgehog formation suffer from disorder, the whole formation is considered disordered.

Columns

Units arranged into a column are not permitted to make ranged attacks. A column represents a unit prepared to move and manoeuvre rather than fight, so we do not permit such units to use ranged attacks. On the whole, columns are vulnerable formations and must be used with care; infantry in particular will suffer very badly if caught whilst unprepared to fight. Cavalry can be luckier, as they are allowed a broader range of response moves when charged as described in the rules for Hand-to-Hand Combat.

'Breaking and entering' Border Reivers style...

Shooting and Skirmishers

Skirmishers can direct their ranged attacks in any direction. Unlike formed units, which shoot to their front, skirmish order units can see and shoot all round. Range is therefore measured from the closest model in the unit to the closest part of the target, although this can be a different model each time the unit shoots. This makes skirmishers very flexible as it is usual to have a choice of targets depending on which model is the designated firing point.

Pick a model from the outside of the formation and calculate shooting from that position. Skirmishers can divide their shots between different targets if you wish – so long as closer targets are shot at first.

Units in skirmish order are obliged to target the nearest enemy they can see in a comparable way to other units. Alternatively, skirmishers can spread their fire against different targets if the player wishes. All shots must be allocated before rolling any dice to hit. In such cases we deem it appropriate to divide the unit's ranged attacks against all of its potential targets in what seems the most proportionate manner.

As skirmishers are so flexible it is possible to arrange units so that only a handful of the models in the unit are positioned to fire whilst the majority of the unit is plainly unable to do so, for example, if the unit is peeking out from behind a friendly unit. In these cases it is not sensible to allow the unit to shoot with full effect. We shall therefore reduce the number of dice rolled by such units in rough proportion to that part of the unit facing its foes. For example where a unit has three shots in total, this is reduced to one shot if no more than a third of the unit can reasonably fire, and two shots if no more than two-thirds are able to do so. Now this does require judgement, but the application of common sense should suffice.

Here we have a bunch of skirmishers hiding behind a friendly infantry unit in the most craven fashion. As we can see it is possible for the model at the end of the line to draw a bead on the enemy but most of his compatriots are out of sight because of the interposing unit or because they are in each other's way. This is a pretty clear case for a maximum one dice out of the usual three – and note that the shot will also count as 'not clear' as less than half the enemy unit is visible. In extreme examples of this sort of thing one might not expect the skirmishers to shoot at all. Such matters may be left to the conscience of the players (a minimum 'one sixth' of the unit in sight for one shot to count from a unit with three shots is recommend to those in search of moral guidance).

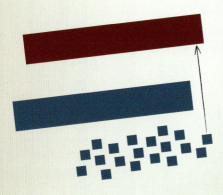

'Father' Tilly leads his men to war.

Enfiladed Targets

Only troops armed with firearms or artillery firing directly at a target can enfilade their enemy. Troops with bows, thrown weapons or crossbows cannot do this, and nor can cannons firing overhead at a target, or mortars who lob their shots upon their target. Units in skirmish formation also cannot shoot enfilading fire – their firepower is too scattered to take advantage of the situation.

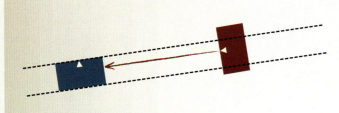

The red unit is clearly positioned so that the leader model lies within a corridor extended from the target's flank.

A target is deemed enfiladed if the shooters are shooting into the flank or side of any infantry or cavalry unit, and the shooter's leader model (centre front rank) lies within a corridor extended to the target's flank in such a way that a direct line extended from the leader strikes the target in the side. This mouthful is much more simply and satisfactorily explained by the diagram above.

A target is also enfiladed if it is in column and is shot at from the front or rear. This is simply the same situation turned through 90°.

Skirmish and hedgehog formations do not have flanks or a rear. These units cannot suffer enfilading fire from any direction.

When shooting at an enfiladed target the total number of dice rolled is doubled – so a unit with a shooting value of 2 will roll four dice. This can cause a certain amount of consternation in your opponent and, as such, is highly recommended.

Closing Fire

When an infantry unit armed with firearms is charged to its front it can deliver a volley of closing fire against the enemy as described below. Only an infantry unit in battle line or within a hedgehog can deliver closing fire in this way – skirmishers, warbands, and troops in column cannot deliver closing fire. We'll deal with cavalry, cannons and closing fire separately.

A unit shoots closing fire exactly as it shoots in the Shooting part of its own turn. Work this out once the charging unit has engaged its enemy and before moving any other units.

Chargers that suffer so many casualties from closing fire that they are *shaken* must take a break test counting the unit as engaged in combat (see Break Test, page 74). If the result of this test is to force the unit to retire then the chargers are moved back the requisite distance without hand-to-hand combat being fought. Should chargers be unfortunate enough to be broken by closing fire, the unit is removed altogether. In both these situations the charge has failed – the attack has faltered without the two sides actually making contact. If insufficient casualties are caused to merit a break test, or if a break test is passed, the opposing units become engaged and both sides take part in the following round of hand-to-hand combat (See Hand-to-hand Combat on page 58).

A unit can only shoot closing fire once during any turn. A unit that shoots closing fire and breaks its target, or forces its enemy to retire, can't shoot again if charged by a different enemy in the same turn.

If a charger attempts to engage more than one enemy unit at once, as can occasionally happen, then each unit can shoot closing fire at the charger, but the charger is not considered a clear target to either (and therefore -1 to hit).

Bear in mind that hits inflicted on chargers can potentially cause them to become disordered. This means they will suffer a combat penalty during subsequent rounds of hand-to-hand fighting.

Closing Fire with Cannons

Cannons can shoot closing fire in the same way as infantry – and will always shoot at their closest range using hailshot. There are times when cannons and infantry are placed together, and then chargers will find themselves facing closing fire from both infantry and cannons. This can be rather messy! When a charger takes closing fire from two or more units at the same time, it is always treated as a 'not clear' target and therefore -1 to hit. See comments under 'Closing Fire' above.

Closing Fire with Cavalry

A common tactic with some types of cavalry armed with pistols or carbines would be to receive a charge and deliver closing fire upon their enemies. This tactic was popular with cavalry units that would caracole (see section on Pike & Shotte tactics page 13) and there are cavalry units in many of the armies include in this book that must react in this way. The merits of such a tactic are a subject of controversy, but it does provide an interesting counterpoint to the cavalry units that will react to charges with a *Cavalry Countercharge* (page 66).

Traversing Targets

Sometimes you will get a situation where an enemy unit moves across the front of one of your 'Shotte' units, thus presenting a target as it passes. This is similar in concept to closing shots, except that it occurs as the enemy moves past your unit's front rather than into hand-to-hand combat with the shooter.

Shooting at a traversing target is a *response* to an enemy move and therefore usually takes place in the Command part of the opposing side's turn. It can also take place following combat during a *sweeping advance* as described on page 73.

A unit can shoot at an enemy traversing its front that crosses half or more of the shooter's frontage and which comes within 12" range as it does so, or within the unit's

maximum range for its weapons if this is less than 12". Range is measured from the centre-front or leader position in the usual way. This is shown on the diagrams below.

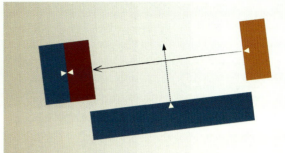

The red cavalry charge the blue cavalry – this is a perfectly good move but it takes the charging unit straight past the blue infantry. Because the red cavalry move across at least half the frontage of their unit, the infantry are allowed to shoot at them as they charge.

A unit can only shoot once during a turn in this way and if subsequently charged it cannot give closing fire. Basically, if the unit shoots as described then it has discharged its fire and won't be ready to shoot again until its own turn.

It can also happen that an enemy unit – often a small fast moving cavalry unit – traverses the front of a unit and moves right around its flank. This only tends to happen when units are isolated, but in situations like this we will allow the unit to shoot if the enemy moves within 12", moves across at least half of the unit's frontage, and moves out (or mostly out) of the firing unit's front quarter. In this case work out the firing as soon as the unit has moved, and apply casualties, disorder and any break test required at the end of the target's move.

These situations are also seen where you have infantry in buildings and hedgehog formations. In these cases units can shoot from the side of the building, or from the hedgehog, if it is traversed in the manner described above – although only with the number of shots allowed to a single facing of a building or a unit within a hedgehog (normally only one shot). See the separate rules on buildings and hedgehogs.

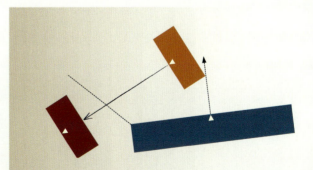

This diagram shows the position where the cavalry move across exactly half of the infantry unit's front – if the cavalry had started further to the left, it could have moved without attracting the infantry unit's fire.

Artillery

Although great technological and tactical advances were made throughout the 16th and 17th centuries to the 'Ordnance' of many armies, artillery was still unreliable at best throughout the period, if not downright dangerous to be around. Cannons did make an impressive noise however, and were useful psychological tools for any battlefield commander. Heavy and siege guns were rarely used to any great effect on the open field, but were vital to breaching fortified positions.

It is convenient that we deal with cannons before going on to describe the part played by mortars and petards. We will cover those shortly.

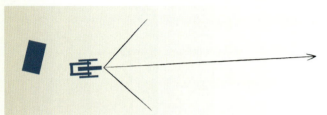

A gun can engage a target to its front – worked out from the position of the gun barrel.

As we have already discussed, each gun forms a unit together with its crew, limber and horses as appropriate. Shooting is therefore worked out for each gun at a time. A gun can only shoot when it is deployed for action. Cannon can shoot at a visible target from within a cone projecting 45° either side of the direction the gun itself is pointing in. This is shown in the diagram below.

Visibility and range is drawn from the barrel of the gun in the same way as from the centre-front rank of an infantry or cavalry unit except as noted below. If there is a visible target within half range or less, a gun must shoot at the closest target in the same way as described for infantry shooting. If there is no such visible target then the gun does not have to shoot at the closest target but can choose any visible unit as a target.

A cannon can shoot at a suitable target excepting enemy units engaged in combat and units visible through extremely narrow gaps as described on page 47. Even though a cannon may be free to choose any visible target, it still suffers the -1 'to hit' penalty against units that don't present a clear target (see page 47).

Unlike both foot and horse units, a cannon is allowed to shoot over the heads of other units when either gun or target lies on higher ground in such a way that a line of sight can be drawn over the heads of intervening formations. Bear in mind that a gun must still be able to 'see' even though there are troops in the way. This sort of thing can only be judged by crouching over the table to get a model's eye view of things. Regardless of whether a gun can see its target, it can only shoot over the heads of units that are both further than 6" from the gun *and* further than 6" from the target. This 6" gap represents dead ground – too close to either the gun or target to permit a clear shot.

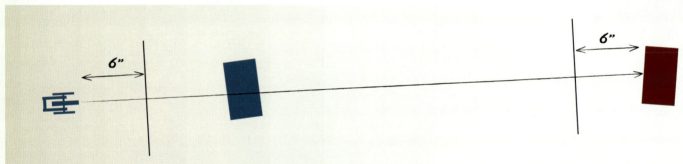

The gun is positioned on a hill facing the enemy unit on the right – a friendly unit lies between but the gun can 'see overhead' in this situation (a good squint over the gun barrel confirms that this is so!). The unit that is being fired over is not within 6" of either the gun or its target – so the shot is allowed.

And a side view of the same shot showing the gun's line of sight over the heads of the intervening unit.

The table below summarises maximum ranges for artillery.

MAXIMUM ARTILLERY RANGE TABLE	
Light guns: Falconet, Leather Gun, Frame Gun	24"
Medium Guns: Minion, Saker, Demi-Culverin	36"
Heavy & Siege guns: Culverin, Demi-Cannon, Cannon Royal, Mortar	48"

As with the weapons covered in the Shooting section, we have set our ranges in convenient steps relative to each other, to other weapons, to the movement of our troops, and the size of the tables we typically use. We would encourage players to adjust these to suit your own needs or to reflect any specific details that have a bearing on a particular conflict.

Shooting Cannons

To shoot a cannon the player rolls the number of dice equivalent to its shooting value. Most cannons have different shooting values at short, medium and long ranges. This is indicated as 3-2-1 where '3' is the value at short range, '2' is the value at medium range, and '1' is the value at long range.

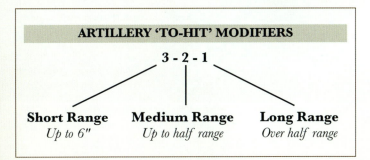

ARTILLERY 'TO-HIT' MODIFIERS

3 - 2 - 1

Short Range	**Medium Range**	**Long Range**
Up to 6"	*Up to half range*	*Over half range*

Short range is always 6" for all cannons. Long range is greater than half the weapon's maximum range. Medium range is greater than 6" and up to half maximum range.

Roll the appropriate number of dice for the weapon's range. Each dice that scores a 5 or more indicates a 'hit' on the target unit. Rolls of 6 also indicate that the target is disordered. All the usual 'to hit' modifiers apply together with the following additional modifiers:

ARTILLERY 'TO-HIT' MODIFIERS	
Dice Roll	**Situation**
+1	Artillery shooting at a unit in column or hedgehog formation.
-1	Artillery at long range (over half maximum range).
-1	Cannons shooting over other units as described earlier.

As with all shooting, regardless of adjustments, a roll of a 1 always misses and a roll of 6 hits and disorders the target.

As you can see, with modifiers, artillery is often only hitting the enemy on rolls of a 6, which represents the general inaccuracy of artillery at the time. However, as rolls of a 6 cause disorder this means that should your artillery hit they usually make an almighty mess of things. Remember to apply the morale modifiers listed earlier to those morale saves!

Artillery cannot move and shoot in the same turn; the only exceptions to this are 'light' artillery pieces which were designed to offer infantry support. Light guns can move twice and shoot.

Hailshot

The Shooting Value given for short range assumes that hailshot is being employed in these situations. Instead of a single cannonball the cannon would fire a hail of smaller metal balls, or nails, rocks, glass etc. This would be employed when the enemy closed in and would give a similar effect to a giant shotgun, devastating to tightly packed troops. It goes without saying that hailshot can never be fired overhead as it can only ever be used at short range.

Guns as Targets

If an artillery piece is shot at, the 'nearest point' of the unit is whatever portion of the gun model is nearest – crews, horses and limbers are ignored in this case. The reason for this is that artillery pieces are disproportionately huge compared to foot and cavalry regiment;, simply treat the gun model as though it were the whole unit.

'The great Guns began to play about eleven of the clock, and before six had made a breach in the middle of the wall, that ten men abreast might enter, and had beaten down one of the Towers which much disheartened the enemy'

Assault on Sherborne Castle in 1645

The Trouble with Big Guns

As already mentioned, artillery of this period was not the most reliable. They were largely cumbersome, required well trained men to operate well and often poorly supplied and maintained. To represent this any artillery pieces, including mortars, that roll two or more '1s' on their 'to hit' dice will be considered to be out of action for the rest of the battle. This represents many of the perils of an artillery commander; lack of ammunition, poor powder, travel damage etc. rather than a catastrophic explosion, but the effect is much the same for the commander on the day.

Note that at short range it is possible for a gun to roll two '1s' and a hit in the same turn. The hits (and any disorder caused) are still calculated in the usual way before the gun is put out of commission. At long range you obviously cannot roll two 1's as only a single dice is rolled to hit. This does not represent an increase in reliability of the gun, but a more measured approach on behalf of the crew to get things right when the enemy are far away. The chance of crew error is greatly increased as the enemy draw nearer, especially with inexperienced crews.

Guns that are put out of action in this way are not considered destroyed and should remain on the tabletop. Make sure you mark them in some way that is easy to see they can no longer fire – we generally turn them to face away from the enemy. They **do not** count as 'lost' for calculating broken battalias (see Victory and Defeat on page 78).

Petards

Although not ranged artillery, these rather devastating bombs are activated in the Shooting phase and fit here better than anywhere else. Petards are effectively artillery pieces moved into position by particularly brave – or foolish – souls and then detonated to breach fortifications.

Units armed with a petard can place it next to any wall, building or fortification in their move, and must finish their move with it. It will automatically detonate in the Shooting part of the next turn, giving them an opportunity to get out of harm's way – a good thing (unless the commander fails his command to move the petardiers in the next turn!). Upon explosion the petard will remove 3" of terrain from the board! In addition any units within 3" of the blast point will take three hits with a -3 to their morale save. Petards cannot be used to target enemy units specifically; they can only be placed against terrain pieces (which might well contain enemy units).

Units carrying a petard can move normally. There is no limit to the number of moves they can make, unlike other manhandled artillery.

Should a unit 'blunder' while carrying the device – a bad thing – it will explode prematurely, thus 'hoisting them on their own petard'. This will take place immediately after completing any movement the blunder initiates. The unfortunate unit carrying the petard and any other units within 3" of the ensuing explosion will take damage as outlined above.

Mortars

The maximum range for mortars and the impact on morale when they actually manage to hit their intended target have already been covered. Mortars are always classed as Heavy Siege artillery, and as such must be placed on the battlefield during set up and are then considered immoveable. The visibility, target choice and range calculation are also the same as cannons, however there are a few notable rules that apply to these weapons that need to be covered separately.

As mortars have a high trajectory when they fire they can always shoot over the heads of other troops, not being restricted in this regard as cannons are. Due to this trajectory of shot, all mortars have a minimum range of 6"; therefore they can never benefit from close range and can never use Closing Fire. It is worth noting that mortars can target units that cannot be 'seen' by other missile troops as they can shoot over intervening units. However mortars are restricted in the same way as other missile troops when it comes to shooting over hills, buildings, woods etc. That we will not allow; we can't have gunners magically picking out targets they would have no chance of viewing.

This is going to hurt! A mortar gives fire...

Mortars have an explosive shell and so inflict the same amount of damage regardless of range. These weapons therefore have 2 attacks at all ranges as shown on their profile.

Mortars only ever hit on a roll of a 6, so modifiers are something of a moot point. As usual, rolls to hit of a 6 will cause disorder – and not a little discomfort – and this reflects the general panic and confusion that being hit by a mortar shell will cause.

Note that Mortars will also be put out of commission on a roll of two '1s' just like all other artillery.

Roaring Meg

Roaring Meg was the largest mortar made during the English Civil Wars. Cast in 1646, it had a barrel diameter of 15.5" and was instrumental in bringing the siege of Goodrich Castle to an end. The Parliamentarian commander, Col. Birch, was so impressed with his monstrous gun he insisted on firing the final shots of the siege himself.

A tough nut to crack - a border fort on the Scottish border in the 16th century.

17th century matchlock and rest (also makes a very good club!) (Stallard collection)

Royalist dragoons on the hunt for supplies.

1551 - The Ottoman Turks and Barbary pirates invade the Mediterranean Island of Gozo, enslaving all inhabitants.

HAND-TO-HAND COMBAT

This section covers combat when it gets up close and personal. When we speak of combat we also tend to use the terms 'hand-to-hand' combat, 'close' combat and occasionally 'melee' combat to describe exactly the same thing. Whatever term falls to hand, it represents decisive man-to-man fighting with pike, swords, and such-like weaponry, and the exchange of pistol fire at point of impact.

How Combat Works

Units begin hand-to-hand fighting by charging their enemy in the Command part of the turn as described below. Once opposing units have moved into touch they are 'engaged in combat' and will exchange blows as described in the rules that follow. In addition to units that touch, we allow nearby units to lend their weight to the fight even though they are not 'engaged' as such – these are referred to as 'supports'. In this way we can represent the mass of mayhem and confusion that constitutes a general engagement at close quarters.

A combat engagement consists of opposing units that are fighting each other plus all those nearby units judged to be supporting. The role of supporting units is described in depth later. For now the important thing to remember is that both **fighting** and **supporting** units form part of the same combat engagement as shown in the example, right.

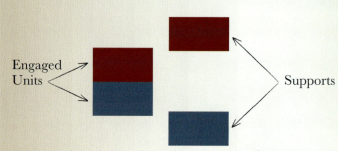

Engaged Units — Supports

The left hand units have moved into touch – they are 'engaged' in combat. The right hand units are not engaged but are close enough to offer support to their respective sides – these are referred to as 'supports' (nothing to do with the surgical variety!). We shall explain how units support in more detail later.

Charge!

A charge move is a move intended to bring a unit into contact with its enemy. Often a charging unit will make

Without the safety of a nearby pike block, these musketeers are in trouble...

1552 – War breaks out between France and Charles V's Holy Roman Empire.

several moves one after the other, but only the **final move** into touch is a charge move as defined here. This final move does not necessarily represent a headlong dash at the awaiting enemy; a charge can also represent a steady advance to a few paces followed by an exchange of fire. We therefore employ the term charge because it is useful, dramatic and memorable rather than because it is a literal description of how a unit moves.

State your Intention to Charge!

A player who wishes his unit to charge must be sure to say so when giving orders in the Command part of the turn. He should also indicate the target unit or units he intends to engage. A player who wishes a unit to charge using *initiative* must state his intention before moving. It is important to remember this because the enemy might be allowed to react and this can potentially affect the charger's own movement in some cases.

Remember, unless a unit is specifically instructed to charge it will not do so, although note that such an instruction can sometimes result from a blundered order or a special rule (see page 34 for *Blunders* and *A Selection of Useful Rules* section on page 86 for instances of compulsory charges.)

Before we proceed further, it is worth saying that a unit **can** be ordered to charge an enemy beyond its maximum reach as this saves excess measurement and gets troops moving in the right direction without any fuss. However, no advantage is ever allowed to a unit doing so. Any bonuses to command or free moves that otherwise apply to charging units are only taken into account where the enemy is within reach, i.e. where the charge is possible. This rule isn't intended to stop players taking a casual approach to such things, only to ensure that no unfair advantage is conferred, or embarrassment caused, when they do!

Troops Forbidden from Charging

In the following cases troops are forbidden from charging regardless of any instruction they are given to do so:

- **Units that are already engaged in combat.** Units that are already engaged in combat, whether fighting or supporting, cannot be given orders or use their initiative, and cannot charge in any circumstances even where the opportunity might present itself.

- **Disordered Units.** Units that are disordered cannot be given orders and can only retire on their initiative. Even where an exception applies permitting movement in some situations, disordered units cannot charge.

- **Shaken Units.** A unit that is shaken cannot charge. Shaken units are those that have suffered casualties equal to their Stamina value as described on page 77. Such units cannot initiate hand-to-hand fighting even if

they are normally obliged to charge by special rules described elsewhere.

- **Column.** Units that are in column formation cannot charge the enemy. Columns can be given an order to reform into a fighting formation and then charge, but cannot charge whilst they remain in a column.

- **Artillery.** Artillery units cannot charge in any circumstances.

- **Hedgehog:** Units in a hedgehog formation cannot charge. It is a static defensive formation and they won't initiate hand-to-hand combat even if normally obliged to charge by special rules described elsewhere.

- **Skirmish Order.** Units in skirmish order formation are not allowed to charge enemy infantry or cavalry unless these are also in skirmish order. There are some exceptions and further special cases as noted in 'Skirmishers and charges'.

Note that, contrary to the expectations of some students of battle, there is no rule that forbids infantry from charging cavalry; however, in most situations this will prove a very unwise move indeed. Cavalry units can easily avoid infantry by evading or counter charging (usually with devastating results for the infantry). We will come to the rules for counter charges and evades in a moment.

Measuring the Charge

In order to complete a charge home upon the enemy, the unit's leader must be able to see the enemy being charged – remember it is only the final move to contact that is counted as the charge move. We have already talked about what a unit can 'see' when discussing the rules for Shooting on page 47.

When beginning a charge, measure the distance from the centre of the front rank of the charging unit (ie, the 'leader model' position) to the closest part of the enemy formation. Measure base edge to base edge in exactly the same way as for shooting. If the unit's leader model is within one move of the enemy formation then the whole unit is allowed to charge. Some models will often end up moving further than their normal move allowance. This does not matter. Think of the unit quickening its pace as it approaches the enemy.

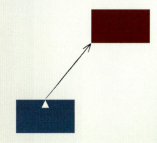

Measure the charge from the unit's leader model to the closest model in the enemy unit – base edge to base edge – this is exactly the same as measuring range for shooting.

Position the Charging Unit

In most cases opposing units will be facing each other and the charger will align against the front of the target in a straightforward manner. We'll consider situations where a unit charges against the flank or rear of an enemy in a moment. For now just imagine the charger is heading for the front of its target.

The charging unit must bring its own centre-front **and** as great a portion of both units' frontages into touch as possible). In most cases this will simply result in the units aligning against each other.

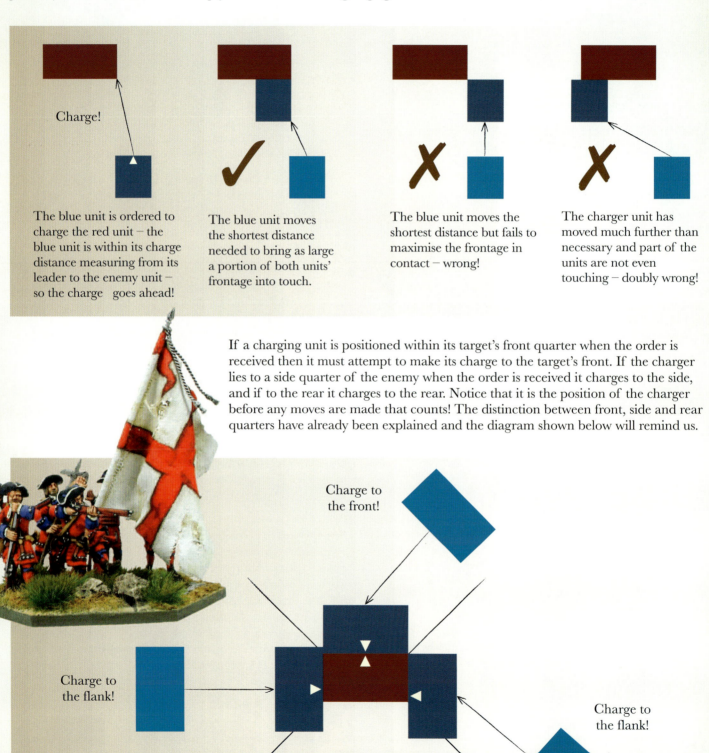

Charge!

The blue unit is ordered to charge the red unit – the blue unit is within its charge distance measuring from its leader to the enemy unit – so the charge goes ahead!

The blue unit moves the shortest distance needed to bring as large a portion of both units' frontage into touch.

The blue unit moves the shortest distance but fails to maximise the frontage in contact – wrong!

The charger unit has moved much further than necessary and part of the units are not even touching – doubly wrong!

If a charging unit is positioned within its target's front quarter when the order is received then it must attempt to make its charge to the target's front. If the charger lies to a side quarter of the enemy when the order is received it charges to the side, and if to the rear it charges to the rear. Notice that it is the position of the charger before any moves are made that counts! The distinction between front, side and rear quarters have already been explained and the diagram shown below will remind us.

Charge to the front!

Charge to the flank!

Charge to the flank!

Here are three examples of charges – a charge to the front and two charges to the flanks of a unit. Notice how in both cases the flank charges move the shortest distance to bring the greatest portion of both units into touch.

1554 - Queen Mary marries Prince Philip of Naples; England lurches back towards Catholicism.

There are times when a charger will not lie wholly within any quarter of the target unit, but will straddle two quarters: for example, the front and side. In such cases the charger counts as in the quarter occupied by its front-centre or leader position. This should be easy enough to decide, but if in doubt players must defer to the umpire or roll a dice for it.

There will be occasions when a unit begins its turn to the front of an enemy but is unable to charge to the front of the enemy formation because of the constraints of terrain or because the enemy unit is engaged to its front. In these cases a unit ordered to charge is not able to do so.

How Many Units Can Contact?

A unit can charge the enemy if there are no friendly units already fighting the same facing – be that front, flank or rear. If there are already friends fighting against the same facing, then the unit *cannot* charge unless there is room for at least half of the target unit's face to fight, *and* the charger can get at least half of his own frontage into touch. This is shown on the diagram, right.

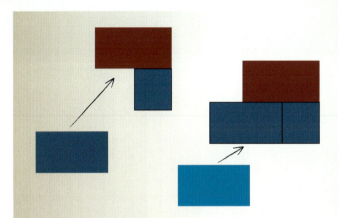

The larger blue unit wishes to charge an enemy already engaged by another blue unit. In this case there is at least half of the target's frontage exposed and at least half of the charger's frontage can be brought into contact – so the charge is allowed! In practice this is quite a rare occurrence but it can happen so we must make allowances.

Imperial regiment of foot

Units that can't charge due to insufficient room may still be able to lend their support to the combat. The role of the supporting unit is described on page 70. Most engagements take place between one unit on each side with other units lending support.

Charging More than One Unit at Once

In some situations enemy units will be positioned in such a way that charging one will automatically bring another into touch. The most common instance of this is where an artillery piece is accompanying infantry, cavalry or another artillery piece, although it can also occur amongst different size units.

In these cases the obligation for a charger to bring as large a portion of its frontage into touch as possible extends to all enemy units. This is best illustrated by the examples below.

Adjacent units are drawn into an engagement if the charger covers *at least half* of their facing – bearing in mind that chargers must maximize their contact as described earlier. When a charger covers at least half the facing of an adjacent unit then the adjacent unit fights in the ensuing combat and can deliver closing fire or make any permitted response to the charge where able to do so. If less than half the adjacent unit's facing is covered by the charge then the unit is not engaged, does *not* fight in the ensuing combat round and cannot deliver closing fire or make any other response to the charge. Where a unit is touched but does not become

engaged, it is a good idea to move it back slightly to show this – about 1" should suffice to make the situation clear. Such a unit is still eligible to provide support during the combat in the usual manner, but it is not engaged and won't fight.

It is worth pointing out that we take a fairly lax attitude to the exact number of models in our units, and the widths of different units do therefore tend to vary within certain limits. Where this is the case it is important not to confer an unintended advantage when it comes to two-on-one engagements simply because of a unit's width. Likewise players are encouraged to take an easy going approach as far as exact alignments of units are concerned.

One must remember that this is an entertainment amongst peers, and as such does not lend itself to pettiness regarding the exactitude of a unit's position to the fraction of an inch. Such things are not worth sullying one's reputation over and where doubt arises it is always best to be generous.

Charging Units and Support Units

It is important to note that orders to charge are different to orders to support. The benefits of support units in combat are covered later, but are an important aspect to the game. If a battalia order is given to charge (or multiple units are ordered to charge) only units that can engage the enemy will be affected by such an order. To move supporting units into place a separate order is needed.

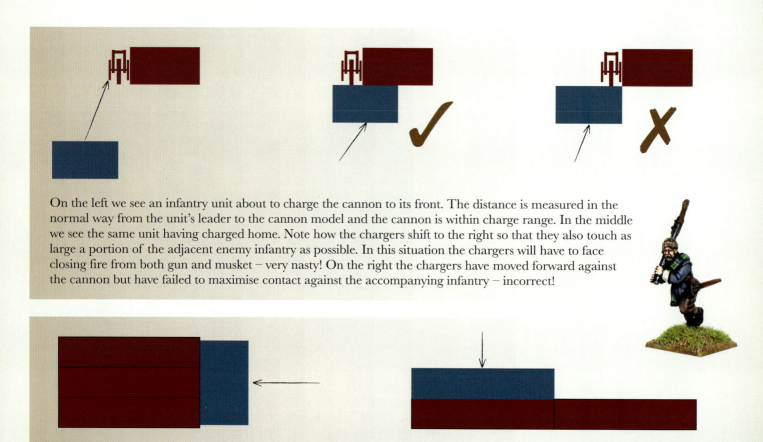

On the left we see an infantry unit about to charge the cannon to its front. The distance is measured in the normal way from the unit's leader to the cannon model and the cannon is within charge range. In the middle we see the same unit having charged home. Note how the chargers shift to the right so that they also touch as large a portion of the adjacent enemy infantry as possible. In this situation the chargers will have to face closing fire from both gun and musket – very nasty! On the right the chargers have moved forward against the cannon but have failed to maximise contact against the accompanying infantry – incorrect!

Here are two situations where chargers touch adjacent enemy when they charge. Left – the blue unit charges the middle of three enemy units arranged one behind the other, contacting all three enemy at once. Right – in this case the chargers are the same size as their enemy and therefore cannot avoid touching the adjacent unit corner-to-corner. However, the adjacent will not be engaged as less than half its facing is in contact but it is ideally placed to support the combat.

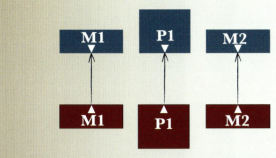

A Battalia order is given to charge. In this case, all the units must engage an enemy unit where possible. Be careful when issuing Battalia orders to charge that your cavalry don't get thrown against pikemen by mistake.

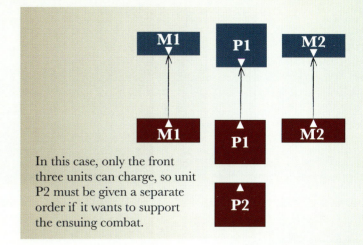

In this case, only the front three units can charge, so unit P2 must be given a separate order if it wants to support the ensuing combat.

Skirmishers and Charges

As we have already covered, units that are skirmishing *cannot* normally charge units in a battle line, pike blocks, warbands or hedgehog formation. However, there are some exceptions that we will deal with here.

- Skirmishers can charge units occupying buildings, artillery, units in column and other units in skirmish formation

- Skirmishers *cannot* charge a permissible enemy if they would be obliged to also charge an adjacent enemy that they are not allowed to charge. For example, they cannot charge a gun if a unit of line infantry is adjacent and would become engaged as a result of the charge.

- Skirmishers *can* charge an enemy they are not normally allowed to charge if that enemy is already engaged in combat.

- Skirmishers *can* charge an enemy they are not normally allowed to charge if that enemy is already shaken or disordered. (See sections on shaken and disordered troops on pages 77 and 50.)

Most charges by units in skirmish order will therefore be against other units in skirmish order. The rules that follow explain how to move such units into combat. The same method is used whether open skirmishing units charge or are charged.

When a unit in skirmish order charges, pick the closest model to the intended target and measure the charge from that model. It doesn't matter which direction the model is facing in as troops in open order can see all round. As skirmishing units can sometimes be quite dispersed, a charge may result in some models moving considerably further than others. We feel this is perfectly acceptable for troops unencumbered by a rigid formation and moving as individuals.

When either charging or being charged, skirmishers are brought into contact with their opponents in as satisfying a manner as possible. This is best achieved using the method shown below for an open order unit charging another; however, the same method also works if only one unit is in open order. Begin by moving the chargers up against the opposing models as shown in the diagram. The normal rule that obliges open order troops to maintain a distance between the models is waived for the duration of hand-to-hand combat, this results in the units closing ranks and forming tighter bodies.

Combat between units of skirmishers can get a bit messy. If other units are to become involved the players may be called upon to judge where a unit's flank lies, so it helps to think of the combat as taking place between two units in a rough line. A useful tip is to draw a line between the models on the extreme edges of the formation, ignoring those between, but common sense must prevail and we leave it to players to make whatever arrangement they feel best fits the circumstances.

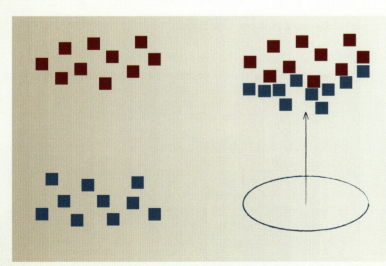

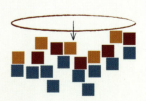

Combat between skirmishers is not that common, but this shows the best method of arranging the lines into an engagement. On the left the blue unit is shown before it charges forwards – notice how the models are kept within the width of the enemy's formation in the middle diagram. On the right the red unit is brought into a rough line by moving models directly forward.

Parliamentarian Ironsides

Charge Responses

Depending upon the situation, a unit that has been charged can opt to make **one** of the responses listed below. Only units that are not already engaged can respond in this way. Units that are already engaged will always 'stand'. In the case of skirmishers, they will automatically close ranks ready to fight as described in the previous section unless they decide to evade or countercharge as described below.

Here are the charge responses open to our troops:

- **Stand:** This is the default response and sometimes the only option available. The unit remains where it is. In the case of a unit in skirmish order it will close up its ranks as already described.

- **Closing Fire:** An artillery piece or an appropriately armed infantry or cavalry unit that is charged to its front can respond with closing fire as explained in the Shooting section.

- **Evade:** Cavalry units that have been charged by infantry can choose to avoid combat by evading. Infantry skirmishers charged by non-skirmishing infantry, or cavalry skirmishers charged by non-skirmishing cavalry, can also choose to evade. This is all explained under 'Evades' on page 66.

- **Fire and Evade:** Some troops have the special rule that allows them to shoot and then evade. To do so they must pass a Command Test based on their battalia commander's command level. If successful they shoot with closing fire and then evade. If the command test is failed they can only 'Stand' as explained above and lose the option of closing fire.

- **Hedgehog:** Non pike armed infantry troops that are charged can elect to 'hedgehog' with any pike block from the same battalia within 6". For full details see the section 'Hedgehog as a Charge Reaction' below.

- **Countercharge.** A cavalry unit that has been charged to its front can elect to countercharge assuming it would otherwise be allowed to charge the enemy concerned, and also assuming it does not have a special rule preventing it from counter charging. This is explained under Countercharge on page 66.

- **Turn to Face.** A cavalry unit or pike block formation that is charged to the flank or rear can turn on the spot to face the charging enemy. This is explained under Turn to Face below.

1557 - The Battle of St. Quentin, the French are defeated by the Spanish.

Turn to Face

A cavalry unit can turn on the spot to face a charging enemy unit regardless of whether the enemy is charging the front, side, or rear of the formation, assuming the unit is free to move in the fashion described. This allows a cavalry unit to present its front to an attacker and reflects the natural mobility of cavalry formations compared to closely packed infantry.

Pike and other infantry block formations can also turn to face a charging enemy in the same way. This obviously does not represent any natural mobility on behalf of the troops, but rather the formation's ability to present a solid wall to a new direction very quickly, the product of hours of training and drill.

There must be room for the unit to turn to face its foe – if there is not room for it to do so then it cannot move. Similarly if the unit is disordered it is not normally allowed to move and therefore cannot react by turning to face.

Bear in mind that a unit that turns to face one enemy may well present a flank to another!

Hedgehog as a Charge Reaction

Non pike armed infantry troops that are charged can elect to 'hedgehog' with any pike block from the **same** battalia. The pike block formation needs to be within 6" of the unit, measured from the unit's leader model. A maximum of two units can seek shelter in any pike block at any one time. If the only eligible pike block already has two other units converged with it, forming a complete hedgehog, further units cannot join and must take their chances with a different charge reaction – such as stand or closing fire.

A unit cannot form a hedgehog formation with a pike block that is engaged in combat or disordered.

In order to hedgehog a unit must pass a Command Test based on their battalia commander's command level. If successful they reach the sanctuary of the pike block and form a hedgehog with it. If the command test is failed they can only 'Stand' as explained above and lose the option of closing fire – this outcome is generally met with some colourful language. Should the hedgehog move be successful, the charging unit has a choice to continue its charge into the combined units of the hedgehog or – more sensibly – to pull up 6" short.

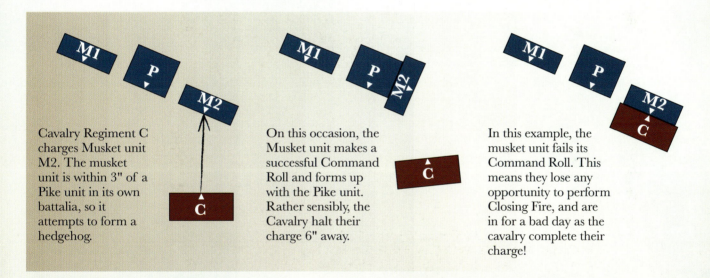

Cavalry Regiment C charges Musket unit M2. The musket unit is within 3" of a Pike unit in its own battalia, so it attempts to form a hedgehog.

On this occasion, the Musket unit makes a successful Command Roll and forms up with the Pike unit. Rather sensibly, the Cavalry halt their charge 6" away.

In this example, the musket unit fails its Command Roll. This means they lose any opportunity to perform Closing Fire, and are in for a bad day as the cavalry complete their charge!

Hampden's Greencoats come under pressure. Both wings of musket have successfully formed a hedgehog as a charge reaction from enemy cavalry. Both Royalist cavalry units have wisely chosen to rein in their attack.

Evades

As noted previously, some units can respond to a charging enemy by evading. Evading units move away from their enemy thereby avoiding hand-to-hand fighting. Units can evade whichever direction they are charged from, front, side or rear. However, units cannot evade if they are disordered.

To work out the evade move begin by moving the charging unit in the usual way. The opposing player then declares his unit is evading. The evading unit is retired one full move directly away from the charging unit. The unit that has charged remains where it is and its movement ends for the turn regardless of its orders.

Evading units retire one move exactly as described under Break Tests and are treated in all respects like units retiring from combat. See the Break Tests rules on page 74 for a description of how this works.

A cavalry unit in column *can* evade if charged by infantry. If it is a skirmish unit it will automatically change to skirmish order. Such a unit is automatically *disordered* once it has moved. In effect the evading unit has made two moves: a move and a formation change. As with units that retire twice from combat it therefore becomes disordered as a result (see *Combat Results* on page 71).

A unit can only evade once per turn, this includes units that have used the 'Fire & Evade' special rule.

The Cavalry Countercharge

A cavalry unit that is charged to its front by another unit of any kind can respond with a countercharge. Counterchargers must be of a type and status normally allowed to charge the enemy bearing down upon them. For example, units that are already disordered or shaken are not

"You might feel a little prick". Doctor's surgery open for business. South-west England 1643.

1559 - The Peace of Cateau Cambresis, France makes peace with England and Spain.

allowed to countercharge, and units in skirmish order cannot countercharge formed units. Skirmish order units can countercharge other skirmishing units assuming they are otherwise able to do so.

When a countercharge has been declared, both the chargers' and counterchargers' move simultaneously. Establish a point equidistant between them and move both units so they contact at that position. Both the charger and countercharger are treated as having charged and both units receive all the combat bonuses as if charging.

If a cavalry unit countercharges against charging infantry then the infantry are automatically disordered and receive no bonuses for charging. In reality, no infantry unit in control of its faculties would contemplate engaging a cavalry unit in hand-to-hand combat unless the cavalry were in serious trouble already. We feel that this rule offers a serious enough disincentive for such madness.

Cavalry Charges against Pike

No right minded cavalry commander would contemplate ordering a charge into a fully formed and ordered unit of pikes. Fortunately, history is full of people not of the right mind, and such things did happen – mostly unsuccessfully it must be said.

If a cavalry unit charges an infantry unit armed with pikes that is not already engaged in combat or disordered, it will receive **no** bonuses for charging or any special rules that unit could normally employ on a charge (including weapon bonuses). In addition, the pike unit will receive **double** its normal combat dice. Ouch!

Should the pike unit be disordered or already in combat then the cavalry charge can be completed as normal, with all the associated bonuses and the pike unit will fight with its usual combat value.

Cavalry charges into formed pike formations really should only be a last resort, but could be a glorious affair for the particularly fortunate.

Note that should a pike unit decide to charge cavalry, then it is perfectly acceptable to countercharge if applicable as the infantry unit will become automatically disordered – see The Cavalry Countercharge section previous – and as such be **vulnerable**.

Combat Engagements

A combat engagement describes any situation where one or more opposing units are fighting each other. Most engagements are fought between one unit on each side. Some engagements can include several units on one or both sides either because of incidental contacts or because units are fighting to front, flanks and rear at the same time. All units that are interlinked by enemy units they are fighting are part of the same engagement.

Units already engaged in combat cannot move further except by the result of a combat as described in the Combat

Results section. Nor can they shoot. They are committed to the fight and must stick it out from one turn to the next until one side retires or breaks.

During the Combat part of each side's turn, each engagement is fought in its entirety, one at a time. It is possible that there will be several separate engagements to work out. The player whose turn it is decides the order in which such engagements are fought.

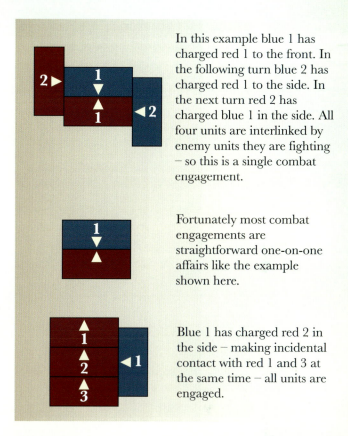

In this example blue 1 has charged red 1 to the front. In the following turn blue 2 has charged red 1 to the side. In the next turn red 2 has charged blue 1 in the side. All four units are interlinked by enemy units they are fighting – so this is a single combat engagement.

Fortunately most combat engagements are straightforward one-on-one affairs like the example shown here.

Blue 1 has charged red 2 in the side – making incidental contact with red 1 and 3 at the same time – all units are engaged.

Fighting Combat

Regardless of which side's turn it is, every unit engaged in combat takes part every turn. All units that are engaged in combat fight and all units that are supporting contribute as supports. Because combat happens every turn, we often refer to combat in terms of 'rounds'. So, in Blue's turn fight a round of combat, in Red's turn fight a round of combat, then in Blue's turn another round of combat, and so on until the engagement is over.

During each round it is usual to work out one engagement in its entirety, then another, and so on until all engagements on the tabletop have been fought. So, if opposing cavalry are fighting each other on the western side of the table whilst two groups of skirmishers are engaged on the eastern side, it would be usual to pick one engagement (say the cavalry) and work that out completely, including any results and break tests, before turning to the skirmisher battle and resolving that in the same way. The player whose turn it is can decide the order in which to tackle engagements. Note that this can be quite an advantage as units victorious in one engagement can potentially move into or influence another.

Attacks

In reality units in hand-to-hand combat obviously strike at the same time; however, for the sake of our game it is convenient to work out all the attacks from one side and then all the attacks from the other side. It doesn't strictly matter which side strikes first as all units fight with the status they had at the start of the combat round. We usually allow the player who charged or who is winning the fight to strike first, but this is by no means essential.

Combat attacks are worked out in the same way as described for shooting attacks. The number of dice rolled equals the unit's Hand-to-Hand combat value (henceforth referred to as simply 'combat value'). Roll a dice for each attack and establish the number of hits inflicted on the enemy, the enemy makes morale saves if he has them, and any hits that are not saved become casualties recorded against the unit's stamina value.

If the unit is a small or large unit by the standards already discussed, then the following modifiers apply. Where a unit's combat value is 6, units roll six dice if they are standard sized, eight if they are large, four if small and one dice if tiny. These adjustments are usually made to the basic Fighting Qualities values (or stat line) and are included in the example stats for appropriately sized units throughout this book.

UNIT SIZE MODIFIERS FOR HAND-TO-HAND COMBAT

Combat Value	Formation Modifiers
+2 Dice	**Large Unit.** The attackers are a large unit.
-2 Dice	**Small Unit.** The attackers are a small unit.

We also make a few allowances for units in specific formations and situations as follows.

FORMATION MODIFIERS FOR HAND-TO-HAND COMBAT

Combat Value	Formation Modifiers
1 Dice	**Column.** Units in column have a combat value of one dice regardless of their size.
2 Dice per Face	**Buildings.** Units occupying buildings are limited to two dice from any face up to a maximum equal to its Hand-to-Hand value - see the rules for buildings page 82.
Total of all units' combat values	**Hedgehog.** A hedgehog formation combines all the component units' Hand-to-Hand values.

To make your attacks roll the appropriate number of dice. Any dice scoring 4, 5 or 6 indicate that the attackers have inflicted a hit on their target. For example, six dice scoring 1, 3, 3, 4, 5 and 6 = 3 hits.

In some situations it becomes easier or harder to score a hit. These situations are taken into account by adding or subtracting from the dice rolls as noted below. For example, if a unit is charging it is considered more effective and so a +1 bonus is added to the chance of scoring a hit – so dice rolls of 3, 4, 5 or 6 will hit.

Regardless of these modifiers a dice roll of a 1 is always a miss and a dice roll of a 6 is always a hit. There is no such thing as an automatic hit or miss.

1561 - 'The Red Sagums', Shane O'Neill scatters an English rearguard in a bloody encounter in Monaghan.

'TO HIT' DICE ROLL MODIFIERS IN HAND-TO-HAND COMBAT

Dice Score	Situation
+1	**Charging.** If the unit has charged or countercharged into combat the bonus applies in the first round of fighting. Charging units will therefore usually hit their enemy on the roll of a 3+ rather than a roll of 4+.
+1	**Winning.** If the unit fought and won the previous round of the same combat engagement then this bonus applies during the following round of fighting. As with chargers these units will usually score hits on a roll of 3+.
-1	**Combatants are Shaken and/or disordered.** This applies if the unit is either shaken, disordered, or both. Essentially the same as we have described in shooting.
-1	**Skirmish Order.** This applies if the unit is in skirmish formation. Such units prefer to skirmish rather than get stuck in and will generally require a 5+ to score hits rather than the usual 4+.
-1/face	**Engaged in the Flank/Rear.** This applies to all of a unit's attacks if it is engaged to either flank or to the rear, including any attacks made to its front.

A unit normally fights to its front, but if attacked in the side or rear, or when it is attacked from several directions at once, then its own attacks are distributed as noted below. Where the player has a choice, it is necessary to declare where all the attacks will be made before rolling any dice – otherwise confusion will surely reign!

At least half of a unit's attacks must always be allocated to its front if it is engaged to the front. If engaged to the front by more than one unit then attacks must be divided as equally as possible amongst them. Whatever the situation, a unit cannot allocate more than half of its attacks against either flank or rear.

For example, a unit has seven attacks and is attacked to the front and a flank. It could make three attacks against the flank as this is the most it can allocate to a flank, whilst it is obliged to make at least four attacks to its front as any fewer will be less than half.

The Hedgehog in Hand-to-Hand Combat

As we have already covered, a hedgehog formation is a convergence of a pike unit and one or two other (usually musket) units from the same battalia. Whilst in the hedgehog formation these units fight as one body, the musket retiring behind a defensive wall of pikes. Hedgehogs have no rear or flanks and all attacks are deemed to be made from the front. They cannot receive support from any other units due to them not having flanks or rear to support.

Hedgehog formations fight using the combined combat value of all the units within it. All close combat attacks against the hedgehog are directed against the pike element of the formation.

Any break tests that are required by the formation are made on behalf of all the converged units; they are all affected in the same way. If the hedgehog breaks and is destroyed, remove all the units that comprise it.

A hedgehog formation that takes a break test ignores results that oblige it to retire and will hold its ground without becoming disordered instead. This makes a defensive hedgehog exceptionally hard to shift as a Break result is needed to destroy it.

Stand aside! Cuirassiers on the move.

"I came, I saw,
God conquered"

Holy Roman Emperor Charles V

1562 - The Battle of Dreux. Catholic and Huguenot forces fight out a draw.

69

Supports

Supporting units are a very important aspect of combat so it is worth spending a little time on the subject.

Some non-engaged units can contribute to a nearby combat engagement by adding a bonus to the combat results as noted below. This reflects the unit offering support fire or relieving fighting troops. Only units that are not themselves engaged in combat can support in this way.

A unit can support any single engaged friend within 3" (this is measured to the closest point of both units). A unit cannot support more than one friend, even if it is positioned so it could potentially support several different units.

There are some limitations on what units can be supported within a combat and these are noted below:

- Artillery cannot be supported

- Skirmishing units cannot be supported

- Hedgehog formations cannot be supported as they have no rear or flanks

- Units within buildings also cannot be supported for the same reason

- Units engaged to their side or rear cannot be supported even if they are also engaged to their front

Most units are able to offer support, regardless of formation or size. Once again there are exceptions and these are noted below:

- Units in column cannot offer support

- Units of limbered artillery cannot offer support

- Units shaken or disordered cannot offer support

Where two or more units are positioned to offer rear or flank support to the same engaged friendly unit, then the bonus is still +1 in total; ie, the unit receives +1 because it has a supported flank or rear and not +1 per supporting unit. The maximum bonus to a single unit is therefore +3 (both flanks and rear)

To support a flank or rear a unit must be within the appropriate quarter and within 3" of the supported unit. A unit's sides and rear quarters have already been defined for other purposes, but we shall remind ourselves with the aid of the following diagram.

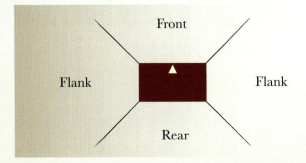

When a combat includes two or more units fighting on the same side, add all the casualties and bonuses together and work out a single result. For example, if two units are fighting alongside each other and each has a rear support then add +2. In multiple combats only the extreme flanks of the combat can be supported.

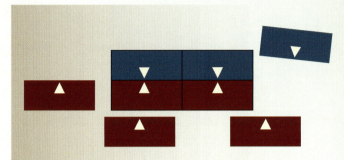

In this example the red force has +3 supports and the blue has +1 support.

Units that have friends fighting on their flanks as part of the same combat cannot be supported on that flank. This is most easily demonstrated with a further diagram.

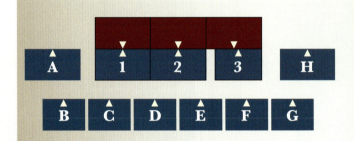

How many supports? Units 1, 2 and 3 are engaged in the same combat because they are all interconnected as a result of touching common enemies. A and H can only support to the flanks of 1 and 3 respectively – so they give +1 each and +2 in total. 1, 2 and 3 can all be supported from the rear by a choice of units, so +1 for rear support for each engaged unit = +3 in total from the rear. But can the flanks of 2 be supported by, say, G or B if they are within 6" of 2's flank quarter? The answer is NO because unit 2's flanks are already covered by other units engaged in the same combat. No bonus is added for the flanks of unit 2 or for the inner flanks of units 1 and 3 even though there happens to be a bit of a gap between units 2 and 3. The total value of support for this combat is therefore 5. This is the usual way support works: +1 for each flank and up to +1 rear support for each engaged unit.

Morale Saves

We have already discussed Morale saves at some length in the section on Shooting. Morale saves in hand-to-hand fighting are the same in all respects and you might wish to refer back to remind yourself how this works. See page 48.

Modifiers to the Morale save are also the same as for ranged attacks. In hand-to-hand combat the +1 bonus for *cover* and the +2 for *buildings* apply to any stationary unit that has been charged. These bonuses continue to apply from round to round until the unit loses a round of combat. Once the unit loses a round of combat, the enemy is assumed to have broken through any intervening cover, and the Morale save bonus is lost during further rounds.

For the avoidance of doubt, a unit that charges an enemy behind (or in) cover does not benefit from the cover itself, even where a barrier physically separates both units. Only units that take up a position within cover receive the bonus, this rule also includes fighting within woods. This should be obvious enough, but let us be clear and dispel any lurking confusion at this stage.

Casualties

After Morale saves have been taken, any hits that have not been saved are recorded as casualties on the unit. As with shooting, casualties inflicted in hand-to-hand-fighting represent men killed or wounded as well as other factors that we might expect to affect a unit's ability to fight such as exhaustion and loss of nerve. Casualties are recorded on the unit using markers as already discussed in the section on Shooting page 49.

During a combat round it is important to keep a separate tally of the casualties inflicted on a unit in the current round. This can most easily be done by carefully keeping any fresh markers separate from casualties inflicted previously, or by means of a dice placed face up to indicate the number of casualties suffered that round. Players can use these or any other method to keep track of the casualties in the current round.

Once the combat has been worked out, the result established and break tests taken, all casualties suffered in excess of a unit's stamina value are removed.

Combat Results

Combat results are worked out for each combat engagement as soon as all units taking part in that combat engagement have fought. To work out which side wins, add up the number of casualties inflicted by each side during that round (do not include any casualties inflicted by closing or traversing shots prior to the round of combat itself). Then add the following bonuses to each side where they apply:

The side that has inflicted the most casualties is victorious and the other side has been defeated. If both sides suffer the same number of casualties then there is no clear winner or loser and the result is a draw.

COMBAT RESULT BONUSES	
Bonus	**Formation Modifiers**
+1	**Rear Support.** This is explained under Supports opposite.
+1	**Flank Support.** This is explained under Supports opposite
+2	**Cavalry versus non-pike block infantry.** Any cavalry unit that is fighting an infantry unit that is not a pike block gains +2 combat bonus.
+2	**Pike versus Cavalry.** Any infantry unit armed with pikes gain a +2 combat bonus when fighting any cavalry unit. This bonus cannot be used in conjunction with to the Hedgehog versus Cavalry bonus, it's one or the other.
+3	**Hedgehog versus Cavalry.** Hedgehogs are an ideal defense against cavalry units and receive a +3 bonus against them. This bonus cannot be used in conjunction with the Pike versus Cavalry bonus, it's one or the other.
+3 or +2	**Occupied Buildings.** If units are fighting from buildings they count +3 if large or standard sized, or +2 if small. This is explained under the rules for Fighting from Buildings on page 82.

Cuirassiers

After Combat

After any break tests have been taken and units retired or removed as appropriate, any units remaining in contact with the enemy are locked in combat and will fight again in the following round. Some units may be allowed to turn to face their enemies if they are not already doing so. See the section on Break Tests for more about these moves.

Defeated Troops

Each engaged unit on the losing side must take a break test and abide by the result (see Break Test on page 74).

Supporting units are not engaged and therefore don't need to test unless friends break nearby as described later in the Break Test section.

Draws

In the case of a draw, all engaged units that are *shaken* must take a break test and abide by the result. This means that units on both sides could have to test in some cases.

If the combat is a draw then *all cavalry units on both sides* that are not shaken, and which therefore do not have to make a break test, must automatically retire one move. This rule reflects the volatile nature of cavalry engagements – cavalry who do not win will inevitably retire in order to regroup, assuming they are not forced to flee and are destroyed as a result. The rules for retiring units are given in the rules for Break Tests on page 74.

Victorious Units

If all the units on one side of a combat either retire or break, each unit on the other side can do any of the following:

- Hold – the unit stays where it is.

- Change formation as described in the section on Formations (page 39).

- Fall back as described shortly.

- Make a sweeping advance as described shortly.

- Occupy buildings/positions as described shortly.

If all the enemy forces touching a unit retire or break, but other enemy are still engaged in the same combat against other friendly units, then a victorious unit can do any of the following:

- Hold – the unit stays where it is.

- Change formation as described in the section on Formations (page 39).

- Fall back as described shortly.

- Move back into the combat as described next.

Move Back into Combat

If the unit is able to move back into combat with an enemy unit already engaged in the same combat then it can do so. It can move up to a normal move as directly as it can back

1564 - William Shakespeare is born in Stratford-upon-Avon.

into the fight. It can do this even if shaken or disordered. This doesn't happen very often – as in most cases there won't be any enemy left to fight!

Fall Back

This move represents a unit regrouping around its colours, away from immediate danger.

A unit that falls back can make one move to its own rear up to its usual move distance. It can do this even if disordered. The unit cannot use the move to charge another enemy. The unit is free to reorient itself as it moves – for example, if fighting enemy to its flank it can turn to face as long as it has room to do so.

Sweeping Advance

This move represents a unit breaking through a gap in the enemy's lines or pursuing a retiring enemy in a running fight. It is especially useful for cavalry units because it gives them the opportunity to move further and hit harder.

A sweeping advance is only permitted in specific cases which we will cover next. A disordered unit is never allowed to make a sweeping advance, even if meets other requirements to do so.

If a unit charges or countercharges, wins the ensuing round of combat, and all the enemy units engaged are either broken or retire, then the victorious unit can make one move to its own front up to its normal move rate. This is

called a sweeping advance. The unit *cannot* use this move to charge unless it is a cavalry unit.

If the unit is a cavalry unit then it *can* use its sweeping advance to charge so long as it is not shaken. It can charge any enemy units just as if it were charging in the Command phase of the turn. It can even charge an enemy unit that has retired from the same combat engagement – think of the cavalry pressing home the attack on their fleeing foes! If a cavalry unit charges in this way, fight a further round of combat that turn.

A cavalry unit can only charge on a sweeping advance *once* during a turn. Horseflesh can only stand so much and will need time to recover. It is possible for a cavalry unit to charge, defeat its enemy and then charge again as a sweeping advance, fight a further round of combat and defeat its enemy, and then make a second sweeping advance, but this second sweeping advance cannot also be a charge.

When a cavalry unit charges on a sweeping advance, the enemy can only respond by holding their ground, they are not allowed any other charge reaction (not even those covered by special rules) as the onslaught is far too rapid to counter.

Occupy Buildings

In a fight where units are attacking buildings or similar fortifications, then victorious infantry units can move in and occupy buildings if all the units defending them are broken or forced to retire. The unit just makes a standard move into the building as described under the Terrain rules (page 40).

A skirmish in Bohemia – Catholic League troops advance on the Swedish Yellow Guards.

1565 - The Siege of Malta. The Knights of St. John survive the Ottoman assault.

Break Tests and Shaken Units

A break test is taken to determine how a unit reacts in perilous circumstances. Most commonly, tests are required when defeated in hand-to-hand fighting. Troops will also be called upon to take a break test if they are shaken by shooting, and in other situations as noted below. A unit that fails a break test by a sufficient margin is removed from the game; its soldiers turn tail and flee in disarray. This is often how units are defeated and destroyed in our game, so it is an important part of play as can readily be imagined. Break tests don't always result in a unit's destruction. Sometimes units will be obliged to retreat, they might become disordered, or they could simply hold their ground.

There are five situations when a break test is required:

- Units suffer **excess casualties** from shooting.
- Units are **shaken** by closing fire.
- Units are **defeated** in hand-to-hand combat
- Units **draw** hand-to-hand combat and are **shaken**
- Supporting units have **friends Break**.

Tests from Shooting

A unit is shaken once it has suffered casualties equal to its stamina level, adjusted for unit size as noted elsewhere. Once a unit has suffered sufficient casualties it becomes shaken. See Shaken Units on page 49.

After each turn's shooting is complete, units must take a break test if their total number of casualties is **higher** than their stamina value. Any casualty markers scored in excess of the stamina level are discarded once the test is taken –

a unit never has more casualties than its stamina value once break tests have been taken.

Tests from Closing Fire

Any chargers must take a break test if their total number of casualties stands **equal to or higher** than their stamina value once closing fire is completed – ie, if the unit is shaken by closing fire.

Break tests from closing fire refer to the results table as if the chargers were engaged in hand-to-hand combat. Note that this is different to (and more dangerous than!) break tests from other shooting, which are worked out from the 'shooting' line of the break test table. In all other respects the test is exactly the same as for shooting.

Tests by Units Defeated in Combat

Once each engagement has been fought and results calculated, each unit engaged on the losing side must take a break test. In most cases there will be a single unit fighting – so only one test is taken, but it is possible for two or more units to be engaged in the same combat in which case each unit must test individually. In such a case the player whose units are taking the test can decide which to test first.

Units that lose a combat must take a break test regardless of whether they are shaken or not. However, units will have penalties applied to the test score if they suffer casualties in excess of their stamina in the same way as units testing for shooting. This means that excess casualties must be temporarily recorded and then removed once break tests are complete, exactly as described for tests from shooting.

A mule train laden with precious supplies.

1566 - Riots over religious disputes begin the 80 Years' War in the Netherlands.

Tests by Units in Drawn Combats

If a combat engagement results in a draw then *all* units that are shaken must take a break test. Units on both sides may have to test. It doesn't matter which side tests first. Otherwise this is the same as described for units defeated in combat.

Tests for Supporting Units

Supporting units do not have to test simply because their side has been defeated in hand-to-hand combat. However, supporting units *do* have to test if friends they are supporting *break* as a result of a break test.

Supporting infantry or cavalry units ignore engaged artillery units that break. The loss of such units does not impact on the willingness of other troops to fight on.

Supporting units read their results off the 'hand-to-hand combat' line of the break test chart in the same way as units that are actually engaged.

For purposes of this test, supporting units are considered to be such if they are theoretically able to support regardless of whether they actually contributed a support bonus or not. For example, if a unit is positioned so it could support two different friends from the rear then it must test if either breaks regardless of the fact that it can only support one of them.

Regardless of the number of friends who break from an engagement, a supporting unit only has to test once.

Note that engaged units usually break because they get a 'break' result on the break test. However, it is also possible for a unit to break if it is unable to retire for whatever reason (see the *Break Test Result Table* on page 72).

The Break Test

To take a break test roll two dice, add the scores together and apply the following modifiers to the total.

BREAK TEST MODIFIERS	
Modifier	**Situation**
-1	**Excess Casualties.** Deduct -1 for each excess casualty suffered by the unit, either from shooting or hand-to-hand combat.
-1	**Disordered.** Deduct -1 if the unit is disordered.
-1	**The unit has suffered at least one casualty from artillery** that turn if testing as a result of shooting or closing fire.

Break Test Result Table

Modified Dice roll	Combat Type	Outcome		
4 or less	Shooting and Hand-to-Hand	**Infantry, Cavalry & Artillery** The unit *breaks* and is deemed destroyed – remove the entire unit from the field.		
5	Shooting and Hand-to-Hand	**Infantry & Cavalry** The unit *retires* one full move to its rear without changing formation and at all times avoiding contact with the enemy. Once it has moved, the unit becomes *disordered* if it is not already so. If unable to comply, the unit may make two moves to its rear if this enables it to reach a tenable position. If unable to comply with this further requirement, the unit *breaks* as described for 4 or less above.		**Artillery** The unit *breaks* and is deemed destroyed – remove the entire unit from the field.
6	Shooting	**Infantry & Cavalry** The unit *holds its ground* – it stays where it is and does not move.	**Artillery** The unit *breaks* and is deemed destroyed – remove the entire unit from the field.	
	Hand-to-Hand	**Infantry & Cavalry** The unit *retires* one full move to its rear without changing formation and at all times avoiding contact with the enemy. Once it has moved, the unit becomes *disordered* if it is not already so. If unable to comply, the unit may make two moves to its rear if this enables it to reach a tenable position. If unable to comply with this further requirement, the unit *breaks* as described for 4 or less above.		**Artillery** The unit *breaks* and is deemed destroyed – remove the entire unit from the field.
7 or more	Shooting	**Infantry, Cavalry & Artillery** The unit *holds its ground* – it stays where it is and does not move.		
	Hand-to-Hand	**Infantry** If the unit is infantry then it *holds its ground* – the unit remains where it is and will continue fighting in the following combat round.	**Cavalry** If the unit is cavalry the unit *retires* one full move to its rear without changing formation and at all times avoiding contact with the enemy. If unable to comply, the unit becomes *disordered* and may make two moves to its rear if this enables it to reach a tenable position. If unable to comply with this further requirement, the unit *breaks* as described for 4 or less above.	**Artillery** The unit *breaks* and is deemed destroyed – remove the entire unit from the field.

1568 - The Battle of Heiligerlee. Louis of Nassau defeats a Spanish army led by Count Aremberg.

Retiring Units

A retiring unit must move a full move, or in some cases two full moves, as described on the results chart. Units generally retire to the rear, except that units fighting *only* to one flank, or *only* to their rear, must retire in the opposite direction instead. For example, a unit fighting to its left flank will retire to its right side quarter.

A 'retire' move is a normal move in every respect, but it must be made entirely within the confines of the unit's rear (or opposing) quarter. Remember that troops don't have to turn around as they move, just move the entire unit backwards. Units can move through friends as long as they can move all the way through their formation. Troops retiring thus through an infantry pike unit or a heavy cavalry unit may disorder that formation (see *'Moving through Friendly Units'* on page 38).

A unit that is unable to retire as required will break instead. Remove the unit as if it had been destroyed. This can happen because enemy units or impassable terrain block its rearward movement. Friendly units can also block a unit's move if the defeated unit is unable to move all the way through their formation. It is wise to bear this in mind when positioning supporting troops.

Units that retire from the table are deemed to be destroyed, dispersed, routed, surrendered, or fleeing and take no further part in the battle. Remove the unit from the field as if it had been broken. This places units in a certain amount of danger if they are fighting with their backs to the table edge. Although we consider this entirely appropriate, we would not wish it to come as a surprise to anyone.

Troops in column who are obliged to retire will automatically form into their standard formation. As this formation change requires an additional move the unit automatically becomes disordered if it not so already.

Units that Hold their Ground

A unit that holds its ground will, generally speaking, stay where it is and will continue to fight in the following turn if still in contact with the enemy.

There are some situations where a unit that holds its ground must move as described below. This covers troops who are caught in the flank or rear, or whilst in column and allows them to turn to face their enemy for the next round of combat. This means that if they can hold out for a turn, we can allow them to turn if there's room for them to do so.

Troops in column who hold their ground will automatically form into their standard formation. As this formation change is an extra move, the unit automatically becomes disordered if not so already.

Other units fighting exclusively to their rear or one flank will automatically turn to face their enemy where there is sufficient room to do so.

Units that are fighting in more than one direction at once, say to their side and rear, are stuck as they are and must do their best in the following round. This will usually mean they are unable to bring all their fighting potential to bear. Quite honestly – they are lucky to have survived thus far!

Defeated Cavalry

As you can see from the Break Test Results table, the best result that a defeated cavalry unit can get is to 'retire'. This is deliberate. This means that cavalry are more brittle than infantry in hand-to-hand combat. Cavalry versus cavalry fights do not become bogged down, but are resolved quickly, often leading to one side retiring and the other making a sweeping advance. This is as it should be!

Shaken Units

Casualties accumulated on a unit represent the results of mounting fatigue, loss of officers and men, expenditure of ammunition, falling morale, and a multitude of other factors that erode a unit's ability to carry on the fight in a cohesive manner. Once a unit has accumulated casualties equal to its stamina value it is deemed to be shaken. A shaken unit is no longer able to fight at full efficiency and is likely to break and flee if further casualties are inflicted upon it as already described.

As should be clear by now – casualties suffered in excess of a unit's stamina value are always discarded once the necessary break tests have been taken. A unit that is shaken is indicated by the number of casualty markers equal to its stamina value, and this is about as bad as it gets for our troops! The rules that affect shaken units are covered throughout this rule set because they affect shooting, hand-to-hand combat, and, in some cases, moves. We summarise these rules here for ease of reference:

- Shaken units are removed from the battle for good if they leave the table – they are over the hills and far away!

- Shaken units suffer a -1 'to hit' penalty when shooting.

- Shaken units suffer a -1 'to hit' penalty in hand-to-hand combat.

- Shaken units cannot charge or countercharge an enemy unit.

- Shaken cavalry units that win a round of combat cannot use a sweeping advance to charge an enemy unit.

As described in the rules for The Rally Order on page 36 it is possible for officers to restore a unit's fighting efficiently by rallying flagging troops and thereby removing casualty markers. This rule applies to all units that have suffered at least two casualties, including units that are shaken. If a shaken unit is successfully rallied in this way, it loses one casualty marker and is no longer shaken.

Victory & Defeat

This section of the game is where we look at victory and defeat – how we adjudge where one army has emerged victorious from the conflict. In our game there is no set way on deciding when a battle is over, or which side has won; such considerations may differ depending on scenario played, time allowed or number of turns allocated for the game. Often in our games, we play until a general consensus to stop is reached – this is normally when the fridge is empty.

Certain conventions have certainly evolved over the years and these form the basis for the rules in this chapter. Players need not feel bound by these particular rules; we are happy to ignore or change them dependant on the types of game we are playing. We suggest you do the same.

Battalia Morale

Once a battalia has suffered a great deal of casualties, or if it has partly abandoned the battlefield, the fighting spirit of its remaining units is likely to be affected. Surviving troops are considered too disheartened to carry on the fight effectively. This is called the 'Battalia Morale rule' and it works as follows...

If at the start of any side's turn, *more* than half of the total infantry or cavalry units in a battalia are lost then the whole battalia is deemed to be 'broken'. All the remaining units in the battalia are then obliged to follow the rules for broken battalias as described shortly. Once a battalia is broken it remains broken for the rest of the game – it cannot recover.

A unit is considered 'lost' for the purposes of calculating battalia morale if:

- It has been removed from the battlefield because it has been destroyed, or

- It has left the battlefield either deliberately or otherwise, or

- It is 'shaken' at the start of the turn (ie, if it has suffered casualties equal to its stamina)

We usually ignore artillery pieces when working out whether a brigade is broken, although artillery pieces will be affected by the rules for broken battalias along with the other units. The exception to this is where artillery forms the majority of units in a battalia, such as a 'grande battery', where guns are counted along with any infantry or cavalry.

For example, if a battalia consists of four infantry units, one cavalry unit and two guns then it is broken once three infantry/cavalry units are lost – three being 'more than half' the total of five. In this case the two guns are ignored. If the battalia consists of four guns and two infantry units it is a 'grande battery' and is broken once any four units are lost including guns – four being the lowest number 'more than half' of the total of six units.

Units from Broken Battalias

The following rules apply to units from broken battalias.

- Units that have already left the table, or which leave the table from that point on, cannot return and are deemed to be out of the battle for good.

- Units that are shaken cannot be rallied even if they are allowed to recover by means of some special rule. Once shaken, units remain shaken.

- Units that are disordered remain disordered from turn to turn. Units that have a 'save' against disorder or a special rule that normally allows them to recover can do so.

- Shaken units are allowed to make a single 'retire' move in the command phase instead of using their initiative or receiving an order. They can do this even if disordered – in which case it is the only move they are allowed to make. Retiring units must attempt to withdraw from the fighting in the most practical way possible. Artillery crew that retire in such circumstances are deemed to abandon their guns.

- Shaken units within 12" of the enemy and not already engaged in combat must retire as described above unless occupying buildings or other defendable position, or in hedgehog formation in which case they can hold their ground instead. Infantry units that are hopelessly surrounded and unable to retire can form a hedgehog if normally able to do so.

- Unshaken units in a broken battalia can be given orders normally, but will have their morale reduced to 6+ for the remainder of the game. If they become shaken or disordered they will follow the above rules for shaken/disordered troops in a broken battalia.

Army Morale

Once half the battalias in an army are broken then all the other remaining battalias are automatically broken as well, and all the rules for broken battalias will apply to the whole army.

This is often time to call an end to the game, although this depends to some extent on the nature of the game and its victory conditions. If matters are very close it can happen that a retreating force can mutually drive its opponent from the field, leaving neither in possession.

The Prince of Waldeck directs the defence of Walcourt.

Winners and Losers

Once the morale of one side's army has collapsed, it is usually considered to have lost. On occasion it is worth carrying on for a turn to see if the retreating army can inflict a similar condition on a fragile enemy or achieve some other overall objective. Such a fighting withdrawal, if successful, may salvage a draw from the situation should the players feel such things important.

Driving the enemy from the field is obviously pretty decisive. Sometimes a battle will rage long into the night without either side being broken and circumstances demand an end to play. Such undecided games can only be resolved in terms of relative success, for neither side has 'won' whilst each has achieved at least part of its objective (in so far as it hasn't 'lost' either!). In such a situation the army with the largest proportion of intact battalias is deemed to have the advantage and, bearing in mind what other objectives have been set, is the winner.

Objectives

We commonly set objectives for both sides prior to the beginning of the battle. These objectives invariably go above and beyond the simple destruction of the opposing army. A battle may be fought for possession of a village, hill, bridge or other point of strategic importance. Another common objective is the 'running battle' in which one side's objective is to reach the far side of the table and 'escape' – usually over an area covered by ambushing enemies and

tricky terrain. The other side has to catch and destroy the enemy – or some key element of it – before they have time to escape.

When setting an objective it can be useful to impose a time limit – for example, you must take the defended position within eight turns. This ensures that players don't get bogged down, though it is important to allow long enough for the game to progress in a sensible fashion. What you are aiming for is a nail biting conclusion that could easily go either way – not a task that's so obviously impossible there seems little point in trying!

Summary

A battalia is broken once more than half of its units are lost.

Units from broken battalias:

- Cannot return to the table

- Stay disordered once disordered (barring special rules)

- Stay shaken once shaken

- Can automatically retire one move (even if disordered)

- Shaken units must retire one move if any enemy are within 12" unless defending or in hedgehog formation

- Unshaken units can be given orders normally, but once shaken or disordered will remain so.

An army is broken once half of its battalias are broken.

Advanced Rules

This section of the rulebook is used to describe in more detail some of the more complex rules for special formations, troops, and characters you will find in the armies of the period. All of these will be covered in other parts of the book, but deserve a little more attention here to ensure clarity. These rules have been developed in order to increase the scope of games played within the Pike & Shotte era, but are certainly not exhaustive. Hopefully this section can also show how the main body of rules can be adapted and added to by players seeking to represent specific battles, tactics and situations.

Hedgehog Formations

The supporting relationship between pike and musket armed units was a key feature of warfare throughout the pike & shotte period. As we already discussed, the pike elements of your army are fairly secure from cavalry if not shaken or disordered. Other infantry, particularly musket units, are vulnerable to rampaging cavalry especially and even specialist melee infantry enemies. They would look to the pike for sanctuary should such opposing troops threaten.

Non pike armed units can seek support and withdraw into a friendly pike block – a pike unit with at least three ranks - and thus form a 'hedgehog'. The pike unit must be of the same battalia and within 6"; this move can either be made

in the Command phase or as a reaction to an enemy charge. If the move is attempted as a result of a charge reaction, a successful command roll must be made. If this is failed the unit does not reach the sanctuary of the pike block and is caught in the open. The unit does not get to use closing fire in these circumstances and can only stand. The choice to attempt to hedgehog removes the option to offer closing fire.

Each shooting unit within a hedgehog formation has its shooting value reduced to '1', although this shot can be made in any direction as the formation does not have flanks or a rear.

Once formed, a hedgehog cannot move. It is a static defensive formation. As it has no flanks or rear, all combats are regarded as being from the front. In any subsequent turn a successful command roll is required to move units out of the hedgehog. This can only be attempted if no enemy cavalry are within 6" of any part of the formation, and such units will only move once regardless of the margin of success of the command.

A maximum of two units can converge with a pike block to form a hedgehog, no more. Once a hedgehog is formed all the units effectively fight together, so the combat value of the formation is equal to all the units' combat values added together.

Prince Rupert's regiment of foot

1572 - The Battle of St. Ghislain. The Spanish crush French Huguenot reinforcements marching to aid Louis of Nassau.

A Parliamentarian battalia in action – one of its musket wings has formed hedgehog in the face of Royalist cavalry. The remaining wing of musketeers, being unthreatened, maintains a firing line.

An enemy that declared a charge against a unit that successfully hedgehogs as a charge reaction can either continue with the charge – and therefore engage in combat with the complete hedgehog formation – or can, probably more wisely, pull out of the charge and stop 6" short of the formation.

All shooting hits on a hedgehog formation are allocated amongst the composite units by the defending player; this represents troops seeking shelter behind their comrades when they start to waver. In effect the player has the opportunity to spread the casualties across the formation, which can prove a very useful, if somewhat short term, defence.

All artillery shots, with the exception of mortars, receive a +1 bonus to hit a hedgehog formation.

Should any unit within a hedgehog formation suffer from disorder, the whole formation is considered disordered.

Hedgehog formations cannot receive any supports in combat as they have no flank or rear quarters.

All hand-to-hand combat hits must be allocated against the pike unit element of the formation.

Hedgehog formations receive a +3 combat bonus when fighting against cavalry.

As hedgehogs are comprised of pike armed troops, cavalry will lose all charge and special ability bonuses should they charge a hedgehog that is not disordered. In addition the pike unit within the hedgehog receives double its normal combat value against charging cavalry if it is not disordered.

Any break tests that are required by the hedgehog formation are made on behalf of all the converged units; they are all affected in the same way. If the hedgehog breaks and is destroyed, remove all the units that comprise it.

A hedgehog formation that takes a break test ignores results that oblige it to retire and will hold its ground without becoming disordered instead. This makes a defensive hedgehog exceptionally hard to shift as a Break result is needed to destroy it.

"Put your trust in God but keep your powder dry"

Oliver Cromwell

Rules for Fighting from Buildings

Formulating rules for fighting from buildings is no easy matter and must inevitably rely upon gamers to interpret matters which best suit their own model buildings and tabletop set-ups. As described in the section on terrain (page 40) our own approach is to consider buildings as 'blocks' that are roughly squarish. A typical block might be a single largish house or a group of small buildings, perhaps delineated by walls, gardens and what-not.

It is important to note that a building on the tabletop is representative, we assume that one building can equate to a small settlement or a number of buildings that could hold hundreds of men. This is the same principle we use when we build a unit of troops numbering 10-20 models representing some hundreds of men.

A single infantry unit of small, standard, or large size can occupy a building block. In addition we also allow a building to shelter a single cannon – thus a supporting weapon to take up defensive positions without hogging the entire area represented by a single block. Commanders can be placed within buildings already occupied by friendly troops, but not otherwise.

Generally speaking, infantry units occupying buildings are treated in a similar way to units in a hedgehog. Although such units have no formation as such, it is best to think of a unit as having four facings represented by the periphery of the building block. In the same way as for hedghogs, visibility and range are calculated from the centre of each facing. Cannons can be placed anywhere around the periphery and fire is calculated from the position of the cannon model in the usual way.

A unit in a building has a shooting value of 1 per facing up to a total maximum equal to the unit's shooting value. It is up to the player to divide this as he wishes in cases where enemy are approaching from different directions. As with a hedgehog formation it is usually necessary to calculate the shooting for each facing separately. Cannons shoot with their normal value.

A unit in a building has a hand-to-hand combat value of 2 per facing up to a maximum total equal to the unit's combat value. Only those sides of the building engaged by enemy units will fight. Cannons fight with their normal values.

A unit in a building has a +2 morale bonus as already noted in the rules for shooting and fighting.

A reinforced Northumbrian Peel tower. Word arrives of Border Reivers nearby.

1573 - Spanish forces under Alva capture Haarlem after a lengthy siege.

Dragoons

In hand-to-hand fighting a standard sized or large infantry unit in a building has a +3 combat result bonus and a small unit has a +2 bonus. Artillery receive no bonus to their result. Note that units in buildings cannot receive support from other units, but are effectively self-supported by their combat results bonus in the same way as a hedgehog.

A unit in a building that takes a break test ignores results that oblige it to retire and will hold its ground without becoming disordered instead. This is the same as for a hedgehog formation and means that units occupying buildings must be broken before they can be shifted.

Dragoons

Dragoons are listed as horse, or cavalry units. In truth they fought more like mounted infantry than true cavalry, and so do not fall neatly into the role of cavalrymen. For this reason we will cover them and their rules in more detail here.

All dragoons are classed as skirmish order units, with the exception of dragoons covered in the Sun King section of the book (post 1660). By this time the role of this troop type was beginning to evolve and dragoons were more often asked to fight from horseback. Post 1660 dragoons are fielded as Battle Line troops who have the ability to skirmish if desired.

Dragoons are allowed one free mount or dismount move per turn so long as they are not disordered. For example, a

unit could move mounted 9" and then dismount to shoot on foot for one move. Unlike their Harquebusier comrades who were trained to shoot from the saddle, dragoons will only fire dismounted for the purposes of these rules; in reality they did occasionally shoot from horseback, but this was so ineffective it does not warrant a shooting value, so in order to benefit from their shooting value they must dismount to shoot. This means that mounted dragoons cannot give closing fire if charged; only those on foot can do so.

When mounted, skirmishing dragoons are classed as skirmish order cavalry, and as such benefit from and suffer the consequences of being cavalry. They can counter charge as cavalry (within the limits for skirmishing cavalry), and take any break tests as cavalry.

When skirmishing dismounted they are classed as skirmish infantry with all the advantages and disadvantages this incurs, and will take all tests as infantry.

Dragoons that have the 'Fire and Evade' special rule may do so if dismounted and not disordered. This allows them to offer closing fire and make an evade move when charged if they make a successful command role. The evade move includes the free move to mount their horses, so they will retire 9" and be classed as mounted for their next turn. A failed command roll means the unit must simply stand against the enemy charge as they lose the option to give closing fire. A unit of dragoons that is mounted when charged by an enemy unit can either stand or evade.

Generals and Other Commanders

Within the basic rules section we have already discussed the role of commanders and provided suitable rules to represent them. In this section we cover further rules for commanders and, in particular, risks to command models from shooting and hand-to-hand fighting.

Commander Models

In your army each commander can be represented by a suitably sized base bearing the man himself plus his staff or scenic elements as are deemed appropriate. We shall not specify dimensions for bases. We merely require that they should be of a size that is convenient. Hopefully this will give you the scope to make a base worthy of the men leading your troops. Measurements are always drawn from a commander's head so there is no confusion with larger, elaborate bases.

Vulnerability of Commanders

Commander models cannot be shot at or attacked in hand-to-hand fighting and are always ignored when it comes to determining the presence of friends or enemy. For example, a command model within 6" of an enemy unit does not entitle the unit to use its initiative. Similarly a commander immediately in front of an infantry unit or cannon does not stop it shooting straight through him! This is partly because the size of our models is huge in proportion to the ranges of weapons and movement of troops, but also because we assume participants in the battle to be in a state of constant motion – it is merely a convenience that we divide our game into formal periods of movement and firing.

Where the desire to lead from the front is too great, the Commander is still only one very small element of a large body of men. In most circumstances, Commanders are therefore invulnerable to enemy action. However, there are some exceptions that apply when commanders have joined units.

- If a Commander has joined a unit and that unit is destroyed either as a result of shooting, hand-to-hand fighting, or any other reason, then the Commander is also removed as a casualty. He may not necessarily be dead. There is always the chance that he has been captured or merely wounded; in any case, he is out of the battle and the model is removed.

- If a Commander has joined a unit and that unit is 'shaken' then any further casualties inflicted on that unit can potentially result in the Commander also falling casualty. For each casualty inflicted on a shaken

Montrose Irish

unit roll a dice – any dice score of a 6 indicates that the Commander has also fallen casualty and the model is removed.

- If a Commander is obliged to join a friendly unit because enemy troops have displaced him, then the Commander falls casualty if he is unable to reach a friendly unit within a normal move (18" for Commanders on foot and 27" for mounted Commanders).

A Commander unfortunate enough to fall in battle will have his role passed on to a trusty subordinate, who is assumed to have been within the commander's base. This reserve Commander is placed within 6" of any unit in the same division. He can also be placed with any unit if you wish, even a unit that is already fighting a combat.

Reserve Commanders have a command rating one less than their predecessor. So, if the original Commander has a command rating of 8, then his replacement has a rating of 7.

If you are careless enough to let a replacement Commander fall in action then the next in line takes over in the same way, with the associated reduction in command rating. A replacement Commander will never have a command rating lower than 5.

Commanders Joining Units

A Commander can voluntarily join a friendly unit by moving into base contact with it when the Commander moves in the Command part of the turn. The model can then be arranged amongst the unit's ranks if required. A Commander moves as part of the unit he has joined during the enemy's following turn and remains with it either until the unit moves in the following Command phase or, if it doesn't move, until the Commander himself moves. Commanders who have already joined units do not generally move with them when orders are issued – unless the order is a follow me order as described in the Command section.

Commanders are obliged to join units if they issue follow me orders or rally orders. Commanders are also obliged to join a friendly unit if they find themselves displaced by the movement of enemy troops. Note that only enemy troops can displace a Commander – not other Commanders!

Bear in mind that the movement of enemy troops cannot displace a Commander who has already joined a friendly unit – he is considered to be part of the unit. Should it prove necessary the model can be rearranged within the unit's formation as is convenient.

Commander Bonuses

Many players will want the drama of their Commanders getting stuck into the fight. When Commanders join a unit,

A Catholic League general leads his troops through a Bohemian town.

they can add a bonus attack to the unit's combat value. This doesn't necessarily represent the commander wading in personally with sword and pistol – though he might do just that, brave chap that he is! Rather, the bonus accrues from the heightened enthusiasm and determination of the troops themselves. The Commander's example acts as a spur to their natural heroism, inspiring them to ever greater deeds of valour.

Unfortunately not all leaders are especially inspiring, so Commanders with a Command Rating of 8 or more will have a combat value of +1, those with a Command Rating of less than 8 will not confer this combat bonus.

Named Commanders or Dramatis Personae

In the army list sections of these rules we have included some of the 'great and the good' of Pike & Shotte warfare – and also some of the not so great or good. Having Oliver Cromwell or Prince Rupert leading your cavalry charge certainly adds flavor to a battle, so each army has a selection of historical figures at your disposal.

Each of these characters have special rules attached to them, which encapsulate their strengths – or weaknesses – on the battlefield. These rules override those covered in the Commander Bonuses section above. These characters do not get the +1 combat value in addition to their special abilities.

A Selection of Useful Rules

The pages laid down so far provide us with a general framework of rules that cover around 200 years of warfare. Needless to say, whether refighting an historical battle or putting together an army based upon a particular historical force, we will wish to properly represent the unique characteristics of the troops under our command. This is already covered in broad terms by the different fighting qualities represented by each unit's hand-to-hand combat, shooting, morale and stamina values, but this still leaves plenty left unsaid! Just what was it that set the Swedish musketeers in the Thirty Years War apart from their Imperial adversaries, or made the French Gendarmes such a potent force in the Italian Wars? The rules that follow are used to represent a number of factors that contributed to how certain troops actually performed in battle, including specific weapons, tactical skills, training or even cultural inclinations.

These rules are intended as examples of how such factors can be interpreted with modifications to the basic rules, but are certainly not a definitive 'tool set'. As such they can be changed, added to and developed to suit your own games. Players who have collected particular forces for the period may well have expert knowledge of the forces, battles and tactics of their chosen subject; such players should feel free to create rules to reflect these qualities. In fact, we hope a great deal of enjoyment can be garnered by bringing such knowledge to the battlefield.

There is no need to be slavish about how these rules are applied either. We see no need to be entirely consistent in how we achieve our aim and will happily ascribe different rules to similar troops – or even the same ones – depending upon the nature of the game being played.

Some of the following rules may be routinely applied without danger of blunting our game: others will prove more effective when brought out occasionally to represent more unusual situations. Looked at as a whole there do appear to be lots of quite complex rules here; but please remember, the idea is not to use all of them in the same game!

Bad War

- Re-roll missed combat attacks against landsknechts

The unit can re-roll all failed hand-to-hand combat attacks in every round of each and every combat when it is in combat against a Landsknecht unit.

This rule represents the savagery of the fighting when one Landsknecht force would face another in the pay of their enemy. In such circumstances there was no quarter asked for or given.

Bows and Short bows

- +1 Morale saves
- Cannot offer closing fire

Units hit by shooting from bows gain +1 to their morale saves. This cannot improve any unit's morale save to better than 2+. Units that normally receive no morale save will receive a save of 6+.

Like all non-firearm shooting weapons, troops with bows cannot give closing fire on charging enemy.

Bows were still used by some troops in this period, but the days of the archer dominating the battlefield were gone for good and they were often a symptom of a lack of firearms rather than well trained archers.

Brave

- Shaken units rally without an order

If the unit is shaken (ie, it has sustained its full quota of casualties) it can attempt to rally at the end of the Command part of the turn if it is more than 12" from any enemy. Roll a dice. On the score of 4 or more the unit recovers one casualty in the same way as if the unit had received a 'rally' order.

This rule effectively allows units to 'come back' to the fight, and as such should be used sparingly on all but the smallest games as it can prolong a game unduly.

English Elizabethan Archers.

1578 - The Battle of Gembloux, the Spanish smash the Dutch State's army in an hour and a half.

> "But such is their beastliness and arrogance that unless they are commanded by a captain of their own nation whom they know to be generous and courageous, and who holds a commission from the Emperor, they are rather a firebrand and a source of trouble than any real advantage"

On Henry VIII's German mercenary troops

Caracole

- Cannot countercharge enemy cavalry.

This rule is used to represent those troops that used the caracole tactic of engaging the enemy at the trot while discharging firearms. If charged by enemy cavalry the unit can only offer closing fire or stand. Caracole units can countercharge enemy infantry as usual.

Clansmen

- Cannot offer support in combat

Any unit that has the Clansmen rule cannot support any other unit in hand-to-hand combat.

This is used to represent troops, particularly Highland Clans, who are far more concerned with getting to grips with the enemy than helping out 'that' clan.

Crack

- Re-roll one failed morale save if you have no casualties already

This unit can re-roll a single failed morale save each time the unit suffers casualties so long as it has suffered no casualties already. Simply roll the save again. As soon as the unit has suffered a casualty then all future re-rolls are lost.

Crossbows

- Cannot offer closing fire

Although crossbows could offer the punch of many of the firearms of the day, like the bow they were on the wane. Like all non-firearm shooting weapons, troops with crossbows cannot give closing fire on charging enemies.

Double-handed Infantry Arms

- -1 Morale save

Units hit by troops with double-handed infantry wepaons suffer a -1 penalty to their morale save.

This is a catch-all term for a whole range of weapons from billhooks and halberds to swords and axes wielded in both hands. Although these weapons were being phased out in favour of the pike, which offered more protection against enemy cavalry, they were ideal for combat.

Dragoons

- Free mount or dismount move
- Fire and evade
- Count as skirmish cavalry when mounted, skirmish infantry when dismounted.

Dragoon troops were introduced in the early 1600s and soon saw service in most armies, ideal as they were for scouting, foraging and grabbing key objectives until relieved. See the section on dragoons on page 83 for the complete description.

Eager

- Free move on charge order

Units given a charge order to charge an enemy within charge range always make one move even if they fail their order, assuming they don't blunder. If a blunder is rolled the result is always taken as a 6 on the blunder result table – Uncontrolled Advance! If a battalia order encompasses units that are eager and units that are not, then only the eager units are entitled to a free move.

This rule is used to represent headstrong, rash or impetuous troops, eager for battle and difficult to hold back once the enemy are close by.

Elite

- Overcome Disorder dice roll

Elite units can be graded 2+, 3+, 4+, 5+ or 6+ with 2+ being the best and 6+ the least 'elite'. However, for practical purposes, elites are generally rated at 4+. At the start of the Command phase, before any units are moved or orders given, the player rolls a dice for each Elite unit that is currently disordered and which is not already engaged in hand-to-hand fighting. If the dice scored equal to or more than the unit's elite rating the unit overcomes its disorder. The disorder marker is removed and the unit can use its initiative to move or be given orders as usual that turn.

Storming Party

Fanatic

- Morale Save +1 until shaken

Fanatic troops have a Morale value bonus of +1 regardless of type – they are so intoxicated by righteous zeal or fervour that they ignore all but the most fatal wounds and fight with utter disregard for their own safety. This effect lasts until the unit is shaken. Once the unit is shaken it loses its special Morale save bonus and reverts to whatever Morale value it would normally have for its type.

Ferocious Charge

- Re-roll missed combat attacks following charge

The unit can re-roll all failed hand-to-hand combat attacks in the first round of each and every combat when it charges or countercharges. Note that this bonus only applies when the unit charges or countercharges and not when it is charged.

This rule simply makes charging units even more dangerous – especially so because they also receive the usual dice bonus for charging.

Fire and Evade

- Can give closing fire and then evade when charged.

This rule is designed for troops that are best suited to scouting ahead of the main force and not engaging in combat. Troops with this ability can give closing fire if charged and then evade by making a move to the rear, thus avoiding combat. A successful command roll is needed to achieve this when charged, should the command roll fail the unit can simply hold.

Firelocks

- Short range extended to 12".

Firelock armed units get the +1 to hit bonus for short range extended from 6" to 12". This represents the increased effectiveness of the weapon over its matchlock counterparts.

More accurate and reliable than muskets, firelocks were initially restricted to mounted troops and units assigned with guarding the baggage train. Not having to keep a lit match at all times meant that the firelock was also less susceptible to the weather, being able to function perfectly well in the rain.

First Fire

- +1 Dice on first shot

The first time the unit shoots in the game, it gets +1 shot (ie, three dice rather than two if it normally has a value of 2).

Throughout the Pike & Shotte period, there were many limitations to firearms, such as poor equipment and lack of powder. For this reason a greater emphasis was beginning to be placed on fire discipline – it being all too easy to waste a significant portion of a unit's firepower by beginning to shoot too early. The rule simply encourages players to 'hold fire'

Freshly Raised

The unit's capabilities are uncertain: it is freshly raised, its loyalty may be in doubt, training may be poor, etc. Its effectiveness is open to question. We establish how effectively the unit performs either the first time it shoots at

1579 - Maastricht falls to the Spanish army of the Duke of Parma.

an enemy, or the first time it fights hand-to-hand combat. Up until this point the unit behaves as any other unit – it is not until the unit is tested in the heat of combat that its true mettle is revealed!

The first time the unit shoots at an enemy or at the start of its first round of hand-to-hand combat roll a dice:

1	**Terror!**	The unit is momentarily overcome with terror. For this turn only all shots and hand-to-hand attacks need 6s to hit. In addition the unit is immediately disordered if it is not already so.
2-3	**Panic!**	The unit is momentarily overcome by panic. For this turn only all shots and hand-to-hand attacks need 6s to hit.
4-5	**Sterling Job!**	The troops do their duty – no effect.
6	**Huzzah!**	The unit performs unexpectedly heroically. It gets an extra bonus shot or attack this turn only.

This rule is a more practical way of representing armies that have large numbers of newly raised troops compared to the rather more extreme 'untested' rule.

Galloper

- Must countercharge if able to do so.

- Will always engage the enemy on a sweeping advance where able to.

- Standard move of 12" as if Light Cavalry

This rule is used to represent cavalry that are headstrong and not completely controllable, likely to get carried away in the heat of battle. Such units will never back down from a fight and must countercharge when able to do so. If a combat results in the unit being able to make a sweeping advance the unit must follow up and engage the enemy once more with this move if able to.

Grenades

- Enemy ignores all morale bonuses for cover when engaged in combat

Grenadiers were introduced onto the battlefields of Europe in the second half of the 17th century. Their ranks were drawn from the biggest and strongest and were usually at the forefront of any assault. This rule is used to represent grenades being thrown as combat is engaged, disrupting the defenders who cannot gain the benefit of their cover as explosions disrupt their lines.

Heavy Cavalry

- +D3/+1 Combat result on a charge

When heavy cavalry charge or countercharge into combat their side receives a bonus on combat results equal to half the roll of a dice rounding up (ie, between +1 and +3). If more than one heavy cavalry unit is involved on either side just make the roll once for each side. This bonus only applies in the turn the cavalry charge or countercharge. It will also apply if the cavalry make a sweeping advance and charge their enemy as they do so.

Hedgehog

- Immovable

- Combined formation of pike and shotte elements

- No flanks or rear

- All shooting units in the hedgehog have a shooting value of 1

- Combat value is equal to the total of all the component units' values

- Cannot be supported in combat

- +3 combat bonus against cavalry

- Charging enemy cavalry receive no combat bonuses against the formation

- Pike element of the hedgehog receive double combat value against charging cavalry

- Will hold ground instead of retreat as a result of break tests

The hedgehog is the key formation for fighting with armies consisting of pike and firearm elements, for full rules see the section on Hedgehog Formations on page 81.

Swedish cavalry with commanded shot.

Scots Lancers – unpredictable but deadly on their day!

Lancers

- -1/-2 Morale save on the charge

When lance armed cavalry charge or countercharge, any hits they score upon their enemy are inflicted with a -1 morale save if they are cavalry, and -2 morale save if they are infantry or artillery. This only applies during the turn when the lancers charge or countercharge. It will also apply if lancers make a sweeping advance and press their attack by charging an enemy as they do so. Bear in mind that morale saves never get worse than 6+ if they are at least 6+ to start with – so charging lancers cannot erode an enemy's morale save altogether.

Large Unit

- +1 Shooting value (only if the unit has ranged weapons)
- +2 Hand-to-Hand
- +1 Stamina
- May ignore disorder by taking one damage (unless this will cause the unit to become shaken)

Some forces were able to call on extra manpower for certain aspects of their armies, and can field 'Large' units as specified in the Size of Units section on page 23. Such troops gain the above benefits to their fighting qualities; they also can use sheer weight of numbers to push on through when smaller units would become disordered. Note, this rule can only be used by large units to overcome disorder from Shooting, not from disorder caused by other factors.

Marauders

- Ignore distance modifiers for command

When giving orders to a unit of marauders, or to a battalia made up entirely of marauders, the normal distance penalty is ignored. This means that a commander can give an order to marauders who are 48" away as easily as if they were only 6" away.

We normally employ this rule to represent semi-independent units that are used to scout ahead or capture key battlefield objectives, dragoons being an ideal example.

Mercenary

- Will quit the battle if a rally test is failed when shaken

When a mercenary unit is shaken and the Command roll is failed to rally them, the unit will remain shaken for the remainder of the battle. No more attempts to rally them can be made and the unit will retire from the battle via the quickest route and not engage the enemy – even shooting – unless charged.

There is only so much loyalty that money can buy. Mercenary troops should not be expected to stick around when the going gets tough and this rule reflects the chances of such units drifting away to seek their fortune elsewhere.

Militia

- No move on equal command roll

Militia units will fail a Command roll equal to the Commander's staff rating. Otherwise they move exactly as other units. If militia units are included in a group order with other units this means it is possible for other units to move whilst the militia elements remain staunchly immobile.

Pikes

- Can form a hedgehog formation with other (non pike) units of the same battalia.
- Cavalry receive no combat bonuses when fighting an ordered pike unit
- Pike unit gets double combat value when fighting charging cavalry

The pike armed man was the master of the battlefield for much of the Pike & Shotte era, affording excellent protection against enemy cavalry as well as hard-hitting combat ability.

Pike Company

- Cavalry receive no combat bonuses when fighting a unit with a pike company that is ordered
- The unit containing a pike company receives double combat value when fighting charging cavalry

Infantry units that can have a pike company have the option included in the army list. In such cases, a pike company is added to the unit (it is usual to place them behind the centre of the unit) and should number 4 to 8 models.

After 1660 the use of the pike was in decline. Large blocks of pike armed men were largely a thing of the past, However most armies still kept small numbers of pike-armed troops within their infantry regiments.

The addition of a pike company is of particular value when defending against cavalry.

Plug Bayonet

- +2 Hand-to-Hand value
- +1 Combat result against enemy Warband infantry

Plug bayonets add +2 to the hand-to-hand value of the unit when fixed, units are assumed not to have their bayonets fixed at the start

of the battle. Once fixed, they cannot be removed for the remainder of the battle, which will prevent the unit shooting again. Fixing bayonets requires a successful command and takes one action or can be completed automatically as a charge reaction instead of Closing Fire. Units with plug bayonets as standard have the hand-to-hand bonus included in parenthesis as part of their Fighting Qualities.

Rabble

- Every unit must receive a separate command
- Cannot act on a battalia or group order

This is used to represent certain militia that are ill trained and given to look after their own interests first with no inclination to obey general orders. Units will not move as part of a battalia or group order, they have to receive specific orders. Where there are more than one rabble unit, each unit must be issued a separate order even if the instructions are the same.

Used with the Militia rule, this will give you an ideal 'Clubmen' unit from the English Civil Wars.

Reliable

- +1 Command

When giving an order to a reliable unit, or to a group of reliable units, add +1 to the commander's command rating. The bonus only applies if all units in a group are reliable. This means that it will be easier to give such units orders and they will often move further than other units.

Sharp Shooters

- Re-Roll one missed shot

The unit can re-roll a single missed shot each time it shoots.

This rule makes shooters more predictable and is a very good way of representing troops who are remarkably well schooled in fire drill or more than averagely effective.

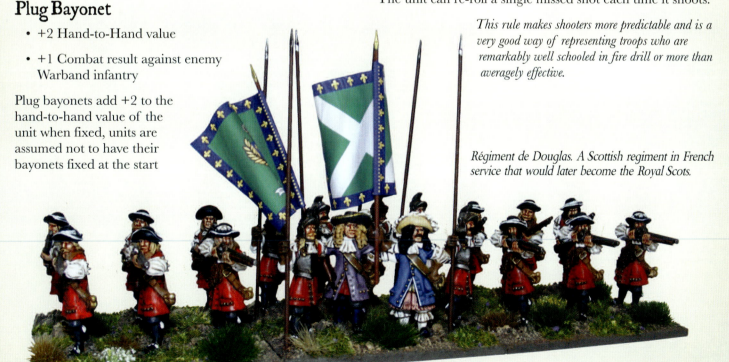

Régiment de Douglas. A Scottish regiment in French service that would later become the Royal Scots.

1583 - The Sea Battle of Terceira; the Spanish defeat the combined English, French and Portuguese fleets.

Small Unit

- -1 Shooting value (only if the unit has ranged weapons)
- -2 Hand-to-Hand
- -1 Stamina

Some forces were faced with severe manpower shortages for certain aspects of their armies, and so can field 'Small' units as specified in the Size of Units section on page 23. Such troops suffer the above reductions to their fighting qualities.

Steady

- Passes first break test

The unit automatically passes the first break test it is called upon to take by scoring the maximum possible value. Note that this might still result in the unit retiring or even breaking in some situations – if it is defeated cavalry or artillery in close combat for example.

Stubborn

- Re-roll one failed morale save

The unit can re-roll a single failed morale save each time the unit suffers casualties. That means the unit can re-roll a failed save each time they are shot at in the enemy's turn and once during each round of hand-to-hand fighting.

This is a significant bonus. In practice 'stubborn' can often be more beneficial than an extra 'pip' of stamina. It can be used to mark out the very best troops in large battles.

Superbly Drilled

- Free Move

If the unit is given an order and fails then it can still make one move.

This rule is useful where a long march or extraordinarily lengthy manoeuvre forms a key part of the game and you want to introduce an element of predictability into the moves. It should be reserved for professional, drilled and disciplined troops and ideally for situations where their opponents are anything but.

Swordsmen

- +D3 Combat result against enemy infantry.

When swordsmen are in combat against enemy infantry their side receives a bonus on combat results equal to half the roll of a dice rounding up (ie, between +1 and +3). If more than one swordsmen unit is involved on either side just make the roll once for each side.

Well trained swordsmen were deadly to other infantry, capable of disrupting even the ablest of pike formations at close quarters.

Terrifying Charge

- Charged enemy must take a break test

Charged enemy units must take a break test as soon as the chargers contact and before working out closing fire. Finish making any moves resulting from the order, assuming an order has been given, before taking the test (ie, if the order was for two units to charge then move both in contact before taking tests). If tests are failed then treat the situation as if the enemy had won a combat round. Work out all resulting moves (eg, retreat, rout and pursuit moves) before continuing the player's Command.

Tough Fighters

- Re-roll one combat hit

The unit can re-roll a single failed hand-to-hand combat attack in each turn of hand-to-hand fighting.

This rule makes hand-to-hand fighters more predictable and is a good way of representing units that are undeniably better than their combat value but not quite worthy of an extra pip of attack. We consider it a nice rule for veterans and 'hard' fighters without making them disproportionately effective.

Untested

- Randomise Stamina

The unit starts the game with no fixed Stamina value. The first time a standard-sized infantry or cavalry unit takes a casualty roll a dice – this determines the unit's Stamina value for the game. 1=1, 2-3=2, 4-5=3, 6=4. Large units add one to the dice score and Small units deduct one.

This rule is useful for representing untried troops who might be equally expected to run off at the first shot or stand toe-to-toe and die to a man. A game can't absorb too many units like this without becoming hostage to the roll of a dice – reserve this rule for a single unit. For troops likely to be poor and only average at best, re-roll 6s.

Valiant

- One free break test re-roll

The unit can re-roll any one failed break test, but only once during the whole game.

This is a minor but potentially critical bonus – it's a good way of giving an otherwise perfectly ordinary unit a chance to shine on the day.

Wavering

- Break test when you take a casualty

The unit must take a break test whenever it takes a casualty. If the unit takes one or more casualties from shooting it must take a break test. If it takes one or more casualties in combat then it must take a break test, regardless of whether it wins the combat or otherwise.

An Imperial tercio moves into position during the Thirty Years War.

A brace of Dutch or German wheel-lock pistols with winding spanner (Stallard collection)

"God made them as stubble to our swords"

Oliver Cromwell after
Marston Moor - 1644

Looks like horse for breakfast... again

Italian Wars 1494-1559

The Italian Wars were a series of conflicts that tore Italy apart for over six decades. The main protagonists were France and Spain, or to be more precise the noble houses of those two Empires, and the largely mercenary armies they raised. What started off as yet another dispute between the Duchy of Milan and the Kingdom of Naples soon attracted French and Spanish interest and escalated into a conflict that dragged in many of the European powers.

Italy in 1494 was a collection of City States, Duchies, Republics, Papal territories and a Kingdom. The kingdom, Naples, covered a third of what is now modern day Italy. Warfare in Italy had developed into a highly ritualised business fought in an awfully civilised manner between contracted warlords, the 'Condottieri'.

Despite many internal squabbles amongst the Italian States, care was always taken that these conflicts did not affect trade and commercial interests, as that would be bad for business. This was to change when the rest of Europe discovered what a prize the region could be. France and Spain soon turned the place into their personal battleground. Key players in the battles that were to come were foreign mercenaries which were used by all sides. The Swiss were the dominant fighting force at the beginning of the war, and as such were the mercenaries of choice to those who could afford their services. To combat the Swiss a new breed of soldier, the Landsknechts, were recruited by the Holy Roman Emperor Maximilian I and they too were soon in the pay of all who could meet the price.

Trouble started in earnest in 1494 when Ludovico Sforza, Duke of Milan, called upon the aid of French King, Charles VIII, to get even with the Republic of Venice. Sforza has since taken much of the blame for what was to follow, as it was claimed that he was the man "who set loose a lion in his house to catch a mouse".

Charles VIII was a young man keen to make an impression on the European scene, and France had consolidated its power base as it no longer faced constant risk of invasion from the English and had managed to centralise control of territories that had been run autonomously in the Middle Ages. Bold and confident, Charles led an invasion into Italy with 25,000 men, including 8,000 of the feared Swiss mercenaries. A string of rapid victories saw the overthrow of the Medici government in Florence, a march on Rome and the sack of Naples.

Pope Alexander VI was apoplectic and quickly moved to galvanise support. Spain was an obvious place to turn, and Ferdinand of Aragon was more than happy to curtail French ambitions. Sforza of Milan, seeing the error he had made inviting the French in, quickly jumped on board this 'League of Venice' along with the Venetians (naturally) and the Holy Roman Empire under Maximilian I. Maximilian had ensured the consolidation of a Hapsburg Holy Roman Empire with his succession earlier that year and had added

motive as his wife was Bianca Sforza (niece of Ludovico). England was to join the league shortly after and it was clear that Europe was aligning against the overly ambitious French.

An army was raised and command given to Condottiero Francesco II of Gonzaga with instructions to eject the French forces. Battle was joined at Fornovo in July 1495, and despite the French winning a tactical victory inflicting more casualties, the strategic victory belonged to the League troops and Charles was forced back into France without gaining a thing from his campaign.

Charles never made it back to Italy, meeting his end two years later when he smashed his head against a door lintel! Without an heir he was succeeded by his cousin, Louis XII, who had claims on Milan himself and soon started looking at conquest. Italy was now a desired property and the cork was truly out of the bottle.

An Uneasy Truce

Louis XII wasted no time in getting his French army ready for war once more and he was soon eyeing up Milan and Naples. This time the French had Papal support as Pope Alexander saw an opportunity to increase his own and his family's (the Borgia's) power. The Papal army marched to war with the French under the Pope's son Cesare Borgia (Alexander had several children, and I would thoroughly recommend further reading on the Borgia family; certainly an interesting bunch).

Milan was first to get the treatment and quickly fell, Ludovico Sforza himself being captured and he was to die in French captivity. The Pope and Cesare Borgia were keen to strike fast in the Papal States, and actually harboured ambitions of a Borgia controlled Italy. The Kingdom of Naples was next, and the Treaty of Granada had been signed between France and Spain effectively splitting the Kingdom between the French and Spanish crowns. Cesare Borgia's forces, along with the French army, stormed into the city of Capua and looked set for the city of Naples itself.

At this stage, unsurprisingly, the truce between France and Spain broke down and normal service resumed.

A new player was about to enter the stage; Gonzalo Fernandez de Cordoba, a military genius of his time. It was his force that marched triumphantly into Naples, not the French or Borgia. His Spanish armies crushed the French at the Battles of Cerignola and Garigliano, both during 1503. At Cerignola the Spanish managed to defeat a much larger French force by using the new tercio formations and massed firepower. This battle is regarded as the first to be won with firearms.

As a result of these defeats France was once more ejected from Italy. Spain, on the other hand, gained control over the Kingdom of Naples, a control they were to keep for centuries. Cordoba himself became the first Spanish Viceroy of Naples.

1586 - The Action at Zutphen. Sir Philip Sidney is killed attacking the Duke of Parma's supply column.

Swiss Infantry Mercenaries

Throughout the later Middle Ages and into the Renaissance, the Swiss Pikeman was the mercenary of choice for European leaders. The Swiss had taken the ancient pike phalanx and adapted it into a stunning offensive weapon. Well trained and disciplined, with an unwillingness to take prisoners, they were rightly feared. It is hardly surprising that they figured heavily on all sides during the Italian Wars.

The ease of hiring an army of these troops also made them very accessible, although expensive; it was possible to raise an entire force by negotiating with the individual Cantons that made up the Swiss region. These forces consisted mostly of pike and halberd armed men supported by skirmishing crossbow and arquebus armed troops. The tactics of mercenary Swiss were brutally effective, massing in two columns at the centre of the army they had been hired by and steamrolling through the opposition. These tactics were actually in stark contrast to the rather sophisticated tactics employed by the Swiss when fighting for their own goals, but effective none the less.

The effectiveness of the Swiss was responsible for the development of the Landsknecht forces by Holy Roman Emperor, Maximilian I to combat them. Rivalry between these forces was bitter, and the savage melees between the two became infamous, with atrocities common on both sides.

The Battle of Novaro in 1513 saw the victorious Swiss sweep all before them in a text book display of their aggressive method of waging war; however the tide was beginning to turn. The advancement of firepower tactics, particularly by the Spanish, and their adoption by Landsknecht regiments was to rid the Swiss of their invincibility over the next decade. The Landsknechts were also becoming the mercenary of choice after 1515 when the Swiss declared neutrality, and therefore became more difficult (and expensive) to employ in large numbers.

The battle of Bicocca in 1522 saw large Swiss formations taken apart by enemy arquebus and artillery and their reputation was never the same again. At the most famous battle of the Italian Wars, Pavia in 1525, the Swiss were once more were neutralised in this way. These setbacks notwithstanding, and the aura of invincibility shattered, the Swiss mercenary infantryman remained the most able soldier in Europe throughout much of the 16th Century.

Today the lasting legacy of the Swiss mercenary is to found at the Vatican where the Swiss Guard remain the last line of defence for the Pope.

Fearsome Swiss pikemen forego subtle tactics.

The War Rages On

1503 saw a reversal of fortunes for the Borgias, Pope Alexander succumbed to malaria and was replaced by Pope Julius II, the Warrior Pope. Cesare Borgia was also struck down by illness and desperately tried to sue for peace with both Spain and the Papacy. This was not to be and Cesare was arrested by Cordoba's Spanish troops and exiled to Spain where he died.

One thorn in his side out of the way, the new Pope turned his attention to Venice which was getting far too influential (in his opinion). Donning his armour, he marched his Papal forces to war after securing a truce with Spain, France and the Holy Roman Empire called the League of Cambrai. Under this treaty the Venetian territory was to be split evenly amongst the League. After initial successes Julius decreed that France were now public enemy number one

Landsknechts

The term Landsknecht means 'servant of the country', and starts being mentioned in historical texts around 1470. The German term Landsknecht literally means 'Land Servant'. Raising them was a reaction to the Swiss mercenary pikemen that had dominated battlefields for the decades leading up to the Italian Wars. They were instigated by Holy Roman Emperor Maximilian I with the help of Georg von Frundsburg, and were very much based on the Swiss model.

The term was initially reserved for those fighting men armed with a pike, but over the course of the war the Landsknechts did develop tactically far more than their Swiss counterparts. The increased use of firearms in conjunction with the pike blocks was to eventually give them the edge tactically.

The most striking aspect of the Landsknecht forces was their outlandish dress. Maximilian was keen to give the men the freedom to wear whatever they wanted, and this resulted in plumes, slashed sleeves and bright colours. A Landsknecht force on the march really could not be missed!

The troops were mostly recruited in Southern Germany and the Tyrol, an Oberst (Colonel) gaining a recruitment commission that led him to taverns and local fairs for manpower. The regiments would be anything from 4,000 to 10,000 men, although the famous Black Band in the service of the French numbered up to 17,000. Most would be armed with a Pike, although Halberds were also common. The front rank would be filled out by 'Doppelsoldners', men on double pay wielding swords in excess of 6' to break enemy pike shafts to force openings for the Landsknecht pike block to exploit.

The brutality of these mercenary forces and especially the carnage of close combat against Swiss forces or opposing Landsknechts was a shock to the Italians who had never seen anything quite like it.

The numbers of firearms grew steadily in Landsknecht ranks from a start point of one in eight, growing to a quarter. This increase in firearms combined with judicious use of defensive positions and artillery were crucial in the tactical edge they were to gain as the Italian Wars progressed.

The major drawback of the Landsknecht forces was that they were mercenaries first and foremost. This meant that their performance in the field varied greatly (generally based on whether they had just been paid). There were amazing feats of bravery as evidenced by the Black Band, a large Landsknecht regiment in the service of France. At Pavia they stood and fought to the last man against their Imperial counterparts. Conversely there were times when whole forces left the battlefield or even changed sides if things took a turn for the worse.

By the end of the 1520's the Landsknechts were in decline as general breakdowns in discipline coupled with more widespread use of firearms and the death of their 'father' von Frundsburg took their toll. Gradually these colourful characters disappeared from the battlefields of Europe to be replaced by the ubiquitous Imperial Foot Soldier.

"No Money, no Landsknecht!"

Landsknecht battle-cry

and formed a new league in 1511, this one including Spain, the Holy Roman Empire and England. England's new king, Henry VIII, was just itching to stake a claim to French territory.

The following year the French defeated Spain at the battle of Ravenna, but their inspirational commander Gaston de Foix was killed attempting to scatter the retreating Spanish tercios. This loss was compounded when Pope Julius paid the Swiss to invade Milan and put Maximilian Sforza back on the throne. Once again the French had to make their way home empty handed. A new plan was quickly hatched to ally with Venice and split Lombardy between them.

1513 was a tough year for France and her allies. The French army's assault on Milan met with failure at Novara, and Holy Roman Empire forces defeated the Venetians. Worse was to follow as the Scots, in keeping with the 'Auld Alliance' with France, were persuaded to march on England to keep the English from French territory. Disaster befell the Scots on Flodden Field and King James IV was killed, the last British monarch to be killed in battle.

One bright spot for the French was the death of Pope Julius, without whom the Holy League began to unravel. His replacement, Leo X, was more interested in looking out for his De Medici family interests in Florence.

By 1515 a new king was on the French throne, Francis I, and he instantly set about rectifying the situation, culminating in a decisive victory over the Swiss at Marignano which allowed him to recapture Milan once more for the French crown. The treaty of Venice effectively gave all the regions of Northern Italy over to French rule and Spain was in no position to retaliate due to the death of Ferdinand of Aragon in 1516.

1587 - The first child of English parents is born in the New World.

Europe in Turmoil

Ferdinand's successor to the Spanish crown was his grandson, Charles, and in 1519 he was to become Holy Roman Emperor Charles V as well as King of Spain. This unification of Spain and Holy Roman Empire was the cause of hostilities commencing with the French once more as Francis I had ambitions on the Imperial throne.

This time the superior Spanish tercio tactics, combining the arquebus firearm with close combat troops, were to prove decisive. The Spanish victory at Bicocca in 1522 was a major turning point as the myth of Swiss invincibility was smashed forever. Francis tried again in 1525 to march on Lombardy, but again the Imperial Spanish were to prove superior and the French army was utterly crushed at the Battle of Pavia and Francis was captured.

In a desperate attempt to turn the tide, France approached the Muslim Ottoman Empire under Suleiman the Magnificent for help. This obviously caused more than a few raised eyebrows! Suleiman, seeing an opportunity, marched into Hungary and defeated a Christian army allied to Charles V at Mohacs. This did little to help the French though and Francis was forced to give up all clams on Italy, Burgundy and Flanders at the Treaty of Madrid.

In the meantime the death of Pope Julius had made way for Clement VIII, and now it was the Papal view that Spain was getting too big for its boots. The League of Cognac was signed in 1526, aligning the Pope, France, Florence, Milan and Venice against Spain. Just how this managed to go through so shortly after the French alliance with the Ottomans is anybody's guess, but successful it certainly wasn't. Two Imperial armies advanced through the northern regions of Italy, one comprising mainly of Spanish, the other mostly Landsknechts. They met up in 1527 and fell on Rome, sacking the city and imprisoning Pope Clement. By now Francis and Charles were running short of men, and not surprisingly were very short of money and sued for peace.

> *"I speak Spanish to God, Italian to women, French to men, and German to my horse."*
>
> *Holy Roman Emperor Charles V*

The End in Sight

Francis was to have another go at Italian conquest (determined chap that he was) and instigated a two year war from 1536 to 1538 when French forces marched on and captured Turin. Again very little was gained, although Turin did remain in French hands as a result of the Treaty of Nice.

In 1542 Francis did the unthinkable and entered into an offensive alliance with the Ottomans. This really did cause outrage all across Europe, especially when a combined Franco-Ottoman fleet captured Nice. As a result both Spain and England launched invasions into France and once again French gains were lost.

It was left to the sons of both kings to bring the Italian Wars to a conclusion, Henry II of France and Phillip II of Spain. The last major battle was fought at Marciano in 1553 and once again the Spanish were victorious. The war was officially brought to a close by the Treaty of Cateau-Cambresis in which France renounced all claims to Italian territory. Spain walked away with Naples, Sardinia, Sicily and Milan as well as controlling influence of the northern regions. France's 60 year campaign to become the dominant force in Italy and curb Spain's expansion had finally ended in failure.

Gendarmes

The term 'Gendarme' is from the French for Men at Arms and was a throwback to the middle ages. By the Italian Wars they encapsulated the resurgence of the medieval fully armoured knight, lance in hand. They were a common sight in most western European armies at the end of the 15th century, but it was the French who made them famous.

Most Gendarmes, especially the French ones, were of noble birth. This fact was to prove both a benefit regarding the élan such formations displayed and a curse as they were notoriously difficult to control. What is clear is that they were an imposing sight on the battlefield being fully armoured, with horse armour too and an array of plumes, velvet coats and other finery. Not only did they look good, they hit hard! They would often (certainly by the French) be used in a very aggressive way, charging *en haye* (in a single rak) with lances smashing aside those unlucky enough to be in the way.

Tactically they were used to crush the opposition cavalry, sweeping them aside, before turning on the enemy infantry which (hopefully) was disordered from melee. Where they performed poorly was against well ordered pike formations with supporting firearms, and as pike and shotte tactics developed the battlefield role of the gendarme was called into question. Late in the Italian Wars each company of gendarmes was supplemented by light cavalry armed with the arquebus, and by the end of the 16th century they had been replaced by pistol armed heavy cavalry, such as the German Reiters.

ITALIAN WARS IMPERIALIST ARMY LIST

At the heart of all Imperial armies in the Italian Wars are the Landsknechts. With their outrageous 'pluderhosen', slashed doublets and feathered hats they are one of the most iconic (and certainly most colourful) units in wargaming. The addition of Gendarmes and other assorted cavalry make a spectacular sight, and also a very formidable force to be reckoned with.

The Imperial army usually went to war with huge pike formations of Landsknechts in the centre with the flanks covered by cavalry. Locally raised troops tended to act as a reserve; after all, those mercenaries need to earn their pay.

Command Ratings

Overall Commander: Random Command Rating (see page 35) .... 40 Points

Roll D6 for rating: 1: Command Rating 7, 2-5: Command Rating 8, 6: Command Rating 9

Infantry/Artillery Commander: Command Rating 8 .... 40 Points

Cavalry Commander: Command Rating 8 .... 40 Points

The Horse

Unit	Unit Type	Weapon	Hand-to-Hand Value	Shooting Value	Morale Value	Stamina	Special	Points
Gendarmes	Heavy Horse	Lance, Mace, Sword	9	-	3+	4	Heavy Cavalry +1, Elite 4+	65

• Maximum of two units of Gendarmes

Unit	Unit Type	Weapon	Hand-to-Hand Value	Shooting Value	Morale Value	Stamina	Special	Points
Men-at-Arms	Heavy Horse	Lance, Sword	8	-	4+	4	Heavy Cavalry +1	53

• Maximum of two units of Men-at-Arms

Unit	Unit Type	Weapon	Hand-to-Hand Value	Shooting Value	Morale Value	Stamina	Special	Points
Reiter	Horse	Sword, Pistols	8	1	4+	3	Mercenary	38

Unit	Unit Type	Weapon	Hand-to-Hand Value	Shooting Value	Morale Value	Stamina	Special	Points
Stradiots & Genitors	Light Skirmisher Horse	Javelin, Sword & Shield	6	1	5+	3	Fire & Evade	35

• Any Stradiot unit can replace Javelins with Lances (reducing the Shooting Value to 0) @ +4 points per unit

Unit	Unit Type	Weapon	Hand-to-Hand Value	Shooting Value	Morale Value	Stamina	Special	Points
Mounted Handgunners	Light Horse	Arquebus	6	1	5+	3	Mercenary	30

• Any unit can replace Arquebus with Crossbow @ 0 points

The Foot

Unit	Unit Type	Weapon	Hand-to-Hand Value	Shooting Value	Morale Value	Stamina	Special	Points
Pikemen	Foot Pike Block	Pike	6	-	4+	4	Hedgehog	34

• Any unit can be upgraded to Large @ 6 points per unit

Unit	Unit Type	Weapon	Hand-to-Hand Value	Shooting Value	Morale Value	Stamina	Special	Points
Arquebusiers	Foot Battle Line	Arquebus	3	2	5+	3		25

• Maximum of one unit of arquebusiers per unit of pikemen

Unit	Unit Type	Weapon	Hand-to-Hand Value	Shooting Value	Morale Value	Stamina	Special	Points
Halberdiers	Foot Infantry Block	Halberd	6	-	4+	4	Double-Handed Infantry Arms	36

• Maximum of two units per army

1590 - Maurice of Nassau captures Breda.

Unit	Unit Type	Weapon	Hand-to-Hand Value	Shooting Value	Morale Value	Stamina	Special	Points
Swordsmen	Foot Battle Line	Sword & Shield	6	-	4+	3	Swordsmen	34

- Maximum of two units per army

Unit	Unit Type	Weapon	Hand-to-Hand Value	Shooting Value	Morale Value	Stamina	Special	Points
Landsknecht Pikemen	Foot Pike Block	Pike	6	-	4+	4	Hedgehog, Mercenary, Bad War	31

- Up to a quarter of Landsknecht pike units can replace pikes with halberds @ 2 points (losing Hedgehog and gaining double-handed infantry weapon ability).

Unit	Unit Type	Weapon	Hand-to-Hand Value	Shooting Value	Morale Value	Stamina	Special	Points
Landsknecht Arquebusiers	Foot Battle Line	Arquebus	3	2	5+	3	Mercenary, Bad War	22

- Maximum of one unit per two Landsknecht pike units
- Any unit can replace arquebuses with crossbows @ 0 pts

From behind the cover of their big guns, the Imperial army advances.

The Ordnance

- Maximum of two artillery pieces per battalia

Unit	Unit Type	Weapon	Hand-to-Hand Value	Shooting Value	Morale Value	Stamina	Special	Points
Artillery	Ordnance	Various Cannon	1	3-2-1	5+	2		Varies

- Light Guns 17 points
- Medium Guns 21 points
- Heavy Guns 25 points

| Siege Artillery | Ordnance | Mortar | 1 | 2 | 5+ | 2 | | 25 |

- Maximum of one mortar

Dramatis Personae

Georg von Frundsberg. Command Rating 9 .... 70 Points
  Special Rule: Father of the Landsknechts.

Grizzled mercenary Landsknecht pikemen

Georg von Frundsberg 1473-1528

The man who would come to be known as the 'Father of the Landsknechts' was born to a family of Tyrolian knights in the town of Mindelheim in 1473. Like many young German noblemen, Georg was called to the service of the Holy Roman Empire at a young age. He then led a life of almost continual campaigning.

In 1499 he was in the service of the Holy Roman Emperor, Maximilian I, fighting the Swiss in the Swabian War. Later that year he was fighting the French on behalf of the Duchy of Milan at the behest of his Imperial masters. He was knighted in 1504 after a display of great valour at the Battle of Regensburg, an honour bestowed on him by Maximilian himself.

Understanding that the Swiss posed a formidable foe, and were a resource the French would call upon at any time, von Frundsberg helped Maximilian found the first Landsknecht forces to counteract the Swiss threat. He, and his "beloved sons", were to play a major role in many

victories in the Italian Wars, most notably La Bicocca in 1522 and Pavia in 1525 where he fought on behalf of the new Emperor, Charles V. Finding time to end the Peasant Revolt in Germany after Pavia, Georg was back in Italy the following year to assist the Imperial cause, even selling off family silver to raise more troops. Much of 1527 was spent campaigning without any major battles and soon the money ran out. Not even von Frundsberg's standing with his men could stop the beginnings of mutiny in the ranks; so shocked was the ageing commander that he suffered a stroke. He was never to recover and died indebted and heartbroken at his Mindelheim castle in 1528.

Georg von Frundsberg: Command Rating 9

Special Rule: Father of the Landsknechts
Von Frundsberg was the founder of the Landsknechts and commands great respect from his men. All Landsknecht units in von Frusberg's battalia receive the 'Steady' special rule.

ITALIAN WARS FRENCH ARMY LIST

The French Army of the Italian Wars really does spoil you for choice. You have the most formidable infantry and cavalry units at your disposal – the Swiss pikemen and French Gendarmes. In addition to these indomitable troops you have an array of additional cavalry choices and can even take 'Black Band' Landsknechts to antagonise your Imperial opponents.

It is hard to argue with the tactic of 'hit hard with the Swiss and the heavy cavalry', and that certainly is in keeping with how the French armies fought at the time. Sometimes such brutally simple methods can come unstuck, but used wisely the French army is a tough one to beat and does allow tactical finesse when needed.

Command Ratings

Overall Commander: Random Command Rating (see page 35)   40 Points

      Roll D6 for rating: 1: Command Rating 7, 2-5: Command Rating 8, 6: Command Rating 9

Infantry/Artillery Commander: Command Rating 8   40 Points

Cavalry Commander: Command Rating 8   40 Points

The Horse

Unit	Unit Type	Weapon	Hand-to-Hand Value	Shooting Value	Morale Value	Stamina	Special	Points
Gendarmes d'Ordonnance	Heavy Horse	Lance, Mace, Sword	10	-	3+	4	Heavy Cavalry D3, Elite 4+	71

- Maximum of three units of Gendarmes d'Ordonnance

Unit	Unit Type	Weapon	Hand-to-Hand Value	Shooting Value	Morale Value	Stamina	Special	Points
Archers & Chevaulegers	Heavy Horse	Lance, Pistol	8	1	3+	4	Heavy Cavalry +1	58

- Maximum of three units
- Archers can replace pistol with Longbow or Crossbow for 1 point per unit

Unit	Unit Type	Weapon	Hand-to-Hand Value	Shooting Value	Morale Value	Stamina	Special	Points
Mounted Arquebusiers	Horse	Arquebus, Sword	7	1	4+	3		39

Unit	Unit Type	Weapon	Hand-to-Hand Value	Shooting Value	Morale Value	Stamina	Special	Points
Stradiots	Light Skirmisher Horse	Javelin, Sword & Shield	6	1	5+	3	Fire & Evade	35

- Any Stradiot unit can replace Javelins with Lances (reducing the Shooting Value to 0) to become Lances Moresques @ 4 points per unit

Unit	Unit Type	Weapon	Hand-to-Hand Value	Shooting Value	Morale Value	Stamina	Special	Points
English or Scottish Cavalry	Cavalry	Spear, Sword	7	-	5+	3		34

The cream of the French army – Gendarmes and Swiss infantry.

1594 - The first tulip bulbs planted in Holland flower.

The Foot

Unit	Unit Type	Weapon	Hand-to-Hand Value	Shooting Value	Morale Value	Stamina	Special	Points
Pikemen	Foot Pike Block	Pike	6	-	4+	4	Hedgehog	34

- Any units can be upgraded to Large @ 6 points each
- Any units can be Italian or German Pikemen. If so they are Mercenary @ -3 points each

Unit	Unit Type	Weapon	Hand-to-Hand Value	Shooting Value	Morale Value	Stamina	Special	Points
Arquebusiers	Foot Battle Line	Arquebus	3	2	5+	3		25

- Maximum of one unit of arquebusiers per unit of pikemen
- Any unit can be Italian or German Arquebusiers. If so they are Mercenary @ -3 points each

Unit	Unit Type	Weapon	Hand-to-Hand Value	Shooting Value	Morale Value	Stamina	Special	Points
Halberdiers	Foot Infantry Block	Halberd	6	-	4+	4	Double-Handed Infantry Arms	36

- Maximum of two units per army

Unit	Unit Type	Weapon	Hand-to-Hand Value	Shooting Value	Morale Value	Stamina	Special	Points
Swiss Pikemen	Foot Pike Block	Pike	7	-	4+	4	Hedgehog, Ferocious Charge, Elite	44

- Maximum of six units per army

Unit	Unit Type	Weapon	Hand-to-Hand Value	Shooting Value	Morale Value	Stamina	Special	Points
Swiss Arquebusiers	Foot Battle Line	Arquebus	4	2	4+	3		30

- Maximum of two units; can only be fielded if there are at least four Swiss pike units
- Any unit can change arquebus for crossbow @ 0 points per unit

Unit	Unit Type	Weapon	Hand-to-Hand Value	Shooting Value	Morale Value	Stamina	Special	Points
Landsknecht Pikemen	Foot Pike Block	Pike	6	-	4+	4	Hedgehog, Mercenary, Bad War	31

- Up to a quarter of Landsknecht pike units can replace pikes with halberds @ 2 points (losing Hedgehog and gaining double-handed infantry weapon ability).

Unit	Unit Type	Weapon	Hand-to-Hand Value	Shooting Value	Morale Value	Stamina	Special	Points
Landsknecht Arquebusiers	Foot Battle Line	Arquebus	3	2	5+	3	Mercenary, Bad War	22

- Maximum of one unit per two Landsknecht pike units
- Any unit can exchange arquebuses for crossbows

The Ordnance

- Maximum of two artillery pieces per battalia

Unit	Unit Type	Weapon	Hand-to-Hand Value	Shooting Value	Morale Value	Stamina	Special	Points
Artillery	Ordnance	Various Cannon	1	3-2-1	5+	2		Varies

- Light Guns 17 points
- Medium Guns 21 points
- Heavy Guns 25 points

Unit	Unit Type	Weapon	Hand-to-Hand Value	Shooting Value	Morale Value	Stamina	Special	Points
Siege Artillery	Ordnance	Mortar	1	2	5+	2		25

- Maximum of one mortar

Dramatis Personae

Francis I. Command Rating 8.. 50 Points
   Special Rule: Rash.

1595 - Shakespeare writes A Midsummer Night's Dream.

Dramatis Personae: Francis I of France 1494-1547

King Francis was one of the most complex of characters of his era, at once being a patron of the arts and humanist but also waging continuous wars against his hated rival, the Holy Roman Emperor Charles , and leaving a legacy of persecution against French Protestants that would scar France for many years.

Francis was an advocate of absolutism in his monarchy, and this, coupled with an over-reliance on personal favourites, led to some hasty actions. Initially his reaction to Protestants in France was protective, but once they started to question his absolute rule then he came down hard on them. His hatred of Charles V led to an array of allegiances and attempted truces; a notable failure being at the Field of Cloth of Gold in 1520 where diplomatic talks with Henry VIII of England finally broke down.

Militarily he was a brave leader, but too rash to be very effective. He led his men from the front at the victory of Marignano in 1515 to capture Milan for the French crown, but was himself decisively beaten and captured at Pavia in 1525. After Pavia he was held in Madrid until agreeing to tough terms which effectively lost France all the gains he had fought for. He was eventually released in 1526 and immediately went back to his expansionist policy despite the terms of his release, but these plans were to fail.

Francis never really recovered from his imprisonment and spent the last 20 years of his life suffering a variety of ailments and eventually wasting away in 1547 when he was succeeded by his son, Henry II. Despite his failings he would be remembered as 'Le Grand Roi Francois' by future French generations who seemed to forgive the poor financial and social state in which he left his country.

King Francis I of France: Command Rating 8

Special Rule: Rash

All cavalry units in the battalia that Francis commands must countercharge if charged when able to do so and will always declare a charge on enemy units to their front and within 9" at the beginning of the command phase. In addition they will always perform sweeping advances to engage the enemy where possible.

Francis adds +2 to the combat resolution of any combat that he engages in.

> "I should like to see the clause in Adam's will which excludes me from a share of the world,"
>
> *King Francis I of France*

Swiss from the Berne canton – it's not all cuckoo clocks and chocolate...

1596 - The English fleet temporarily captures Cadiz.

THE BATTLE OF PAVIA
24TH FEBRUARY 1525.

The Set Up

This encounter is based on the epic battle between the French and Imperialist armies which took place at Pavia in northern Italy in February 1525. An accurate narrative reconstruction of how the battle unfolded is difficult; not surprising in that it consisted of a series of isolated engagements in wooded, boggy country, enshrouded in a mixture of mist and gunsmoke.

The armies of the time were struggling to develop tactics to cope with the new effectiveness of infantry firepower. It is not always clear from accounts of the battle exactly what the proportions of pike and shot were, and how they operated together. So setting up any refight is going to contain a strong element of guesswork - but that need not prevent us using the battle as the inspiration for an exciting and colourful game!

The Holy Roman Emperors and the Kings of France had been fighting over Italy since 1494, but by 1523 the French had been driven out of the country. The current Emperor, Charles V, was also heir to the throne of Spain, and the combined forces of the two realms had created an almost unstoppable superpower. Yet the gallant young French king,

Francis I, refused to give up. In the autumn of 1524 he led a huge and expensive new army over the Alps and drove his enemies out of Milan, then settled down to besiege the nearby town of Pavia. The town was defended by 5,000 German Landsknechts under Don Antonio de Leyva, who held out until a relieving army commanded by Charles de Lannoy, the Viceroy of Naples, arrived early in February 1525. Lannoy had around 18,000 men, including 1,000 cavalry and 6,000 Landsknechts, but even then he did not feel strong enough to attack, and for the next three weeks the two armies faced each other in entrenched positions along the Vernavola River. As the siege dragged on, Francis was losing men daily to sickness and desertion. On February 20th Lannoy learned that 6,000 of the French king's fearsome Swiss pikemen had gone home - leaving their employer with no more than 20,000 troops, of whom only 5,000 were Swiss.

Seeing his opportunity, Lannoy moved his army under cover of darkness to the flank of the weakened French force and launched what was probably only meant to be an exploratory attack to test the French defences. As it happened, the French were caught completely unawares and this is where we pick up the story with our battle report.

The Black Band Landsknechts prepare for a Bad War...

1597 - A third Spanish Armada attempt against England is scattered by storms.

The Imperialists

CHARLES DE LANNOY

General, Command Rating 8

- 1,000 cavalry, under the personal command of Lannoy. (1 unit of gendarmes, 2 units of chevaulegers)

MARQUES DEL VASTO

Command Rating 8

- 200 light cavalry and 1,500 arquebusiers (1 unit of stradiots, 3 units of arquebusiers (2 mounted, 1 foot))

DON ANTONIO DE LEYVA

Command Rating 8

- 5,000 Landsknechts – garrison of Pavia (5 pike units, 1 arquebus unit)

Special Rule: Garrison

GEORG VON FRUNDSBERG

Command Rating 9

- 6,000 Landsknechts (6 pike units, 1 arquebus unit)

Special Rule: Father of the Landsknechts.

ALFONSO DE AVALOS

Command Rating 8

- 3,000 Spanish arquebusiers (4 arquebus units)

Special Rule: For the sake of this scenario the units within this battalia can move through woods as though they are skirmish infantry.

DUC DE BOURBON

Command Rating 8

- Rearguard of 6,000 Spanish and Italian Foot (4 pike units, 1 swordsmen unit, 2 arquebus units)

The French

KING FRANCIS I

General, Command Rating 8

- 1,300 Royal Gendarmes, under the personal command of the king. (3 gendarme units, 1 Men-at-Arms unit)
- 200 light cavalry under Tiercelin. (1 stradiot unit)

Special Rules: Rash

COMMANDER RICHARD DE LA POLE

Command Rating 8

- 4,500 Landsknechts (4 pike units, 2 arquebus units)

Special Rule: Black Band – All units in the battalia gain the 'Brave' special rule.

COMMANDER ROBERT DE LA MARCK

Command Rating 9

- 5,000 Swiss (5 pike units, 1 arquebus unit)

COMMANDER DUC D'ALENÇON

Command Rating 7

- 9,000 French and Italian infantry (8 pike units, 4 arquebus units)

In addition both sides have been given heavy guns – 4 for the Imperialists and 2 for the French – but neither side has had time to get them into position on the battlefield.

> War is my homeland,
> My armour is my house,
> And fighting is my life.
>
> *Soldier's saying, 16th century*

Deployment

The French are deployed facing across the table toward the original Imperial positions. The left is held by the Black Band Landsknechts of de la Pole, positioned within the deer park and close to the French headquarters.

King Francis is positioned with his Gendarmes in the centre, together with the Swiss foot. In the distance on the right flank (and far from the Imperial's initial attack) are the men of the Duc d'Alençon. During the course of the actual battle, these men played no part and headed off to Milan instead of engaging the enemy. Getting them across the table may be a challenge.

After the night march the Imperialist forces are deployed at right angles to the French, at the edge of the park on the French flank. Having the element of surprise, the Imperial army has the first turn.

Victory Conditions

Imperialists

Capture and hold the French headquarters	5 Victory Points
Reach the Imperial Objective on the map to signal the Pavia garrison	5 Victory Points
Capture King Francis	5 Victory Points

French

Secure and hold the French headquarters	5 Victory Points
Break three of the Imperialist battalias	5 Victory Points
Capture Charles de Lannoy	5 Victory Points

If both armies finish with the same total of victory points, the result is a draw. An advantage of 5 points is a minor victory, 10 points is a major victory.

How it Played

Nick Eyre, the owner of North Star Military Figures took command of the Imperial Forces. Nick has a rather large collection of Landsknechts from his own company, but had never actually used them in action before and so was very keen to get stuck in. Due to the element of surprise the Imperialists went first and Nick wasted no time in ordering a general advance. Much to his surprise (and also to everyone else's in the room) these commands were eagerly accepted by the Imperial vanguard which raced toward the deer park and the hated enemy Black Band Landsknechts. The fact that the French headquarters objective was also en-route was seen as an added bonus!

In a daring move to replicate history, Nick tried to move all four units of his Spanish Arquebusier battalia toward the woods flanking the French approach route. This order was received less enthusiastically and they ambled forward cautiously. The safety of the trees was some way off and their timing would need to be right as they crossed the open ground to get into position before the French cavalry could tear them apart.

The Imperial artillery battery opened fire on the Black Band arquebusiers in the deer park and caused the first casualties of the game to much rejoicing among the Imperial commanders.

In response the Black Band took up defensive positions behind the remains of the deer park walls to await the onslaught, hoping that the rest of the army would advance to help them out. The Swiss, assisted by their excellent command rating, did just that, as did the French Heavy Cavalry with King Francis at their head. Somewhat surprisingly, the dubious French/Italian infantry command of the Duc d'Alençon was equally successful in marching to the sound of the guns. This was an added bonus for Bernard Lewis (overall commander of the French forces) as these troops were capable of swamping the Imperial Army with sheer weight of numbers.

Turn 2 did not start well for the Imperialists as the master plan of getting the arquebusiers in position quickly began to unravel, the troops only edging forward once more to block the fire of the artillery whose fire arc they were trying to traverse. On a better note, von Frundsberg was inspirational in urging his Landsknecht 'children' along, although it seemed they needed little encouragement to get to grips with their counterparts in French pay. In the French turn it was clear that the ill-feeling was mutual and the pike block of the Black Band seized the initiative and charged into the advancing Landsknechts and drove the leading arqubus-armed unit back in disorder. The Swiss continued to advance at a frightening speed, only temporarily slowed down by a large bog in the way. At this point the

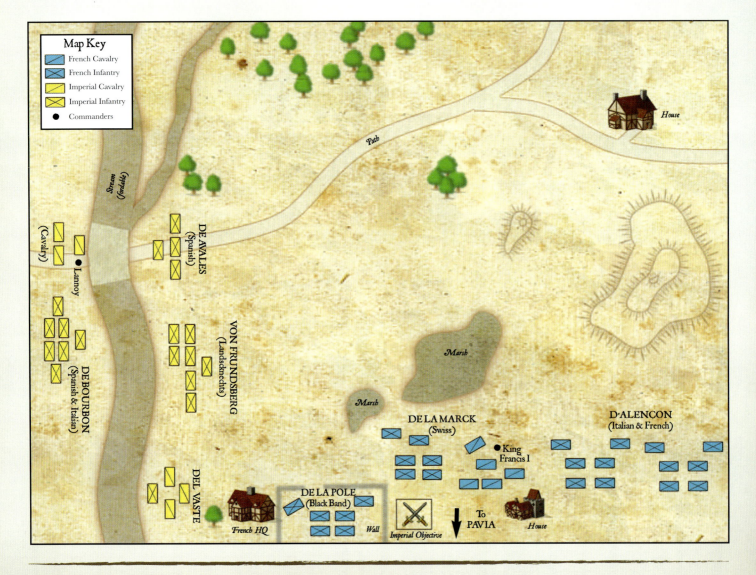

1599 - The Earl of Essex arrives in Dublin with 16,000 men, the largest army ever seen in Ireland.

Von Frundsberg's Landsknechts lead the assault.

French/Italian infantry once more confounded everyone by advancing again! Just as the Imperial commanders exchanged nervous looks they were cheered to see Francis fail to get his elite cavalry to move any further.

Turn 3 was to witness absolute carnage as Landsknecht met Landsknecht in a 'Bad War'. Von Frundsberg's battalia declared charges against four Black Band units that had moved out of the deer park defences. In a devastating attack – with equally shattering dice rolls – three Black Band pike units were destroyed! It was over so quickly their 'Brave' rule was of no use. Von Frundsberg's ability to make his troops 'Steady' was useful and he saved one unit from breaking. The Black Band units were broken, though a few stragglers fought on, while the Imperial Landsknechts were largely intact.

The Spanish arquebusiers were in trouble however. A failed command had left them stranded in front of their own artillery and blocking its fire, while the Swiss marched grimly towards them. The Spanish infantry chose this moment to blunder and fell back toward their starting positions – all the good work of the Landsknechts was in danger of being lost.

The French turn saw the Heavy Cavalry sweep forward once more, now very threatening as the confused Spanish arquebusiers milled around before them. The Swiss got to the far end of the deer park, a little too late to help most of the Black Band but better late than never. With this support,

the Black Band survivors showed their mettle by driving back the Imperial Landsknecht unit nearest to their lines.

Turn 4. A crucial point of the battle was at hand. Nick nervously prepared to attempt to move his Spanish Arquebusier battalia once more and needed some luck. To his relief the imminent peril facing the Spanish seemed to be the spur they needed and they raced off to the woods, sprinting to the safety they offered and turning to provide a corridor of fire the enemy would need to pass through. This move also cleared the way for the artillery battery to open fire once again, and they joyfully targeted the advancing Gendarmes.

The Swiss commander decided to split his force, now moving half to advance on the enemy Landsknechts while the rest moved to cover the deer park approach, attempting to block the way for any cavalry to get into a position to signal the Pavia garrison. The last thing the French needed at this time was another 5000 Landsknechts pouring out of the city to their rear. The Black Band was finally beginning to earn their reputation as the survivors bravely pushed back another enemy pike block.

Turn 5. The vanguard of von Frundsberg's Landsknechts once again charged into the remnants of the Black Band; bolstered by the arrival of the Swiss to their rear the Band held firm once more, to the disbelief of the Imperial commanders. The Imperial mounted arquebusiers on their right flank moved into the deer park in an attempt to break through to the Pavia garrison, but were forced to halt when they spotted the Swiss reserves taking a defensive position in front of them; splitting the Swiss force was proving to be a smart move. The Imperial battery opened fire once more on the leading French Gendarmes, this time blowing huge holes in the tightly packed cavalry formation. With the Spanish arquebusiers also firing from the woods the French cavalry was taking some serious damage.

The French command was determined to get to grips with the enemy; the leading Swiss regiments charged home into the enemy Landsknecht formations and destroy two units utterly. This is enough to break von Frundsberg's battalia, weakened as they had been by the defiant Black Band. King Francis urged his cavalry to charge en masse to the enemy guns and horse; but his men were badly affected by the fire they had received and failed to move. To make matters worse D'Alençon's reserve force blundered and retreated at impressive speed, effectively removing them from the battle.

Turn 6. With the French cavalry caught in the open, the Imperial forces moved to take advantage and strike a critical blow against them. The arquebusiers moved through the woods to get into a position to give enfilading fire – a devastating hail of shot ripped more men from their saddles. The artillery once again target the leading Gendarmes who were forced to retire. In the centre the last of von Frundsberg's command launched a desperate attack to halt the Swiss juggernaut but was destroyed, although they took some of their hated foe with them. (The morale level reduction to 6+ for the broken battalia was to be von Frundsberg's downfall in this combat).

King Francis was faced with the piecemeal destruction of his elite cavalry by an elusive enemy's firepower and could only rally his men as once again they would not charge home. The victorious Swiss moved over the bodies of the slain Landsknechts and spotted their next targets; the combined Spanish and Italian reserve that had advanced into position.

Turn 7. Sensing this was the crucial part of the battle, Nick chose his moment to order his own cavalry to charge into the weakened French Gendarmes. The damage already sustained from the continuous Imperial fire had reduced the French to such a level that the entire cavalry battalia was broken; the cream of the French nobility died in droves and King Francis was cut off from the rest of his army. The entire reserve moved forward, but deemed it sensible not to get too close to the dangerous Swiss, and adopted a defensive position.

On the French side things were looking bleak as their reserve under D'Alençon once more refused to assist their comrades; nearly half of the French infantry strength had decided to stay out of the fight and they started to slip away from the battlefield.

Turn 8. With the cream of his cavalry broken or dead, King Francis of France was surrounded and captured by the victorious Imperial Gendarmes. The remaining Spanish cavalry skirted around the Swiss positions and headed to give the signal for the Pavia garrison to sally forth.

With the collapse of the French cavalry, along with the desertion of the French/Italian reserve, the isolated Swiss were left alone to defend themselves along with the last survivors of the brave Black Band. While the Landsknechts prepared to meet their end (there could be no surrender for these troops against their Imperial brethren) the Swiss began to quit the field in an orderly retreat. As night fell the battlefield of Pavia and the city itself were firmly in Imperial hands.

The Historical Outcome

Lannoy ordered a night attack across the river, with the aim of breaking into the walled deer park of Mirabello which protected the French left and forcing François to abandon his siege lines around Pavia.

It is unlikely that the Imperialists expected to do more than temporarily distract the French while they evacuated the garrison; the weather was wet and cold, food was short, and both armies were fed up and ready to go home. But the Viceroy's move succeeded beyond his wildest dreams. Before dawn on 24th February his Italian pioneers broke down the park wall, and the Marques del Vasto led 200 horsemen and 1,500 arquebusiers through the breach to attack the chateau where François had his headquarters.

The French were taken completely by surprise as del Vasto, followed by three divisions of Spanish and Landsknecht infantry, appeared out of the morning mist and began to roll up their line. However the king was not in the chateau, but had spent the night with his crack mounted gendarmes in the centre, and when he saw the situation he immediately led this, his only mobile reserve, into the fight.

1600 - The English East India Company is founded.

Unfortunately, to get at the enemy advancing from their left the cavalry had to ride across the front of a battery of French guns which had been doing considerable damage to the Imperialists, forcing them to cease fire. With hindsight the gendarmes may seem like an anachronism, but in the early 16th century they were still the most devastating strike force in Europe. Unlike the lighter Imperial horsemen they were true medieval knights, wearing full plate armour, riding armoured horses and equipped exclusively for hand-to-hand combat with their lances and great swords. With the king at their head they broke the Spanish and Italian foot of the Imperial rearguard, then rode over a body of cavalry which bravely attempted a countercharge. At this point Lannoy almost lost his nerve, crying out in despair "There is no hope but in God!"

However the French were now charging on their tiring horses into the heart of the deer park, an expanse of boggy ground dotted with trees, and were falling into disorder. Two columns of mercenary infantry - one of Swiss and the other of Landsknechts - were advancing to support them, but were attacked by the Imperial Landsknechts and

Spanish arquebusiers coming through the park. The Spanish shot were using the tactics which they had developed in previous battles, manoeuvring in small units and taking advantage of cover and natural obstacles, and the Swiss were reluctant to get to close quarters with them. This was not surprising in view of the damage which they had suffered in a frontal attack on arquebusiers three years before at the Battle of La Bicocca, but the unsympathetic French later accused the Swiss of treachery. As their casualties mounted they hesitated and finally fell back, leaving the French Landsknechts (who in any case were their bitter rivals) to be surrounded and massacred by fellow Germans under the famous Georg von Frundsberg. Meanwhile the Duc d'Alençon, commanding on the French left, had received no orders and had no idea what was happening in the centre. Once he had recovered from the shock of the Imperialist attack on the park he set his troops in motion - not towards the sound of the guns, but in the opposite direction, in full retreat, destroying the bridges across the River Ticino behind him.

Now the Spanish closed in on Francis and his gendarmes from all directions, firing and then dodging behind the trees, which prevented the French from charging effectively with their lances. Gradually the horsemen were picked off until Francis was fighting on almost alone, wounded and unhorsed, surrounded by a pile of enemy dead. Eventually he collapsed under a mob of ferocious Spaniards, but Lannoy arrived just in time to save his life. The king was taken as a prisoner to Madrid, leaving 8,000 of his soldiers dead on the field. The Imperialists had lost just 700. The French hopes of dominating Italy were in ruins.

Tudor Warfare in the British Isles

The armies of Henry the Eighth and Elizabeth the First of England are a study unto themselves, stubbornly refusing to modernise en masse despite massive developments taking place on the continent. This rejection of change has many different causes. Although involved in many wars in Europe, the English army's contribution on land was always on a relatively small scale, the work being done by picked troops or as often, with mercenaries. The huge reserves of the trained bands or the militias (there being no fixed standing army), were rarely if ever called upon to serve in great numbers. This meant that some Tudor forces learned new warfare techniques on every campaign, but the majority still steadfastly failed to remodel its ancient tried and tested ways of fighting to suit 'modern' standards. The English additionally had the benefit of being an island nation, defended by a capable and growing navy. England could therefore afford to pick fights that suited its purse and strategic purpose, without plunging the Kingdom into huge wars against more numerous or sophisticated foes.

The Army of Henry VIII

Henry's army was essentially feudal in nature. When it marched, it marched to war in a manner that Henry V would have recognized, and was in many ways still a medieval army. Formed in three components, a vanguard, a main battle and finally the rearguard; it would be led into action by various Earls, Dukes and other dignitaries.

Core was the infantry, the solid Yeomen of England, organised into bands made up of mixed companies from the shires. These Trained Bands and militias were formed by the Lords Lieutenant of the counties. Shortages of manpower could see substitutes being sent in place of good men, the jails emptied and scoundrels sent to the colours.

These men were then marshalled into units fielding bill and bow in various proportions. The 'brown bill' and the longbow had been the traditional English weapons for generations and were still thought quite adequate enough to sort out any invaders of England's green and pleasant land. They proved their worth against the Scots at Flodden (1513) and Pinkie (1547); and in numerous other border clashes and sieges.

The bill and bow bands were supported by continental mercenaries. These could field pike or arquebus and were most often Landsknechts brought over from Germany. When called upon, these professionals generally fought well in their encounters with the enemy.

English cavalry was relatively few in numbers, but generally of good quality. There was an elite body of Gentlemen Pensioners and young nobles in full plate armour and often mounted on armoured great horses. These were supported by the 'Demi-Lancers', who were less well armoured, and also the wild Northern Border Horse. Again, foreign 'sell-swords' were called upon to pad out the English cavalry forces. Solid German 'Ritter' cavalry, heavily armoured and well armed pistoliers; together with dashing units of wild Albanian Stradiots added a touch of the exotic to Henry's forces. Mounted arquebusiers, often from Italy, added to the polyglot force that faced an enemy invader.

Artillery was dear to Henry's heart and he spent much of his wealth on the artillery train. From vast bombards to cannon royal and to the more numerous small guns, 'murderers' and the strange Shrympes (Shrimp Guns) used for the attack and defence of camps.

The Army of Elizabeth I

Elizabeth's armies became involved in what was seen at the time as a true struggle for England's very survival as a

Billmen

The English or "Brown" bill was a time honoured weapon found in many houses great and small throughout the British Isles, though many areas had their own particular version of shape and form. It was a very versatile weapon used both offensively and defensively, though it owes its origins to being a highly useful farming tool for all manner of clearance work.

They would have been the perfect weapon to defend home and hearth with, as they are big enough to intimidate and small enough for anyone to wield aggressively. With its ability to either hack or chop it was also ideal to spear an enemy. For the nervous militiaman, taking along an implement you have worked with all your life is the sort of weapon you want when you march out to join your mustering company!

Billmen formed much of Henry's army at Flodden Field, stopping and then hurling back the Scottish onslaught; then later wading into them to kill their

king and slaughter the survivors. Agricultural tool it may have been, but in capable hands, it clearly was a ferocious weapon.

Elizabeth's troops fielded fewer Billmen, and where deployed they seem to have been clustered around the Ensigns, protecting the colours; perhaps as a remembrance to their noble past or because they still made a useful contribution to guarding the precious flags.

1601 - The Battle of Kinsale. Mountjoy defeats Tyrell as he tries to relieve the besieged Spanish in the town.

Highlanders and Wild Irish

The ferocity of the men of the West and North of the British Isles was well known. Their ferocious fighting skills were acknowledged by all who had met them, with Irish and Scottish contingents found in many armies serving all over Europe. They tended to fight in either long loose lines as skirmishers or in denser mobs with unpleasant hand weapons, the better armed and armoured at the front encouraging the others.

Protestant state. Friction between England and the vast Spanish Empire was bloody and constant. The Spanish Flota treasure ships from the New World would be looted by English pirates, while on the land the Dutch were supported in their wars of liberation against the tercios. It was no wonder that eventually Phillip II of Spain sent the Armada to scratch this itch! Yet he played a similar game to Elizabeth, funding disorder and rebellion in Ireland; while landing Jesuit priests in Britain to continue their works, which incensed English Protestant sensibilities.

Elizabeth's call to arms and subsequent defeat of the Spanish Armada is well recorded, and has become the stuff of legend. If things had been slightly different, perhaps the weather not so fickle, fascinating scenarios can be imagined if the Spanish had actually landed. If the veteran tercios of the Dukes of Medina Sidonia and Parma had set foot on English soil, would the warrior Queen have been able to repel this Catholic horde? As with her father, she had a largely ill-trained and untried force with which to halt the dreaded Spanish tercios. There is no doubt that Elizabeth may have had "the heart of a lion", and her commanders and soldiers were brave, but key military skills were lacking. Although Englishmen had triumphed many times at sea over the hated Don, massed land warfare was a completely different proposition.

In 1588, all the counties answered the blazing beacons. The parishes combed the registers and the Lords Lieutenant and Sheriffs once again called out the Militias and Trained Bands and placed them under their lawful officers and Gentlemen of rank. As before, men arrived hefting a brown bill, the common agricultural wonder tool, and as many again with longbows and a sheath full of cloth-yard arrows. These were particularly to be found in the poorer parishes and counties. The richer areas and towns could find men fully uniformed and armoured at the cost of the local gentry and carrying more modern arms.

The arquebus was a common weapon to be brought to war by this time, although introduced at a frustratingly slow pace in England. The heavy but deadly musket with its accompanying rest, bandoliers and match cord was to be found in increasing numbers amongst the Trained Bands. A few men still brandished swords and bucklers, but increasingly the militias were fielding files of pikemen. These men were well equipped with a sixteen foot ash pike, and back and breast plates; well able to fend of Spanish cavalry or to come to push of pike with the Spanish heavy pike blocks.

The cavalry was still well mounted. There were still a few gentlemen of rank wearing full plate and riding massive horses, carrying lances echoing their forefathers of old. Demi-lancers were the more common heavy cavalrymen armed with a stout lance, back and breast plates and an open helmet, and some now equipped with pistols. The confused fighting in Ireland had seen the Border Horse (with light spear, latch and shield) evolve into excellent light cavalry skirmishers, having crossed swords with the Irish horse and cunning kern. Mounted arquebusiers were also becoming a common sight, men capable of firing from the saddle as firearms improved, giving fire support to their better armoured comrades.

Artillery remained immobile, expensive and a drain on her Majesty's purse, though it is recorded that the Irish particularly feared its destructive blast. In many ways the Elizabethan English army, although infuriatingly old fashioned, was also a complex, flexible and interlinked fighting machine that may well have surprised its Spanish foes. We shall never know.

The Irish Armies

England had many enemies and a few allies in the Tudor period. A rebellion in Ireland was a constant threat in Henry's reign, though thousands also served in his armies at

Border Horse

These men are effectively irregular raiding cavalry rather than more organized close order combat troops. They were excellent skirmishing fighters, well able to remain in the saddle all day if needs be. They fought with the light lance, supposedly so talented in its use that they could spear salmon from a river whilst still mounted.

home and abroad. Elizabeth's experience was much different however, Ireland being a running sore throughout her long reign, in constant uproar and a hotbed of Catholic intrigue fed by Spanish and Papal opportunism.

Ireland was splintered by internal dispute during the 16th century; and alliances did not hold long enough to concentrate the forces needed to eject Elizabeth's garrisons. The nature of warfare in Ireland was characterized by constant raiding and sieges, with only the occasional field engagement. Such pitched battles of a recognizable European nature were rare in Ireland due to the forces being remarkably small, the geography remote and supplies hard to obtain. Irish forces were principally feudal in nature and differed little in how they had fought for centuries - clan versus clan in bitter feuds concerning perhaps some perceived slight of honour, cattle or trading rights.

Longbow

The Longbow was steeped in English tradition and embedded in the nation's psyche. The yeomen of England and Wales had performed wonders in their innumerable battles with the French; and the memory of those glorious episodes was called upon throughout our period to inspire new generations of English soldiers. Against their traditional foe, north of the border, they performed well; the Scots having little to reply with against the massed bow fire and suffering accordingly.

The Longbowmen of Tudor times were not however the men of Crecy or Agincourt. Individually brave or skilled they may ave been, but the foes of the Tudor dynasty no longer feared massed English bow fire as they once had. Bows were still mustered to go to war right up to the English Civil War, but despite efforts being made to repeat their earlier successes, by 1642 they were a relic of previous times and consigned to oblivion in Britain.

They fought under their chief or lord, mustered in the campaign season and then retired to their villages and farms. The Lord and his family would look quite exotic in any social setting other than Ireland, broadly following ancient codes of dress, though some may have adopted more modern continental or English dress. Most of his best men, the most trusted and wealthy, fought from horseback without saddles or stirrups to keep them on their ponies. They wore chain mail shirts and stabbed over arm with cruel spears, tumbling from their horse in melee against the heavier English cavalry only to spring on its back in a trice to carry on the skirmish.

The vast bulk of an Irish host was composed of the kerns, the men who owed fidelity to their lord. They turned out in their hundreds dressed in a flowing shirt with billowing sleeves, barefoot in the main, with shaggy hairstyles mocked by their English foes. They fought with javelins, or darts as they were then called, and had only a light shield for defence with perhaps a long knife or short sword for close quarter work. Fighting from a wood, bog or improvised barricades they could rain down bow fire, javelins or rocks and (in later years) arquebus fire on to the plodding English columns.

If the kern were exotic then the heavy infantry bodyguard that an Irish chief could field was positively a throwback to a long forgotten era. The Gallowglass were men from another era, and were feared by friend and foe alike. Big, burly fellows, originally from the Western Isles, they were effectively mercenaries, selling their renowned fighting skills to those who could afford them and feed them. At times, Elizabeth even took advantage of their skills. They looked to all intents and purposes like Dark Age warriors, clad in long mail shirts, with helmets and huge double handed axes. They fought and died as a warrior elite, bonded by family, tradition and a curious Old World sense of duty and honour. Woe betide any enemy unit that allowed such men to close with them on the field.

The Irish had no artillery, the roads were poor enough for a packhorse and money was scarce enough, though it was seen as a great honour to take cannon from any obliging English troops.

By the end of the Elizabethan period the Irish armies had not only discovered the arquebus but were its master and fire fights became common and deadly. Later Irish armies tried to match the English bill and pike units, but normally came off worst.

1603 - Elizabeth I dies. The coronation of James of Scotland unites the two kingdoms.

Gallowglass (Galloglaigh)

These were an elite class of mercenary originating in the Norse-Gaelic clans of the Scottish Highlands and the Hebrides. They were keenly sought after soldiers in Ireland, with most Irish Chieftains being able to call on their services in times of need - very handy during the Norman incursions of the 12th century.

By Tudor times little had changed, the Gallowglass dress and equipment made them look like soldiers of another era, which in a way they were. By this time though many of the men were native Irish as their forefathers had settled in Ireland.

Armed with their massive two handed 'Sparth Axes' and Claymores (Claidheamh Mor) along with some serious attitude, the Gallowglass caused Elizabeth I's forces some real issues. After the Desmond Rebellions she insisted that over 700 be executed which would imply she was still worried by the threat they posed.

The Gallowglass were on the wane by the early 1600's, but were not a completely spent force. The Swedish Army of Gustav Adolphus contained a few regiments for the invasion of Livonia in the Thirty Years War decades later.'

An Irish army is guaranteed to look wild and exciting on the battlefield and if led well could be an effective, if disturbingly unpredictable force. If some shiploads of hardened Spanish desperadoes are added to stiffen their resolve, then it is a dangerous mix indeed.

The Scots Armies

Whilst Henry's daughter had to watch the Spanish and their wily Irish allies like a hawk, Henry's troubles were with France, of course, and the perfidious Scots!

Scottish armies have a romantic feel about them in many periods, as the men involved were frequently very brave and skilled as soldiers; but most often poorly officered, under equipped and fighting for a lost cause. But their martial skills meant that the Scottish fighting man was to be found serving kings throughout Europe and beyond. The "Auld Alliance" between France and Scotland had existed since the Hundred Years War and would last until the tricorne wars of the 18th century, many generals of Scottish descent even going on to serve Napoleon himself. Various units of Scots would be found on many a foreign field: Fornovo (1495), Seminara (1503), Ravena (1512), Marignano (1513), Pavia (1526), and on both sides at the siege of Boulogne (1544).

Bravery was a watchword with the Scots. It is symbolic that James IV of Scotland died fighting in the front rank at Flodden Field with so many of his nobles, pike in hand. This is testimony to a time when Kings and retinues would fight and die for the cause of their kingdom.

Scottish armies of the period were composed of large blocks of long spear or largely pike armed troops .Formed into schiltrons they were imposing porcupines of well armoured front ranks with lesser armed men in the middle and rear ranks. These formations swiftly marched on their opponents, relying on mass and armoured weight to overawe then overthrow their foe.

Early armies were very well equipped with quality plate armour, and even pavises on occasion. They still proved vulnerable to the English longbow and more so to the heavy hack of the deadly English bill.

Later armies dispensed with full plate and relied on speed with a lighter padded coat of leather and linen while adding more missile troops to their force. But all too often their efforts came to nothing against heavier English firepower.

Scottish cavalry of the period was rare and heavy cavalry rarer still. The nobility dismounted to fight with their infantry and certainly improved their morale by doing so and sharing the inherent risks. An exception was the ubiquitous Border horse, tough men on small nags, who could scout and skirmish with the best in the world. But these hard-nosed border horsemen could take a pragmatic view during a prolonged conflict, changing sides as it suited them.

In artillery however, Scotland was something of a leader. Encouraged by successive kings, despite James II being killed by an exploding cannon, the Scots gun park was huge by English or continental standards. Large artillery trains and innovative casting and design survived through to the English Civil Wars. It sadly never transferred all its potential onto the pitched battles of the period. At Flodden, the heavy artillery of the Scots was famously outshot by the English lighter guns, and there is no record of Scots artillery influencing any land battle of the period.

Highland troops added some colour to an otherwise rather sombre force. They would fight under their own Lairds and in their accepted ancient fashion, spurning the new fangled pike and handguns. They preferred the spear, the sword and the knife and would in appearance look much like their cousins the kern across the water in Ireland. They would make a terrifying sight, wearing loose shirts, barefoot with wild hair flying and accompanied by their skirling bagpipes. While they fought ferociously, they could not be relied upon in prolonged battle or lengthy campaigns.

A Scottish army then is one for the romantic – victories are few and far between, but all the sweeter when they occur.

It can be argued that the Scots' use of French training captains was a bold attempt to transform their old ways of fighting, but the failure to develop combined arms fighting doomed the Scots to defeat after defeat, a sad end to many brave armies.

ENGLISH TUDOR ARMY

The English Tudor armies of the 16th century are a fascinating choice to field on the tabletop. With a breadth of weaponry and troop types along with a host of colourful uniforms and flags, you will not tire of painting your model soldiers. English units can vary in size and formation, while there were accepted ways of deployment it was very much up to the general how he was to muster his men. Units can be in large blocks or composed of many smaller 'building blocks' and formed together into a battalia where the varied weapons could complement each other.

Seemingly old fashioned compared to contemporary Continental armies, the Tudor English armies fought well when provided for by their parsimonious King Henry or the notoriously mean Elizabeth I.

Command Ratings

Overall Commander: Random Command Rating (see page 35) ....40 Points

Roll D6 for rating: 1: Command Rating 7, 2-5: Command Rating 8, 6: Command Rating 9

Infantry/Artillery Commander: Command Rating 8... 40 Points

Cavalry Commander: Command Rating 8 .... 40 Points

The Horse

Unit	Unit Type	Weapon	Hand-to-Hand Value	Shooting Value	Morale Value	Stamina	Special	Points
Demi-Lances	Heavy Horse	Lance,Sword	8	-	3+	4	Heavy Cavalry +1	57

- Maximum of two units in the army.

Unit	Unit Type	Weapon	Hand-to-Hand Value	Shooting Value	Morale Value	Stamina	Special	Points
Border Horse	Horse	Spear,Sword	7	-	4+	3		38

- Maximum of three units in the army.
- Any unit may Skirmish.

1605 - The Gunpowder Plot is uncovered, Guy Fawkes and the other conspirators are executed.

The Foot

Unit	Unit Type	Weapon	Hand-to-Hand Value	Shooting Value	Morale Value	Stamina	Special	Points
Pikemen	Foot Pike Block	Pike	6	-	4+	4	Hedgehog	34

- Any number of pike units can be upgraded to Large @ 6pts per unit
- Up to 25% of the pike units may be Mercenary @ -3pts per unit

Unit	Unit Type	Weapon	Hand-to-Hand Value	Shooting Value	Morale Value	Stamina	Special	Points
Arquebusiers	Foot Battle Line	Arquebus	3	2	5+	3		25

- Maximum of one unit per pike block
- Up to half the units can replace arquebus with muskets @ 2 points per unit
- Any number of Arquebusier units can be downgraded to Small @ -7 points per unit

Unit	Unit Type	Weapon	Hand-to-Hand Value	Shooting Value	Morale Value	Stamina	Special	Points
Swordsmen	Foot Battle Line	Sword & Shield	6	-	4+	3	Swordsmen	34

- Maximum of two units per army

Unit	Unit Type	Weapon	Hand-to-Hand Value	Shooting Value	Morale Value	Stamina	Special	Points
Enlisted Irish Kern	Foot Skirmisher	Sword, Javelin	4	1	5+	3	Mercenary	22

- Maximum of four units in the army

Unit	Unit Type	Weapon	Hand-to-Hand Value	Shooting Value	Morale Value	Stamina	Special	Points
Enlisted Irish Gallowglass	Foot Battle Line	Two-handed Axe & Javelin	6	1	4+	4	Ferocious Charge, Stubborn, Mercenary	40

- Maximum of two units in the army

Unit	Unit Type	Weapon	Hand-to-Hand Value	Shooting Value	Morale Value	Stamina	Special	Points
Billmen	Foot Infantry Block	Billhook or Halberds	6	-	4+	4	Double-Handed Infantry Arm	36
Bowmen	Foot Battle Line	Longbow	3	2	5+	3		27

'I know I have the body of a weak and feeble woman, but I have the heart and stomach of a king, and an English king too'

Queen Elizabeth I

The Ordnance

- Maximum of one artillery pieces per battalia

Unit	Unit Type	Weapon	Hand-to-Hand Value	Shooting Value	Morale Value	Stamina	Special	Points
Artillery	Ordnance	Various Cannon	1	3-2-1	5+	2		Varies

- Light Guns 17 points
- Medium Guns 21 points
- Heavy Guns 25 points

Unit	Unit Type	Weapon	Hand-to-Hand Value	Shooting Value	Morale Value	Stamina	Special	Points
Siege Artillery	Ordnance	Mortar	1	2	5+	2		25

- Maximum of one mortar

1606 - The Union flag is created as a standard for Great Britain.

LATER 16TH CENTURY IRISH ARMY

The Irish army is a real change of pace from most armies in this book. It has the feel of belonging to a much earlier age: the cavalry had changed little from the time of the Norman Conquest, the Gallowglass had more than a hint of Viking about them, while the kerns resembled Celts and Picts. Specialising in hit-and-run tactics, these primitive looking Irish armies were a constant thorn in the side of English ambitions in Ireland, often defeating armies with far more advanced weaponry.

The very rag-tag nature of an Irish army makes it great fun to put together and paint. You will need to be tactically very astute to get the most out of your troops – even the Gallowglass, who must be one of the best infantry choices in the book. Battle flags can also provide an opportunity for some interesting painting projects, although their habit of carrying captured English banners into combat could be emulated.

Command Ratings

Overall Commander: Random Command Rating (see page 35) .... 40 Points

        Roll D6 for rating: 1: Command Rating 7, 2-5: Command Rating 8, 6: Command Rating 9

Infantry/Artillery Commander: Command Rating 8 .... 40 Points

Cavalry Commander: Command Rating 7 .... 20 Points

The Horse

Unit	Unit Type	Weapon	Hand-to-Hand Value	Shooting Value	Morale Value	Stamina	Special	Points
Irish Cavalry	Horse	Javelins, Sword	7	1	4+	3		39

- Maximum of two units in the army
- One Unit can be upgraded to Nobles; gain Elite and Valiant skills for 9 points

Scots Cavalry	Horse	Lance, Sword	7	-	4+	3		43

- Maximum of one unit
- The unit may Skirmish

Irish Horseboys	Light Horse Skirmishers	Javelins	4	1	5+	3		29

- Maximum of two units per unit of Irish Cavalry

1607 - A massive wave sweeps up the Bristol Channel killing 2,000 people.

The Foot

Unit	Unit Type	Weapon	Hand-to-Hand Value	Shooting Value	Morale Value	Stamina	Special	Points
Gallowglass	Foot Infantry Block	Two-handed Axe & Javelin	6	1	4+	4	Ferocious Charge, Stubborn, Double-Handed Infantry Arms	45

- Any unit can have pike instead of Two-Handed weapons at no cost. Lose Double- Handed Infantry Weapon and gain Hedgehog ability.

Unit	Unit Type	Weapon	Hand-to-Hand Value	Shooting Value	Morale Value	Stamina	Special	Points
Bonnachts	Foot Battle Line	Double-Handed Axe, Javelins	4	1	5+	3	Double-Handed Infantry Arms	27

- Any unit can replace Double-Handed Axe with sword and shield for +2 pts. If so the unit loses Double-Handed Infantry Arms and receives Swordsmen ability.

Unit	Unit Type	Weapon	Hand-to-Hand Value	Shooting Value	Morale Value	Stamina	Special	Points
Kern	Foot Battle Line	Arquebus or Javelins	3	2	5+	3		25

- Any number of Kern units can be Skirmisher Infantry instead of Battle Line

Unit	Unit Type	Weapon	Hand-to-Hand Value	Shooting Value	Morale Value	Stamina	Special	Points
The Rising Out	Foot Warband	Javelins, Swords	2	1	6+	2	Rabble, Militia	7

- Unit can be armed with bows @ 2 points each

Unit	Unit Type	Weapon	Hand-to-Hand Value	Shooting Value	Morale Value	Stamina	Special	Points
New Scots	Foot Battle Line	Arquebus	3	2	5+	3		25

- Any unit can replace arquebus with bows for free
- Up to half arquebus units can upgrade to muskets @ 2 points each

'These sort of men be those that do not lightly quit the field, but bide the brunt to the death'

The Gallowglass

The Ordnance

- Maximum of two artillery pieces in the army

Unit	Unit Type	Weapon	Hand-to-Hand Value	Shooting Value	Morale Value	Stamina	Special	Points
Artillery	Ordnance	Light Cannons	1	3-2-1	5+	2		17

IT'S A LONG WAY TO KILLARNEY

The Irish situation had been a thorn in the side of the English Crown since the 12th century, and 400 years had done little to settle the issue. Henry VIII has set his sights on bringing Ireland firmly under his control by a policy of 'Surrender and re-grant', whereby Irish landowners would offer allegiance to the crown in exchange for official titles being issued. It was another attempt to anglicise the country by making English titles and laws take precedent over traditional Irish Brehon law.

Against this policy stood the Irish warlords and chieftains who were determined on keeping their culture intact, and were used to power being granted to them by their people rather than being the birth right of increasing waves of 'Anglo-Irish'.

Being her father's daughter, and certainly not being a lady for turning, Elizabeth I was eager to continue Henry's campaign in Ireland. Luckily for the English the Irish warlords were usually far too busy fighting each other to join forces against a common foe.

The Desmond Rebellions of 1569-83 were typical of the unrest in Ireland throughout the Tudor period. In Munster a conflict had developed between an 'Old English' family, the Butlers of Ormonde and the Irish Catholic Fitzgeralds of Desmond. Such fighting was in violation of Elizabeth's laws and someone was going to get punished; as Ormonde was the Queen's cousin it was no surprise that the Earl of Desmond was detained in the Tower of London. Back home the Earl's men rose in revolt, led by James Fitzmaurice Fitzgerald, who quickly gained the support of the local tribes and many of the feared Gallowglass.

Elizabeth sent more men to quell the uprising and Fitzgerald was soon pushed back into the mountains of County Kerry.

Supplies! Irish troops led by Gallowglass ambush the English supply wagons.

1609 - Spain finally recognises Dutch independence.

The Irish Army

CAPTAIN GENERAL JAMES FITZMAURICE FITZGERALD

General, Command Rating 8

SEAN MACACRTHY

Command Rating 7

- 1 Unit of Noble Cavalry
- 1 Unit of Irish Cavalry
- 2 Units of Horseboys

CIAN O'KEEFE

Command Rating 8

- 3 Units of Gallowglass
- 2 Units of Kern

SEARBHREATHACH FOLEY

Command Rating 8

- 4 Units of Kern
- 1 Unit of Bonnachts

DECLAN MACCONAL

Command Rating 7

- 4 Units of Kern
- 2 Units of the Rising Out
- 2 Units of New Scots

The English Army

SIR HENRY SIDNEY, LORD DEPUTY OF IRELAND

General, Command Rating 9

THOMAS BUTLER, 3RD EARL OF ORMONDE

Command Rating 8

- 1 Unit of Demilances
- 2 Units of Border Horse

HUMPHREY GILBERT

Command Rating 8

- 3 Units of Pikemen
- 3 Units of Arquebusiers
- 1 Unit of Billmen
- 1 Unit of Swordsmen
- 2 Units of Archers

WILLIAM FITZWILLIAM

Command Rating 8

- 3 Units of Enlisted Irish Kern
- 2 Units of Gallowglass
- 1 unit of Pikemen
- 1 Unit of Arquebusiers

The Set Up

The English force under Henry Sidney is marching from the south coast to get desperately needed supplies and men to the beleaguered garrison of Killarney. The road from Kenmare to Killarney is treacherous and many men have been lost to ambushes from Fitzgerald's men in the Kerry Mountains. The English must get their baggage train over the

mountain pass and off the northern table edge and keep Sir Henry alive. The English army is in a March Column formation at the beginning of the game and will remain so until the first Irish troops break cover.

The Irish have the advantage of terrain, local knowledge and the element of surprise. Although not a match for the English force in a straight fight, in this rugged terrain there is a great opportunity to stop Queen Elizabeth's campaign in its tracks. The Irish need to stop the supplies getting through, and if possible force the English to turn back.

The English were to be under the command of Steve Yates whose first decision was to create a marching order for his troops. The English army would start the game at the southern edge of the table, all the units in March Column and would have to remain so until the Irish attacked. As only the vanguard of the army was able to be deployed due to the narrowness of the road, a marching order was needed for the main army and rear-guard. The four wagons had express orders to push on for Killarney as fast as possible, so would automatically be able to move up to their full 18" allowance along the roads along with their baggage guard (one unit per wagon). Once attacked they would become subject to the normal command rules for movement.

The Irish, under John Stallard, would only be able to deploy one battalia on the table at the beginning of the game. The rest of the force was waiting in ambush and hidden from the English, their dispositions noted down by the umpire. These troops could be given commands to move at any time, but would be activated (and therefore revealed) if any English unit moved to within 12" of them. John chose to place the force of Declan Macconal on the eastern road far enough away from the English for them not to affect the English troops, but hoping to force Steve onto the western road.

Victory Conditions

English

Any wagons of the Baggage Train and Sir Henry escape off the northern table edge.	Major Victory
Any wagons of the Baggage Train get through but Sir Henry slain, captured or routed from the field.	Minor Victory

Irish

All wagons of the Baggage Train captured and Sir Henry killed, captured or routed from the field	Major Victory
All wagons of the Baggage Train captured	Minor Victory

Should Fitzgerald be killed or captured by the English the game ceases immediately as the rebellion is effectively over. This will count as a Major English Victory regardless of any other factors.

How It Played

The English vanguard emerged through the mist as they entered the valley, the proud demi-lancers to the fore. The responsibility for the wagons was to fall on William Fitzwilliam's Anglo Irish, and the first two wagons and their guard moved rapidly to the fork in the road and decided to take the western path. Suspecting trouble, the rest of the army was more reticent about moving at such a pace (despite Steve's pleas) and a gap developed between the lead wagons and their support.

In an attempt to provoke a rash move from the noble English demi-lancers, the Irish wheeled out a captured light artillery piece to the edge of the central woods and opened fire on the advancing horsemen. The English cavalry reacted as anticipated, dug in their spurs and charged to the sound of the guns, but drew short as hordes of Irish foot poured out of the woods to their front. The feared Gallowglass of Cian O'Keefe had been found! Supporting kerns hailed down javelin fire on the English horse but with little effect. Although this initial attack had indeed drawn out the English Cavalry, the English infantry were now desperately reorganising their lines. To be caught in March Column would be suicidal in these Irish hills!

Still unthreatened, the two lead wagons and their guard marched on at full pace down the western road. Once again

the remainder of Fitzwilliam's command struggled to keep pace and the gap between the two was becoming a concern. The remaining two wagons were left to the protection of Humphrey Gilbert's battalia, and the decision was made to take these along the eastern road. Splitting the force in the face of your opponent of unknown strength and in a strange land could be the work of genius, or sheer desperation….time would tell.

In the centre, the English demi-lancers were undaunted by the sudden appearance of so many enemies and charged the nearest Gallowglass, pushing them back to the trees. This threat temporarily removed, they then performed a sweeping attack to rout a unit of kern. Stirring stuff indeed, but the Gallowglass had inflicted some terrible damage on the fine English horsemen.

The wagons on the west road had just begun their move when they stumbled across the Irish horse of Sean MacCarthy. This stopped them in their tracks, and desperate cries to the rear were made to bring up support. Luckily, the Irish couldn't make the most of the situation as their horse stubbornly refused to charge, seemingly intimidated by the baggage guard of enlisted kerns. This was a situation that wouldn't

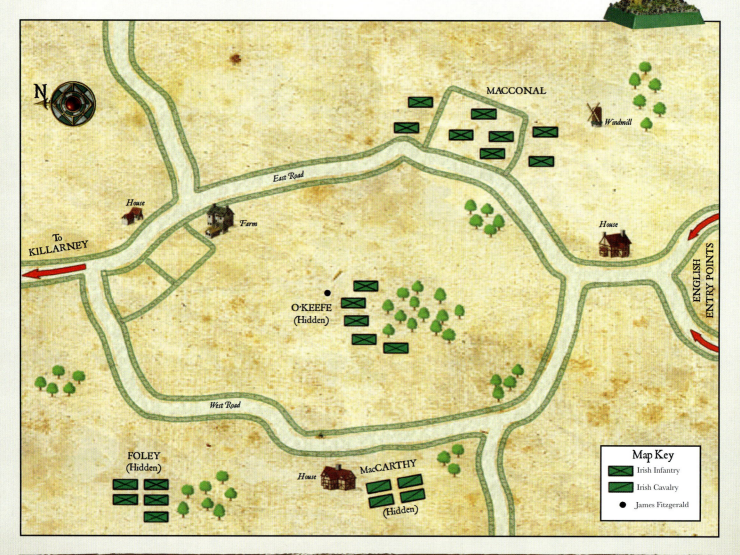

last long and the English struggled to move the rest of Fitzwilliam's command to protect the wagons.

Over on the eastern road the two English units of Border Horse scouted ahead to discover the extent of Macconal's command and came under javelin attack. They fell back and awaited infantry support. Macconal's kerns, New Scots and even the Rising Out, emboldened by their early success, surged forward to press home the attack. Meanwhile O'Keefe's command in the centre had their eyes on the 'western' wagons too, and though the English heavy horse had caused a lot of damage they felt confident to release one of the Gallowglass units to provoke MacCarthy's horse to press their attack.

The English right flank began to form up along the eastern road, Gilbert's men moving the other two wagons forward slowly and pouring fire onto Macconal's men. They quickly put an end to the Rising Out units who fled, but the remaining kerns and New Scots retaliated to cause disorder amongst the English with a sudden outbreak of 6's on the shooting dice. Over on the western road the Irish Horse unit was given heart by the approaching Gallowglass and charged home on the baggage guard. With the Gallowglass attacking the exposed flank of the hapless enlisted kerns the battle was over quickly. The Irish Noble Cavalry used their sweeping advance to rout the kerns guarding the second wagon… maybe entrusting the wagons to Gaelic mercenaries was not such a good idea.

Things were looking grim for Sir Henry Sidney's relief force, and the English Lord ordered a general advance. Over on the eastern road the wagons were moved to the rear as Gilbert's command looked to consolidate in front of the windmill and force the enemy back. In the centre the heavy cavalry rallied and the remaining men of Fitzwilliam tried, unsuccessfully, to get to the lost wagons. It seemed the early recklessness of the English demi-lancers was contagious, as Captain General Fitzgerald gave a 'follow me' order to his fierce Gallowglass, risking himself in a desperate charge at the English cavalry. These attacks were

Shrimp Guns

The curiously named 'Shrimp Guns' were light artillery pieces. They were usually made of brass and were one of many bizarre variants of cannons that became popular in the Tudor age. In this scenario they were hidden in the baggage train to give any potential ambushers a nasty surprise.

brutally repulsed but, luckily for Fitzgerald, the Gallowglass were merely forced to retire and he survived the assault. Despite heavy losses the Gallowglass had caused enough casualties for the cavalry to be shaken, having finally taken them over their stamina level. Even heavy cavalry are susceptible to troops with 'ferocious charge' and double handed weapons!

The Irish right flank pushed on past the wagons to face the oncoming English support, and after savage fighting the English battalia broke, as over half its units were shaken or routed, and William Fitzwilliam fled the field. The Horseboys were in for a shock as they went to take the wagons away; hidden 'shrimp' guns wreaked havoc on them and forced them back. The Gallowglass nearby quickly ended the resistance though and the wagons were led away.

In an act of desperation the remaining wagons were moved forward down the eastern road, their own hidden 'shrimp guns' being used as an offensive weapon (not to great effect). This put them in a precarious position and they were soon surrounded by triumphant kerns. With his left wing gone, his best cavalry under threat of being surrounded and the last wagons looking lost Sir Henry gave the order to retreat. He would live to fight another day, along with whatever men he could extricate from the field. The Irish had captured the entire baggage train, and although Sir Henry got away, they earned a well deserved victory.

'the English bande provoked the skirmishe, and so the bloodie broile began hotter and hotter…and came to hande strokes, where many a Launce was broken, and many a man laie grovelying on the ground, some under their horses, and some strike from their horse backs, suche was the terrour of the tyme, and the furie of the fight'

Elizabeth I army fighting in Picardy

The Thirty Years War

The Thirty Years War was a series of conflicts that devastated large areas of Europe, especially the German provinces, from 1618 to 1648. These conflicts centred on the Hapsburg Holy Roman Emperors, Ferdinand II and Ferdinand III and their opponents. Although perceived predominantly as a religious war between Catholic and Protestant nations, its roots and causes are far more complicated than simple religious differences, as political motivations also played a large role. This is evidenced by the fact that nations changed sides and Bourbon France, a Catholic country, bankrolled many of the Protestant armies through this period as they engaged in a political struggle against the Imperial Spanish.

The war turned much of modern-day Germany into one large battle zone. One of the primary reasons that the German states were so unstable at this time dates back to the Treaty of Augsburg, signed in 1555. This effectively allowed freedom of religion in the provinces which was generally determined by the ruler's preference. The Holy Roman Empire and its Catholic allies, particularly the Spanish, wanted to see a move back to Catholic dominance in the provinces that had moved over to the Lutheran faith. Added to the mix was the emergence of the Calvinist faith, which was not covered by the Treaty of Augsburg at all.

To highlight the religious issues that were arising one only has to look at the Electors, those men who chose the next Holy Roman Emperor during this time. Considered the most powerful of the electors was Frederick of the Palatinate, a Calvinist, as was the Margrave of Brandenburg. The Duke of Saxony was Lutheran and had no love for either the Catholics or Calvinists (or anyone for that matter). The remaining four electors were Catholic however, Maximillian II of Bavaria and the Archbishops of Mainz, Trier and Cologne. Maximillian went on to form the Catholic League to bring Protestant provinces back into the fold.

These powerful men forged alliances, and many German provinces took up arms for or against the Hapsburgs. Many provinces found themselves switching allegiances as the war continued when the political situation and pressures within their borders changed.

Harquebusiers

1614 - In France, the Estates General meet for the last time until the French Revolution.

Johann Tserclaes, Count von Tilly 1559-1632

Johann Tserclaes was born in February 1559 to a devoutly Catholic Walloon family at Castle Tilly, Spanish Netherlands, in what is now modern day Belgium. In his youth he was raised with a deep seated hatred of Protestantism as the Dutch revolt scarred his homeland. The hatred was reinforced by a Jesuit dominated education in Cologne. His devout faith was never to leave Tilly, and he was to become known as the 'Monk in Armour'.

Naturally, for a Catholic Walloon noble, he joined the Spanish army when he was 15 and fought against the Dutch and was present at the successful siege of Antwerp in the ongoing 80 Years War.

In 1594 Tilly joined the forces of the Holy Roman Emperor, Rudolf II, in the 'Long War' against the Ottoman Turks in Hungary and Transylvania. Due to his part in the capture of Stuhlweissenburg in 1601 he gained the rank of Major General, shortly after he bought the colonelcy of a Walloon regiment and in 1604 was made General of Cavalry. By 1605 his meteoric rise was complete, and he was made Field Marshall of the Catholic League forces.

In 1601 Tilly was employed by Duke Maximillian of Bavaria (the future Elector, Maximillian II) to command all Bavarian Catholic League forces. He showed his brilliance in military organisation by transforming this rabble into a professional force. In 1620 he led his army to the crushing victory over Bohemian rebels at White Mountain. By 1622 he had formed a very strong double team with the Spanish general Gonzales de Cordoba and over the next two years won a string of victories against both Christian the Younger of Brunswick and the Margrave of Baden-Durlach. After the successful battle of Hochst he was made a Count. His victory at Stadtlohn was possibly the highpoint in his career and saw the surrender of Bohemia, a collapse of Protestant resistance in Germany and brought to a close the 'Palatinate phase' of the Thirty Years War.

It was during this period that Count Tilly became known as 'Father Tilly' to his soldiers. Although a traditionalist, rather than an innovator, he would use tactics to get the most out of his resources, and made sure his men were taken care of (and heard the word of God). This was not to stop the rampant pillaging that took place from his forces, however, and this was to have serious repercussions on his reputation.

In 1626 the Catholic League was at war with the Danes, and more victories came at the siege of Munden and the decisive Battle of Lutter which forced the Danish King, Christian I, to sue for peace. However, Tilly's rivalry with the other pre-eminent Catholic leader, Wallenstein, was beginning to take its toll. His army was starting to be drained away as Wallenstein offered to pay his soldiers more and supplies were being withheld. It was these circumstances that contributed to the most infamous action of the Count's career. The siege of Magdeburg had dragged on through 1631 and the eventual sacking of the town was brutal. Frustrated and close to starving, the furious soldiers rampaged through the town slaughtering 20 000 civilians. These soldiers were the Catholic forces of Tilly and Pappenheim, and this act led to a galvanising of Protestant resistance and damaged Tilly's reputation across Europe.

The new Protestant resurgence was led by Gustav Adolf, the dynamic Swedish king, and the Catholic forces were put on the defensive. Battle was joined at Breitenfeld in September 1631, where Tilly's force was decisively beaten by the Swedes. Too late, Tilly was to receive reinforcements and supplies, but the Swedish army was rampant. In early 1632 Count Tilly attempted to stop the Swedish army at the Battle of Lech but was wounded by a cannonball and forced to retreat. 'Father Tilly' died of tetanus 15 days later on April 30th 1632 at the age of 73.

Command Rating: 9

Special: Father Tilly
Tilly was renowned for the care he took in looking after his soldiers and they repaid this with their loyalty. Any unit within 12" of Tilly may re-roll any break test they are required to make.

Bourbon France was in a particularly interesting position in the war. For much of the period France was happy to work politically, offering financial support to forces that could oppose the Imperial alliance. The French, concerned that the Holy Roman Empire had become too powerful, saw their country increasingly hemmed in on all sides. When the revolt in the Spanish Netherlands broke out, Spain could not reinforce the Catholic 'obedient provinces' by sea due to the English fleet (relations had not improved since the failed Armada the previous century) and so was forced to use a land route that skirted French territory. This did nothing to improve the political situation and only succeeded in encouraging the French to back the Protestant rebellion.

What is clear is that the Thirty Years War is a fantastic period to wargame. From pitched battles to sieges, a multitude of nations and armies were represented and larger than life characters dominated the battlefields. Although the whole conflict can seem very complicated, history has conveniently broken the 30 year period down into a number of phases and so it would be churlish not to take advantage of this to paint a clearer picture.

Bohemian Phase 1618-1621

War was on the cards when Emperor Matthias announced that he wanted Ferdinand II, the future Holy Roman

Emperor, to inherit the thrones of Bohemia and Hungary. As Matthias was childless this was a political move that ensured that a devout Catholic would be elected to these important seats. Surprisingly this was actually met with support from quite a few Protestant nations, but importantly the Bohemians were not in agreement. Being a Protestant nation themselves they could see a future of religious persecution and wanted the throne to go to Frederick V, Elector Palatine, who was a fellow Protestant.

In anticipation of his rule in Bohemia, Ferdinand sent two Catholic councillors to Prague where they would administer his kingdom in his absence. These men were promptly seized, put on trial, and thrown from a palace window into a midden (waste dump) in the moat some 50 feet below. Unfortunately for the Bohemians, the refuse provided a soft landing and they survived. They also made sure to report back to an irate Emperor-in-waiting.

This action led to outright revolt, and this quickly spread across Europe. Frederick was officially approached to take the throne if he stepped in to help. In order to cover their bases the Bohemians also made similar offers to Transylvania, Savoy and Saxony. News of this duplicity (with the help of the Hapsburgs) quickly got out, at which point Saxony immediately left the fight.

Despite this setback, the early stages of the revolt went well for the Protestant forces and Ferdinand was forced to call on the help of his nephew, Philip IV of Spain. Early 1619 was a mixed bag for Ferdinand, as on the death of Mathias he was officially proclaimed Holy Roman Emperor and King of Hungary and Bohemia, however after revolts in Austria the Protestant forces under Count Thurn were knocking on the walls of Vienna. The siege was lifted when an Imperial army under Count Bucquoy defeated the main Protestant Union army of Count Mansfeld at the battle of Sablat in June 1619, cutting all communications with Prague.

Despite this setback, both Thurn and Mansfeld had strong armies in the field and by August Ferdinand was deposed as the King of Bohemia and Elector Frederick V of the Palatinate took his mantle.

In the east there was more trouble for the Emperor as the Transylvanians had entered into an alliance with the Ottoman Empire, and revolts throughout Hungary were quickly getting out of hand. This alliance led to the Polish-Ottoman War of 1620-21, as the Poles were firm allies of the Hapsburgs, and the Ottomans were fought to a standstill by the plucky Poles.

The turning point came in 1620 as a Spanish army under Ambrogio Spinola left Brussels to add extra manpower to the Imperial cause. He also took the opportunity to grab some key territory and conquered the Lower Palatinate on the Rhine. This move secured a route for the Spanish from Italy to the Spanish Netherlands. Saxony, still mightily annoyed at the Bohemians, also sided with the Emperor at roughly the same time.

In November 1620 the two main Imperial armies, the Emperor's force under Count Bucquoy and the Catholic League under Johann Tserclaes (Count Tilly) joined forces and smashed Frederick's forces at the Battle of White Mountain near Prague. Resistance in Bohemia was crushed and the Holy Roman Empire was quick to ensure that the enforced conversion back to Catholicism was swift. Frederick was stripped of all land and titles and, outlawed, sent into exile where he moved from court to court trying to raise support. This action ended the Bohemian phase of the Thirty Years War.

Palatinate Phase 1621-1624

The Hapsburgs and Spanish had, by 1621, developed a stranglehold on much of Europe. Frederick V, Elector Palatine was in exile and his speedy exit from Prague in the previous November had given him the label 'The Winter King'. His army, still under the command of Count Mansfeld, fought a series of battles against the Spanish to defend his remaining holdings along the Rhine, but ultimately this conflict ended in failure. Mansfeld and his men, along with the other Protestant army in the field led by Duke Christian of Brunswick, decided to go into Dutch service to continue the struggle.

The Dutch had been fighting a war for independence from the Spanish since 1568 and the Dutch army became home to many Protestant soldiers. Although the extra manpower was a short term help, the focus of attention from the rampaging Imperial armies was not.

In 1623 Duke Christian led his force from the Netherlands into Saxony to turn the tide of the war there, but without support quickly began to retreat when he was confronted by Tilly's superior Imperial force and soundly beaten at the Battle of Stadtlohn.

With this final disaster Frederick had to concede defeat and withdrew from the war. The Protestant rebellion was over and this brought the 'Palatinate Phase' of the Thirty Years War to a close.

Danish Phase 1625-1630

With Frederick V out of war, the Holy Roman Empire and its policy of Catholic expansion constituted a very real threat for a number of nations. The Protestant League was formed from a number of German states, Holland, England and Denmark, secretly funded by the (very Catholic) French. This coalition needed a champion and this was Christian IV of Denmark. The Danes were benefitting from receipt of war reparations from Sweden (this had the unfortunate side effect of keeping the Swedes out of the alliance), as well as being bankrolled from England and France. Danish expansion into northern Germany had been aggressive and Hamburg, as well as large tracts of land, was under Christian's jurisdiction.

Unfortunately for the Danish king he was about to run into the 'perfect storm' of the two ablest Imperial generals of the entire war. Count Tilly had already developed a reputation as being a brilliant leader in previous campaigns, now Ferdinand also turned to the Bohemian mercenary, Albrecht von Wallenstein. Wallenstein had grown his power base from the confiscated lands of his fellow Bohemians and had a vast army at his disposal. He offered this army to the Imperial cause in exchange for all the plunder from the conquered territories (this was to be quite considerable) as well as a hefty fee.

In April 1626 Wallenstein defeated the beleaguered Mansfeld at the Battle of Dessau Bridge in Saxony. A further blow hit the Protestant cause as Mansfeld died in the retreat.

By August 1626 the Imperial forces were on the rampage, and Christian's Danes had to rush south to help the German Protestants in the aftermath of Dessau Bridge. They had the misfortune to run into Tilly's army at the

Battle of Lutter and were beaten comprehensively.

These twin defeats left the Danes vulnerable, and Wallenstein marched north to occupy Jutland. He was only prevented from capturing Copenhagen due to the lack of a fleet and the cost of taking his army further into enemy territory; funding the war was becoming an issue on both sides.

With his allied support withering away, and his field armies in pieces, Christian sued for peace. This was concluded with the Treaty of Lubeck in 1629. In exchange for keeping his sovereignty over Denmark Christian had to withdraw all Danish support to the Protestant German States, effectively removing Denmark from the action.

Albrecht Wenzel Eusebius von Wallenstein 1583-1634

Albrecht von Wallenstein was born into a poor Protestant family in Heřmanice, Bohemia (modern day Czech Republic) in 1583. His early years were dominated by the loss of both parents at an early age and his uncle packed him off to Goldberg Protestant grammar school in Silesia before finishing his education at the universities of Altdorf, Bologna and Padua.

Like many young men of his time he found the call to military life was strong, and he joined the army of Holy Roman Emperor Rudolph II. From 1604 to 1606 he advanced his career in campaigns against the Ottoman Turks and Hungarian rebels. Due to the influence of Hapsburg and Jesuit friends in court Wallenstein converted to Catholicism in 1606, and this opened many doors for the young soldier. Not least of these opportunities were two very beneficial marriages, first to an older widow, Lucretia of Landek, and only a few years after her death to Isabella Katherina, the daughter of the influential Count Harrach. Both these unions, along with confiscated Protestant land from the Bohemian revolts, made Wallenstein one of the wealthiest men in Bohemia with vast estates. In fact his holdings were so large that he was able to create the new state of Friedland.

By 1625 Wallenstein had earned the reputation of a powerful mercenary captain and very able politician with an army of between 30,000 and 50,000 men. One of his major innovations was the way he raised taxes in order to wage war, and this allowed him to raise, finance and lead his own forces. The new Holy Roman Emperor, Ferdinand II, turned to Wallenstein to lead a Catholic force in the Thirty Years War. In return for his aid Wallenstein would be rewarded handsomely and be able to keep any plunder from conquered areas. For opposing the Danish forces of Christian IV he also received the title 'Duke of Friedland'.

In 1626 Wallenstein defeated the Protestant army of Mansfeld at Dessau and spent the next twelve months successfully driving the opposition back. In 1627 he joined forces with Count Tilly and defeated the Danes, most notably at Wolgast, which with Tilly's victory at Lutter effectively pushed them out of the war. More titles and territory follow, including Admiral of the North and Baltic Sea Fleet and the Duchies of Sagan and Mecklenburg.

Such successes don't go unnoticed and enemies at court started to plot against him. Not only were Wallenstein's political motives brought into question, many nobles erre dismayed that someone of such humble origins could get so much acclaim. Wallenstein also made enemies on both sides of the religious divide by his uneven pursuit of the 'Edict of Restitution' which set out to bring Catholicism to all those regions back under Imperial rule. Chief among these enemies was Elector Maximillian II of Bavaria and in 1630 he was dismissed as commander of the Catholic League forces. Command of his army fell to Count Tilly and Wallenstein retired to Friedland.

This was a time of consolidation and political manoeuvring for Wallenstein, and his ability to withhold supplies and entice soldiers to his own army with higher pay seriously impeded Tilly's ability to wage war. On Tilly's death the Emperor was forced to call on Wallenstein again and he once more took command of the Imperial forces.

In 1632 the new enemy was Sweden, under the command of Gustav Adolf, and the two leading players met finally at the Battle of Lutzen. Wallenstein was defeated but Gustav is killed. Wallenstein started to initiate peace talks, and improved his negotiating position with victory over a combined Swedish/Saxon force at Steinau in 1633. This was to be his final success.

Alarmed by his political manoeuvrings, once again his enemies turned the Emperor against him. Convinced that Wallenstein was working purely for his own ends and maybe even be about to switch sides, he was accused of high treason. Wallenstein still felt he was in a position of strength and in early 1634 made his men swear loyalty to him alone. It was not enough and on orders from the crown he was assassinated by his own officers in the city of Eger on the 25th February 1634, on the eve of a conciliatory meeting with the Swedes. The assassination was carried out by a unit of mercenary dragoons under the command of an Irish officer, Colonel Butler. The killing blow was struck by English officer, Walter Devereux, in Wallenstein's bed chamber. It was an ignominious end to a great military leader.

Command Rating: 9

Special: Warchest
Wallenstein was able to raise huge numbers of men by using his vast wealth. This wealth also ensured his men stayed in the field, as mercenaries were eager to be paid. Any Imperial units with the 'Mercenary' special rule lose this while Wallenstein is still in command of the army.

1618 - The Defenestration of Prague. Imperial Catholic representatives are thrown from a castle window by Protestants.

Swedish regiment of foot

The Holy Roman Empire now saw an opportunity to demand a return to Catholicism for all the territories that had converted since the Treaty of Augsburg in 1555. Emperor Ferdinand was ruthless in setting about this task. Many German states were forced back into the Papal fold, and finally the Calvinist and Lutheran Protestants had to put their differences aside and unite.

Swedish Phase 1630-1634

A new champion of the Protestant cause was needed, and he was found in 'The Lion of the North' Gustav Adolf (or Gustavus Adolphus, if you prefer) of Sweden. With the Danes out of the picture and a costly war with Poland brought to a close with French help, the Swedish military machine was ready to tip the balance back from the Catholic League.

Sweden, like Denmark before, had concerns about the increased power of the Holy Roman Empire and felt it was only a matter of time before the 'Catholic wave' reached home shores. Also the lure of controlling the important Baltic and German states was a great incentive.

It was not all plain sailing to begin with as divisions in the Protestant camp threatened the whole campaign. However, in 1631 Tilly's Catholic League army had besieged and taken Magdeburg, a major Protestant centre, and over 20,000 civilians had been killed in the subsequent sacking of the city. This galvanised the Protestant League into action.

Initial Swedish gains were impressive. The army itself, although being Swedish led, included many German mercenaries, and not a few Scottish, who had to be paid. French funding, to the tune of one million livres per year, would keep them in the field. By 1632 Gustav had managed to drive the Imperial forces back, conquering about half of the Imperial kingdoms and reclaiming all the German Protestant land lost in the previous few years. Such success took the French aback and they began to see the Swedes as a threat.

These setbacks for the Imperials may have been due, in some part, to the fact that Ferdinand had dismissed Wallenstein in 1630 for political reasons and had to rely entirely on the aged Tilly. Tilly's situation certainly wasn't helped by political intrigues that prevented him from executing his battle plans as desired and he was constantly short of men and supplies.

In 1631 the Swedish army inflicted a stunning defeat on Tilly at the Battle of Breitenfeld, and a year later, following another defeat at the Battle of Lech (or Rain), 'Father' Tilly was dead.

The death of Tilly put the Holy Roman Emperor in a difficult position, and he was forced to recall Wallenstein despite some serious misgivings. In 1633 Wallenstein and Gustav Adolf met on the most famous of all Thirty Years War battlefields, Lutzen. Even though the Swedes prevailed, their king was killed at the moment of victory. Wallenstein was to fare little better as Emperor Ferdinand II had him killed by his own men after accusations of treachery. In reality Wallenstein had simply become too powerful for his own good, and had played the political game a little too often.

The loss of their king, combined with the higher reliance on foreign mercenaries, meant the Swedish army was weakened. Although led by Gustav's trusted lieutenant, Horn, and Bernhard of Saxe-Weimer the Swedes were defeated by Cardinal-Infante Ferdinand's Imperial Spanish at the First Battle of Nordlingen in 1634, losing over 14,000 men and all their artillery. These were losses they could not afford and within a year the Swedish armies had been driven from all the land they had occupied and sued for peace. The Peace of Prague officially removed Sweden from the war (albeit temporarily), and also allowed the Emperor to form a union between the Army of the Emperor and the German States thereby increasing his power base once more. This treaty was to bring France openly into the conflict (perhaps accompanied by the words 'if you want something doing…').

French Phase 1634-1648

Throughout the Thirty Years War up to this stage Louis XIII's France had been happy to intervene indirectly, offering large sums of money to the Protestant allies,

> The Swedes have come,
> Have taken everything,
> Have smashed in the windows,
> Have taken away the lead,
> Have made bullets from it
> And shot the peasants.
>
> *The "Song of the Swedes" - 1625*

particularly the Swedes and the Dutch. Cardinal Richelieu, the real power behind the throne, was a master diplomat, but now was the time for direct action. The Swedes had been knocked out of the war and the Spanish/Hapsburg alliance had become more powerful than ever. With much of France encircled by Imperial lands and forces this situation could not be tolerated.

In 1635 France declared war on Spain; this was opportune timing as the Spanish were facing a financial crisis combined with revolts at home and the Dutch making ground in their fight for independence. In 1636, feeling

King Gustav II Adolf (1594-1632)

King Gustav II Adolf, or Gustavus Adolphus to give him his commonly used Latinised name, was born in Stockholm and went on to become 'the father of modern warfare'. Born of Swedish/German heritage, the son of the future King Karl IX, Gustav was born into a country constantly at war. In his early years he was to lead men into battle against the Danes, Russians and Poles, in fact he was commanding armies from the age of 17 and continued to do so until his death.

Gustav matured into a very striking figure, being tall, blond and bearded. This appearance, as well as his prowess in battle, led to him being known as the 'Lion of the North'. He could also speak several languages and was eager to come to grips with all aspects of leading his country from a backward land to one of immense power. He developed the country's industry to allow him to wage war as well as introducing military innovations such as regional conscription to give him the manpower.

According to contemporaries he was pious, energetic and frugal. His strict Lutheran upbringing was a key driver behind his 'Articles of War' which meant his armies were not marred by the scourge of pillaging, and this helped his cause in conquered territories.

Gustav Adolf had a huge influence on modern warfare which came from his understanding that firepower was the most important and decisive of weapons. Salvo firing from his infantry with mobile artillery support was the cornerstone on which his strategies were built. He abolished caracoling for his cavalry and instead introduced headlong charges that swept all before them. When faced with the Imperial tercio style huge blocks of pikes, he adopted shallow formations, only 5 or 6 ranks deep, which allowed him to redeploy rapidly along with the light artillery pieces that would fire canister into the massed enemy ranks. He also ensured his men were trained, disciplined and motivated.

His one fatal flaw was his insistence on putting himself in harm's way. A Polish sniper shot to the neck at the Battle of Dirscau in 1627 had left a wound that meant wearing metal armour pained him. From this point on he would insist that 'the Lord God is my armour'. In 1632 his horse was shot from under him by a cannonball at the siege of Ingolstadt. The recklessness was to prove his undoing, and at the Battle of Lutzen he was killed by Imperial forces while leading a cavalry charge.

Arguably he was Europe's greatest modern commander until Napoleon. Certainly he founded the Swedish Empire and led them to their 'Era of Great Power'.

Command Rating: 10

Special: Lion of the North
King Gustav was the master of aggressive manoeuvres and was usually seen leading from the front. When Gustav joins a unit and issues a 'Follow Me' order, the order applies to all the units in the battalia, not just the unit he has joined. In addition any unit that Gustav joins receives a +1 combat resolution bonus.

1620 - The Battle of the White Mountain – the Protestants of Bohemia are defeated by the Holy Roman Empire.

confident, France finally declared war on the Holy Roman Empire and launched attacks into the Low Countries and Germany. Looking for allies, France enticed Sweden back into the mix with promises of more money and this ensured that there was another army in Germany to oppose the Imperials.

Despite Richelieu's confidence, the Holy Roman Empire still had three veteran armies available to them and the tables were soon turned. France faced a three-pronged invasion: a force under Cardinal-Infante Ferdinand marched through Picardie, Philip IV of Spain attacked from the South, while a marauding Imperial force under Matthias Gallas came from the east. There were fears that the Cardinal's force would actually capture Paris. It was only at the Battle of Compiegne that a force under Bernhard of Saxe-Weimer, the old Protestant champion now in French service, stopped the Imperial armies' march on the capital.

Meanwhile, by late 1636 the Swedes were making an impression with victories against Holy Roman Empire forces at Wittstock and Brandenburg. With the promise of French money to keep the soldiers paid the Swedes headed into Bohemia, reaching the outskirts of Prague.

In February 1637 Ferdinand II died and he was succeeded as Holy Roman Emperor by his son, Ferdinand III. The new Emperor could see that the costly war was eroding, not increasing, his powerbase and he was keen to find a peace with France and Spain. Unfortunately this peace was a long time coming, as most nations were unwilling to give any ground.

By 1639 King Philip's Spain was facing increased pressure. The Dutch had won considerable ground in the Low Countries, and the Spanish Atlantic fleet was destroyed by Dutch Admiral Tromp. Sensing weakness, Portugal declared independence from Spain in 1640. To make matters worse, France's military position was strengthening despite the death of Bernhard of Saxe-Weimer. This strength was epitomised by two brilliant generals, the Vicomte de Turenne and Louis II de Bourbon, 4th Prince de Conde (the Great Conde), who would both lead France to new military heights.

In 1642 Cardinal Richelieu died, followed shortly after by King Louis XIII. Louis' five year old son, Louis XIV (the future Sun King) assumed the throne, although the country was now being controlled by Cardinal Mazarin. Sensing weakness the Spanish launched an offensive, but this was crushed at the Battle of Rocroi by Conde. The Spanish had by now had enough, and began moves to sue for peace.

1643 also saw a resumption of hostilities between the Swedes and Danes; with those two it was only a matter of time. The Torstenson War, named after the prominent Swedish Commander, lasted two years and ended with Sweden becoming once more the dominant force in Scandinavia and the Balkans. Torstenson then led his Swedish army back through Germany to victory at the Battle of Jankau (near Prague) in 1645. A few months later, Turenne and Conde marched their French army to victory at the Second Battle of Nordlingen over the Imperial Bavarians. The last notable Imperial Commander, Baron Franz von Mercy, died in the fight, and with this loss the Holy Roman Empire also started to look for a way out of the war.

France was having problems of its own, being wracked by civil unrest, and the Fronde civil war meant that France was incapable of continuing the fight and also began to seek a peace agreement.

The final catalyst for an end to the Thirty Years War came in 1648, when Spain and Holland finally ended their 80 Years War, and the Dutch claimed independence at last.

A German Imperial battalia staunchly defending their homeland.

1621 - The truce between Spain and the Netherlands breaks down and war begins again.

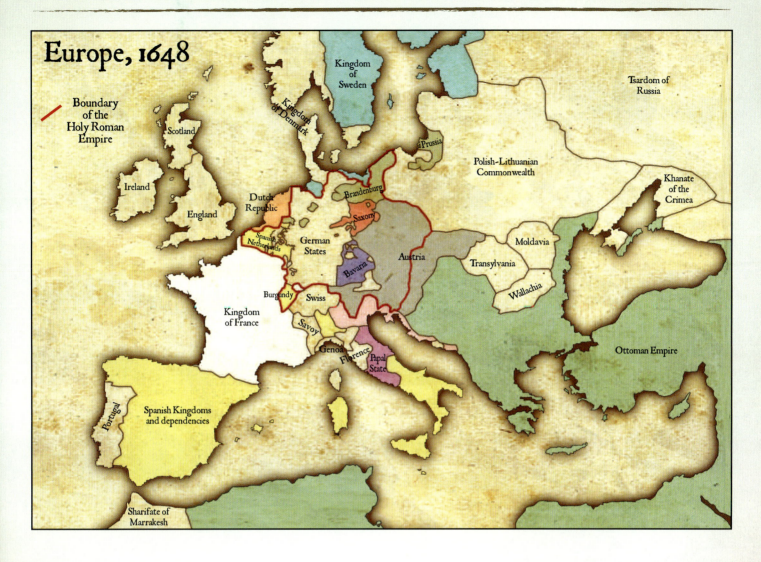

Europe, 1648

Boundary
of the
Holy Roman
Empire

Aftermath

The end of the Thirty Years War was formalised by the Peace of Westphalia, which was actually a culmination of a number of treaties over several months (those of Hamburg, Osnabruck and Munster). Much of Europe was on its knees, with the major Empires facing bankruptcy from decades of fighting. It really was a 'total war' and the impact on civilians was just as apparent as the death toll inflicted on the armies. The German States were ravaged, the male population across them being reduced by nearly 50%, and some regions facing mortality rates of 75% of entire populations. The historian Langer claims that a third of all German settlements were effectively wiped off the map from war, famine and disease. Plague and typhus was rampant and the movement of soldiers only made the situation worse.

The German states were not alone in their suffering as much of modern day Czech Republic (considered at the time as part of Germany) faced a similar situation, and as the Holy Roman Empire asserted its control over Bohemia and Austria the Protestant exiles could never return home.

The political situation had changed too. The Holy Roman Empire faced a reduction in influence as many of the German states gained sovereignty. Spain had lost the territories of Portugal and the Netherlands, while France gained territory but was facing financial ruin.

The longer term impact of the conflict was also massive. The devastation caused by hordes of mercenaries scouring the continent meant that nations began to recruit their own standing armies and this was to see an end to mercenary forces in Europe. The new independent regions would set the benchmark for the modern sovereign state, and this has shaped the Europe we know today. With the decline of the Holy Roman and Spanish Empires a power vacuum was formed and this was to be filled by France under Louis XIV.

Saxon troops in Swedish service.

1622 - The Battle of Fleurus is fought when German Protestants march to the aid of the besieged Dutch at Bergen-op-Zoom.

129

THIRTY YEARS WAR IMPERIAL ARMY

This is a very versatile army list that can cover the entire Thirty Years War through all the phases, and is equally viable for a Holy Roman Empire, Catholic League or Spanish Hapsburg force. Imperial pike troops form the backbone of the infantry but there are many interesting troop types to choose from too.

Although traditionalists were loath to move away from tercio tactics that had served the Empire so well in the past, new tactical formations were in evidence as the war progressed and the Imperial Army was always able to adapt to new challenges throughout the war.

Command Ratings

Overall Commander: Random Command Rating (see page 35) .... 40 Points

> Roll D6 for rating. 1: Command Rating 7, 2-5: Command Rating 8, 6: Command Rating 9

Infantry/Artillery Commander: Command Rating 8... 40 Points

Cavalry Commander: Command Rating 8 .... 40 Points

The Horse

Unit	Unit Type	Weapon	Hand-to-Hand Value	Shooting Value	Morale Value	Stamina	Special	Points
Cuirassiers	Heavy Horse	Sword, Pistols	8	1	3+	4	Caracole, Heavy Cavalry +1	53

- One unit can be upgraded to Lifeguard (as Wallenstein's). Unit gains Lance and Elite 4+ @ + 11 points

Unit	Unit Type	Weapon	Hand-to-Hand Value	Shooting Value	Morale Value	Stamina	Special	Points
Harquebusiers	Horse	Sword, Carbine, Pistol	7	1	4+	3	Caracole	39
Croats	Light Skirmisher Horse	Sword, Pistol, Spears	7	1	4+	3		39
Hussars	Light Skirmisher Horse	Sword, Bow	7	1	5+	3		36
Cossacks	Light Skirmisher Horse	Lance, Axe, Bow	7	1	5+	3	Marauder	46
Dragoons	Horse Skirmishers/Foot Skirmishers	Firelocks	3	2	5+	3	Fire & Evade, Marauder	35

The Foot

Unit	Unit Type	Weapon	Hand-to-Hand Value	Shooting Value	Morale Value	Stamina	Special	Points
Imperial Pikemen	Foot Pike Block	Pike	6	-	4+	4	Hedgehog, Mercenary	34

- Any Pike unit can be upgraded to 'Large' @ 6 points each
- Up to one Pike unit can be 'Elite 4+' for 6 points
- One unit can replace Pikes with Halberds. Unit loses 'Hedgehog' ability and gains 'Double Handed Infantry Weapons' @ +2 pts

Unit	Unit Type	Weapon	Hand-to-Hand Value	Shooting Value	Morale Value	Stamina	Special	Points
Imperial Musketeers	Foot Battle Line	Matchlock Muskets	3	2	5+	3	Mercenary	27

- Maximum of two Musketeer units for every Pike unit
- Any unit can be downgraded to Small @ −8 points each

1623 - The first complete folio edition of Shakespeare's works is published.

Unit	Unit Type	Weapon	Hand-to-Hand Value	Shooting Value	Morale Value	Stamina	Special	Points
Commanded Musket	Foot Battle Line	Matchlock Muskets	3	3	4+	3	First Fire	34

- Maximum of two Commanded Musket units in the army
- Up to one unit can be upgraded to Large for +8 points

Unit	Unit Type	Weapon	Hand-to-Hand Value	Shooting Value	Morale Value	Stamina	Special	Points
Storming Party	Foot Battle Line	Firelocks, Assorted Assault Weapons	4	2	4+	3	First Fire	34

- Maximum of one Storming Party per Army
- Make unit Elite 4+ for +6 points
- Equip unit with a Petard for +20 points
- Equip unit with grenades for 1 point

Unit	Unit Type	Weapon	Hand-to-Hand Value	Shooting Value	Morale Value	Stamina	Special	Points
Swordsmen	Foot Battle Line	Swords	6		4+	3	Swordsmen	34

- Maximum of two units of Swordsmen

Unit	Unit Type	Weapon	Hand-to-Hand Value	Shooting Value	Morale Value	Stamina	Special	Points
Militia	Foot Warband	Mixed	2	1	6+	2	Rabble, Militia	7

- Shooting value of 1 represents thrown weapons

The Ordnance

- Maximum of two artillery pieces per battalia

Unit	Unit Type	Weapon	Hand-to-Hand Value	Shooting Value	Morale Value	Stamina	Special	Points
Artillery	Ordnance	Various Cannon	1	3-2-1	5+	2		Varies

- Light Guns 17 points
- Medium Guns 21 points
- Heavy Guns 25 points

Unit	Unit Type	Weapon	Hand-to-Hand Value	Shooting Value	Morale Value	Stamina	Special	Points
Siege Artillery	Ordnance	Mortar	1	2	5+	2		25

- Maximum of one mortar per army

Dramatis Personae

Wallenstein. General. Command Rating 9 .... 70 Points
   Special Rule: War Chest.

Tilly. General. Command Rating 9 .... 70 Points
   Special Rule: Father Tilly.

Watch out, peasant, I am coming.
Get yourself out of the way, quick.
Captain, give us money,
While we are in the field.
Girl, come here,
Join me and the jug.

Soldiers' song – Thirty Years War

THIRTY YEARS WAR SWEDISH ARMY

The Swedish Army is one filled with excellent troop choices, and it was generally very well led. Formed on the base of elite Swedish and German infantry, the Swedish army of Gustavus Adolphus provided a rude awakening to the Imperialists with a string of victories.

Although weaker than their adversaries in the cavalry arm, the revolutionary tactics that maximized the firepower of its musketeers more than made up from this. The Swedish brigade formation maximised the amount of firepower and epitomised the aggressive nature of this army. To reinforce the need for mobility the Swedish army only went to war with artillery light enough to advance with its infantry and provide mobile firing platforms. The addition of Saxon allies makes this a very rewarding army to play; although usually outnumbered it will generally hold its own.

Command Ratings

Overall Commander: Random Command Rating (see page 35)..................40 Points

Roll D6 for rating: 1-5: Command Rating 8, 6: Command Rating 9

Infantry/Artillery Commander: Command Rating 9 .... 60 Points

Saxon Infantry Commander: Command Rating 8 .... 40 Points

Cavalry Commander: Command Rating 8 .... 40 Points

The Horse

Unit	Unit Type	Weapon	Hand-to-Hand Value	Shooting Value	Morale Value	Stamina	Special	Points
Cuirassiers	Heavy Horse	Sword, Pistols	8	1	3+	4	Caracole, Heavy Cavalry +1	53

- Two units maximum per army

Unit	Unit Type	Weapon	Hand-to-Hand Value	Shooting Value	Morale Value	Stamina	Special	Points
Harquebusiers	Horse	Sword, Carbine Pistol	7	1	4+	3		39

Unit	Unit Type	Weapon	Hand-to-Hand Value	Shooting Value	Morale Value	Stamina	Special	Points
Light Cavalry	Light Skirmisher Horse	Sword, Pistol	7	1	5+	3		35

Unit	Unit Type	Weapon	Hand-to-Hand Value	Shooting Value	Morale Value	Stamina	Special	Points
Finnish Cavalry	Light Horse	Sword, Pistols	7	1	4+	3	Gallopers, Ferocious Charge	42

- Finnish Cavalry units cannot outnumber Light Cavalry units

Unit	Unit Type	Weapon	Hand-to-Hand Value	Shooting Value	Morale Value	Stamina	Special	Points
Dragoons	Horse Skirmishers/ Foot Skirmishers	Firelocks	3	2	5+	3	Fire & Evade, Marauder	34

The Foot

Unit	Unit Type	Weapon	Hand-to-Hand Value	Shooting Value	Morale Value	Stamina	Special	Points
Swedish, German Veteran Pikemen	Foot Pike Block	Pike	5	-	3+	4	Hedgehog,	37

- Any units can be upgraded to Elite 4+ for 6 points each
- Up to two units can be 'Guard' Infantry. Unit gains 'Stubborn' special rule @ 5 pts each

Unit	Unit Type	Weapon	Hand-to-Hand Value	Shooting Value	Morale Value	Stamina	Special	Points
Commanded Musket	Foot Battle Line	Matchlock Muskets	4	3	4+	3	First Fire	35

- Maximum of two Commanded Musket units in the army
- Up to one unit can be upgraded to Large for 8 points

1625 - Charles I crowned king of England.

Unit	Unit Type	Weapon	Hand-to-Hand Value	Shooting Value	Morale Value	Stamina	Special	Points
Swedish, German Veteran Musketeers	Foot Battle Line	Matchlock Muskets	4	2	4+	3	First Fire	33

- Maximum of three Musketeer units for every Pike unit
- Any unit can be upgraded to Elite 4+ @ 6 points each
- Up to four units can be 'Guard' Musketeers. Unit gains 'Stubborn' special rule @ 5 pts each
- Any unit can be downgraded to Small @ -8 points each
- Up to three units can substitute Muskets for Bows (as Scots) @ -2 points per unit

Unit	Unit Type	Weapon	Hand-to-Hand Value	Shooting Value	Morale Value	Stamina	Special	Points
Storming Party	Foot Battle Line	Firelocks, Assorted Assault Weapons	4	2	4+	3	First Fire	34

- Maximum of one Storming Party per Army
- Make unit Elite 4+ for 6 points
- Equip unit with a Petard for 20 points
- Equip unit with Grenades for 1 point

Unit	Unit Type	Weapon	Hand-to-Hand Value	Shooting Value	Morale Value	Stamina	Special	Points
Saxon Pikemen	Foot Pike Block	Pike	6	-	4+	3	Hedgehog, Mercenary	31

Unit	Unit Type	Weapon	Hand-to-Hand Value	Shooting Value	Morale Value	Stamina	Special	Points
Saxon Musketeers	Foot Battle Line	Muskets	3	2	5+	3	Hedgehog, Mercenary	24

Unit	Unit Type	Weapon	Hand-to-Hand Value	Shooting Value	Morale Value	Stamina	Special	Points
Militia	Foot Warband	Mixed	2	1	6+	2	Rabble, Militia	7

- Shooting value of 1 represents thrown weapons

> I will die in t"First (saith he), giving fire unto three little Field-pieces that I had before me, I suffered not my muskettiers to give their volleyes till I came within Pistollshot of the enemy, at which time I gave order to the first rancks to discharge at once, and after them the other three: which done we fell pell mell into their ranckes, knocking them downe with the stocke of the Musket and our swords."
>
> *Lt. Colonel Muschamp, Swedish Brigade*

The Ordnance

Unit	Unit Type	Weapon	Hand-to-Hand Value	Shooting Value	Morale Value	Stamina	Special	Points
Artillery	Ordnance	Light Cannons	1	3-2-1	5+	2		Varies

- Light Guns: 17 pts
- Medium Guns: 21 pts
- Maximum of three artillery pieces per battalia
- No more than one Medium gun per three Light Guns

Dramatis Personae

Gustavus Adolphus. General. Command Rating 10 .... 95 Points
Special Rule: Lion of the North.

Thirty Years War Protestant Colours

Each regiment would carry a number of colours into battle representing companies of foot or troops of cavalry. The role of the ensign was held in high regard and much sought after despite the obvious risks the extra attention would attract.

On the battlefield these colourful standards would act both as regimental identifiers and highly visible rallying points.

The colours on this page are of Holy Roman Empire's staunchest enemies, namely the Swedes and their German mercenary regiments. We have also included Dutch colours as they were a continual thorn in the side of the Imperialist expansion in the Low Countries.

Swedish Infantry Regiment

Swedish Blue Regiment

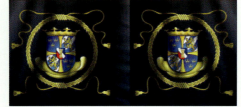

King's Lifeguard (Johan Baners Life Regiment)

Swedish Yellow Regimennt

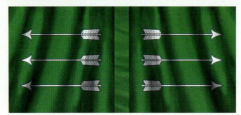

Swedish Green Regiment

Swedish Vastgota Regiment

Upplands Swedish cavalry regt

Swedish Småland Regiment

Holtzmuller's Dragoon Company

Småland Swedish cavalry regt

Karberg Swedish cavalry regt

Ohm's Swedish cavalry regt

King's German Lifeguard regt

Schaffman's Swedish cavalry regt

Swedish Cuirassiers

General Ake Tott's Cuirassiers regiment

The four flags below represent the protestant Dutch who were also fighting against the Imperialists, most notably the Spanish during their 80 years war for independence

Generic Dutch Regimental colour

Generic Dutch Regimental colour

Generic Dutch Regimental colour

Generic Dutch States colour

1627 - The French Huguenots are besieged in the stronghold of La Rochelle by Royal forces.

Thirty Years War
Imperial and French Colours

The Imperial colours on this page represent all corners of the Hapsburg Empire. Foot and horse regiments of the Catholic League, the Spanish Hapsburgs and the Holy Roman Empire itself are all covered.

Although technically not Imperial troops we have also added French standards as they played a pivotal role in the Thirty Years War. Despite being a Catholic nation, France gave financial support to the Protestant cause and even entered the war directly against the Holy Roman Empire towards the end.

Spanish Cavalry cornet

Bavarian cornet 1630-1647

The Imperial Eagle of the Holy Roman Empire

Bavarian Infantry regiment standard

The three colours below are typical of the Spanish armies of Philip IV who fought throughout the Thirty Years War.

Spanish Infantry regiment circa 1643

Imperial Harquebusiers after de Waggky

Imperial Harquebusiers, Piccolomini 1632

The Imperial Eagle of the Holy Roman Empire

Spanish Infantry regiment raised in Italy, 17th century

Imperial Harquebusiers

Bruener's Regiment

The four colours above are representative of typical banners of the Holy Roman Empire and the Catholic League. The Catholic League was led by Elector Maximillian II of Bavaria which explains the preponderance of Baviarian regiments during the war.

Spanish Infantry regiment circa 1643

Imperial Harquebusiers

Croatian Cavalry

The trio of colours below are not Imperial colours. They are French standards of the armies of Louis XIII. Although the French fought against the Holy Roman Empire the armies would have dressed in a very similar manner to Imperialist troops.

Turenne's standard

Imperial Cuirassiers

Calvisson standard

Lyonnais standard

Von Tilly's Dragoons

17TH CENTURY POLISH ARMY

The Polish army of the 17th century was renowned for the quality of its cavalry, especially the iconic Winged Hussars. These troops are probably one of the most popular of any wargaming period, and for this reason we had to include this list in the book. Unlike most armies of the time, the cavalry arm of the Polish forces generally far outweighed the infantry in numbers and importance. They were usually first into the fray and were the main shock troops used. Infantry regiments raised in Poland were musket armed, with axes for close combat. For the pike units common amongst most Western armies at the time the Poles would rely on mercenaries, usually from Germany. It was the Polish army of Jan Sobieski that broke the Ottoman siege of Vienna in 1683, a battle that would immortalise the Winged Hussars and prove to be the high watermark of the Ottoman Empire in Europe.

The Polish army does offer unique challenges for a wargamer given their tactics were so removed from Western European armies of the time, but they are a fantastic looking force on any tabletop.

Command Ratings

Overall Commander: Random Command Rating (see page 35) .... 40 Points

  Roll D6 for rating. 1-5: Command Rating 8, 6: Command Rating 9

Infantry/Artillery Commander: Command Rating 8... 40 Points

Cavalry Commander: Command Rating 9 .... 60 Points

The Horse

Unit	Unit Type	Weapon	Hand-to-Hand Value	Shooting Value	Morale Value	Stamina	Special	Points
Winged Hussars	Heavy Horse	Lance, Sword Pistols	10	1	3+	4	Elite, Stubborn, Heavy Cavalry D3	77

• Maximum of four Units per Army

Unit	Unit Type	Weapon	Hand-to-Hand Value	Shooting Value	Morale Value	Stamina	Special	Points
Pancerni	Horse	Axe, Sword/ spears Pistols	7	1	4+	3		39

• Any unit can be armed with carbines @ 1 point

Polish Winged Hussars – is there a finer sight on the battlefield?

1630 - Gustavus Adolphus leads Sweden into the Thirty Years' War on the Protestant side.

Unit	Unit Type	Weapon	Hand-to-Hand Value	Shooting Value	Morale Value	Stamina	Special	Points
Cossacks	Light Horse Skirmishers	Lance, Sword, Bow	6	1	5+	3	Marauders	44

- Any unit can replace bows with carbines @ 0 points

Unit	Unit Type	Weapon	Hand-to-Hand Value	Shooting Value	Morale Value	Stamina	Special	Points
Tatars	Light Horse Skirmishers	Spear, Bow	6	1	5+	3	Marauders	39
Rajtar	Horse	Sword, Pistols	7	1	4+	3	Caracole	39

- Any unit can add carbines for 1 point per unit

Unit	Unit Type	Weapon	Hand-to-Hand Value	Shooting Value	Morale Value	Stamina	Special	Points
Levy Cavalry	Skirmish Horse	Sword, Spear	4	-	6+	2	Militia	17
Dragoons	Skirmisher Horse/ Skirmisher Foot	Sword, Carbine	4	2	5+	3	Fire & Evade, Marauder	35

The Foot

Unit	Unit Type	Weapon	Hand-to-Hand Value	Shooting Value	Morale Value	Stamina	Special	Points
Hungarian/ Polish Infantry	Infantry Battle Line	Musket, Sword/Axe	5	2	4+	3		33
German Pikemen	Pike Block	Pike	6	-	4+	4	Hedgehog, Mercenary	31
German Musketeers	Infantry Battle Line	Musket	3	2	5+	3	Mercenary	24
Levy Infantry	Warband	Mixed	2	1	6+	2	Militia	12

- Shooting value reflects thrown weapons

The Ordnance

- Maximum of two artillery pieces per battalia.

Unit	Unit Type	Weapon	Hand-to-Hand Value	Shooting Value	Morale Value	Stamina	Special	Points
Artillery	Ordnance	Various Cannon	1	3-2-1	4+	2		Varies

- Light Guns: 19 points • Medium Guns: 23 points • Heavy/Siege Guns: 27 points

Unit	Unit Type	Weapon	Hand-to-Hand Value	Shooting Value	Morale Value	Stamina	Special	Points
Siege Artillery	Ordnance	Mortar	1	2	4+	2		27

- Maximum of one mortar per army

Polish Winged Hussars

Winged Hussars, or Winged Lancers, were originally a mercenary force of light cavalry from Serbia who found their way into Polish service. By the 17th Century they had evolved into an elite cavalry formation attracting the cream of Polish nobility, arguably the best cavalry in the world at the time.

Their 'wings' were usually made of eagle feathers on a wooden frame. Along with the plate armour, kopia lance, two swords, pistols, carbines, gold leaf and other adornments the Winged Hussars certainly looked the part.

The kopia lance was extremely long, being made of two hollowed parts and tipped with steel. It allowed the hussars to provide a devastating impact when they charged in, one that was very hard to face down, even with pikes. It has been claimed that Polish Winged Hussars went over 100 years without suffering a defeat; this may well be hyperbole but they were certainly an incredible fighting force. Their place in history was assured with the charge at Vienna in 1683 where they smashed the Ottoman Turkish army apart and were hailed as saviours of Christian Europe.

1631 - The Battle of Breitenfeld – Gustavus Adolphus defeats the Catholic League.

17TH CENTURY OTTOMAN ARMY

The Ottoman Empire was a serious threat to Christian Europe throughout the 16th and 17th centuries. The expansionist policies of Suleiman the Magnificent in the 1500's had seen a huge Empire carved from Eastern Europe, North Africa and east into Asia. The driving forces behind this army were the expanding Janissary Corps of infantry and the feared Sipahi cavalry. These 'household troops' were backed up by a wide array of feudal troops from across the Empire. This particular list is more in line with end of the 17th Century when Mehmet IV attempted to aggressively expand into central Europe, only being stopped at the gates of Vienna in 1683.

This army is a joy in its sheer diversity, fantastic shock troops mixed with levies offers a challenge to any general, although you can always rely on the very capable artillery. Although certainly not a typical 'Pike & Shotte' army, having no pike regiments, the Ottoman Army was too influential on European warfare of the period to be omitted from the book.

Command Ratings

Overall Commander: Random Command Rating (see page 35) .... 40 Points

Roll D6 for rating. 1-2: Command Rating 7, 3-5: Command Rating 8, 6: Command Rating 9

Infantry/Artillery Commander: Command Rating 7.. 20 Points

Cavalry Commander: Command Rating 8 .... 40 Points

Special Rule: A Class Apart

All units in an Infantry or Cavalry Battalia must be of the same type.

The Horse

Unit	Unit Type	Weapon	Hand-to-Hand Value	Shooting Value	Morale Value	Stamina	Special	Points
Sipahis of the Porte	Heavy Horse	Lance, Sword Pistols	8	1	3+	4	Elite 4+, Heavy Cavalry +1	64

- Maximum of three Units per Army

Unit	Unit Type	Weapon	Hand-to-Hand Value	Shooting Value	Morale Value	Stamina	Special	Points
Feudal Sipahis	Horse	Sword or Spear, Pistol	7	1	4+	3	Elite	45

- One unit can be armed with carbines @ 1 point
- One unit can be armed with lances @ 5 points

Unit	Unit Type	Weapon	Hand-to-Hand Value	Shooting Value	Morale Value	Stamina	Special	Points
Gonullu	Heavy Horse	Lance, Sword, Pistol	7	1	4+	3	Heavy Cavalry +1	48

Unit	Unit Type	Weapon	Hand-to-Hand Value	Shooting Value	Morale Value	Stamina	Special	Points
Light Cavalry/ Delli/Arabs	Light Horse Skirmishers	Sword, Bow	6	1	5+	3		34

- Up to half the units can replace bows with carbines @ 1 point

Unit	Unit Type	Weapon	Hand-to-Hand Value	Shooting Value	Morale Value	Stamina	Special	Points
Tartars	Skirmish Horse	Sword, Bow	4	1	6+	3	Marauder	31

The Foot

Unit	Unit Type	Weapon	Hand-to-Hand Value	Shooting Value	Morale Value	Stamina	Special	Points
Janissaries	Infantry Battle Line	Musket, Swords	5	2	4+	3	Elite 4+	39

- Up to three units can be Guard Janissaries. Gain 'Fanatic' ability @ 5 points per unit

Unit	Unit Type	Weapon	Hand-to-Hand Value	Shooting Value	Morale Value	Stamina	Special	Points
Azabs	Infantry Battle Line	Musket, Axes	3	2	5+	3		27

1632 - The Battle of Lutzen, Gustavus Adolphus is victorious again, but is killed.

Unit	Unit Type	Weapon	Hand-to-Hand Value	Shooting Value	Morale Value	Stamina	Special	Points
Tufekci Fusiliers	Infantry Battle Line	Sword, Musket	3	2	5+	3	First Fire	28
Irregular Infantry	Infantry Skirmishers	Sword/Axe, Bow	3	1	5+	3		25
Levy Infantry	Infantry Warband	Mixed	2	1	6+	2	Militia	12

- Shooting value represents thrown weapons

The Ordnance

Maximum of four artillery pieces per battalia

Unit	Unit Type	Weapon	Hand-to-Hand Value	Shooting Value	Morale Value	Stamina	Special	Points
Artillery	Ordnance	Various	Cannon	1	3-2-1	4+	2	Varies

- Light Guns: 19 pts
- Medium Guns: 23 pts
- Heavy/Siege Guns: 27 pts

Siege Artillery	Ordnance	Mortar	1	2	4+	2		27

- Maximum of one mortar per army

Polish Winged Hussars charge the Ottoman line by Peter Dennis © Osprey Publishing Ltd. Taken from Campaign 191: Vienna 1683.

1634 - The Battle of Nordlingen. The Roman Catholic Imperial army wins a crushing victory over the Swedes and their Protestant allies.

BLOOD ON THE DANUBE

On April 15th 1632 the Swedish army, under the dynamic leadership of their king, Gustav Adolf, won a decisive victory at the Battle of Rain on the river Lech. This victory not only put a serious dent in the army of the Catholic League and Imperial campaign plans, it also opened up the way for a full invasion into the Bavarian heartland. Even worse, early in the battle, the famous Imperial commander Tilly was seriously wounded by a cannonball.

It was left to Maximilian I of Bavaria to organise a disciplined retreat, the aim was to reach the safety of Ingolstadt and stop the Imperial army from disintegrating under the pressure of Swedish attacks.

In this scenario King Gustav has detached part of his army to chase down Maximilian while he pushes south toward Munich; he has given command to his trusted subordinate Nils Brahe who will have the elite Yellow Guards at his disposal, along with a mixed Swedish, German and Saxon force. Maximilian has stopped his Catholic League force at the town of Neuburg an der Donau (Neuburg on the Danube) to offer a rear guard to stop the Swedes in their tracks. Crucially the Imperial war chest is also in the town as no provision has yet been made to get this to safety; the rest of the Imperial army along with the mortally wounded 'Father' Tilly are well on their way to Ingolstadt by now.

Swedish spies have got word to the Swedish Commander Brahe about the gold. He now has even more incentive to come to grips with Maximilian's army and destroy it. The capture of the Imperial treasure will make it far more difficult for the Catholic League to raise fresh mercenary troops for the battles to come.

The Set Up

The Swedish army approaches Neuberg from the west and will deploy its forces according to marching order; as the attacking force it will get to move first.

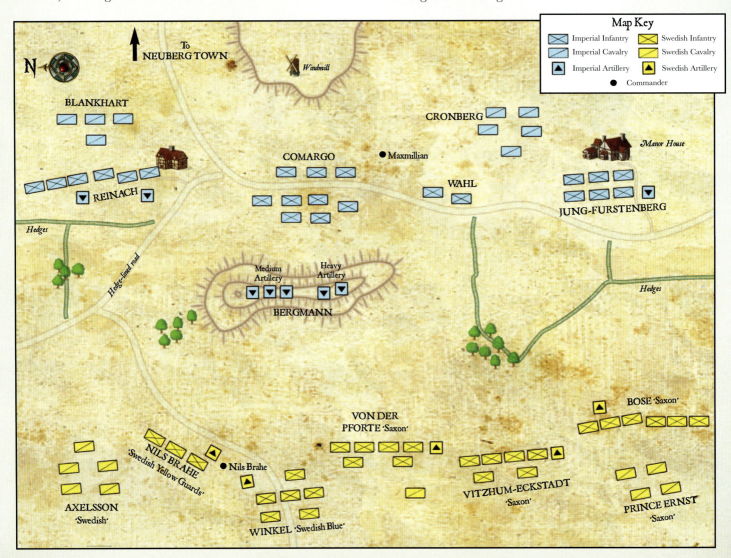

1635 - The Thirty Years' War enters a new phase as France declares war on Spain.

The Imperialist Catholic League Army

Maximilian I, Elector of Bavaria

General, Command Rating 9

Oberst Reinach

Command Rating 8

- 2 Units of Imperial Pikemen
- 4 Units of Imperial Musketeers
- 2 Attached Medium Guns

Oberst Comargo

Command Rating 8

- 3 Units of Imperial Pikemen
- 6 Units of Imperial Musketeers

Oberst Jung-Furstenberg

Command Rating 8

- 2 Units of Imperial Pikemen
- 4 Units of Imperial Musketeers
- 1 Attached Medium Gun

Oberst Wahl

Command Rating 8

- 2 Units of Free Company Commanded Musket

Oberst Blankhart

Command Rating 8

- 4 Units of Cuirassiers

Oberst Gronberg

Command Rating 8

- 2 Units of Cuirassiers
- 3 Units of Harquebusiers

General-feldzeugmeister Bergmann

Command Rating 8

- Artillery battery of 2 Heavy Guns and 3 Medium Guns

The Swedish Army

Nils Brahe

General, Command Rating 9

The Yellow 'Guards' Battalia

- 1 Unit of Veteran Pikemen
  (Guards Infantry – Elite & Stubborn)
- 2 Units of Veteran Musketeers
  (Guards Musketeers – Elite & Stubborn)
- 1 Attached Light Gun

Oberst Hans Georg aus dem Winkel

Command Rating 9

- 2 Units of Veteran Pikemen (Elite)
- 4 Units of Veteran Musketeers (Elite)
- 1 Attached Light Gun

Oberst Carl Bose

Command Rating 8

- 2 Units of Saxon Pikemen
- 4 Units of Saxon Musketeers
- 1 Attached Light Gun

Oberst Hans von der Pforte

Command Rating 8

- 2 Units of Saxon Pikemen
- 4 Units of Saxon Musketeers
- 1 Attached Light Gun

Oberst Damien von Vitzhum-Eckstadt

Command Rating 8

- 2 Units of Saxon Pikemen
- 4 Units of Saxon Musketeers
- 1 Attached Light Gun

Oberstleutnant Isaak Axelsson

Command Rating 8

- 4 Units of Saxon Harquebusiers

Ernst, Prince of Anhalt-Bernburg

Command Rating 8

- 4 Units of Saxon Harquebusiers

Oberst Fredrick Stenbock

Command Rating 8

- 1 Unit of Cuirassiers (Reserve)

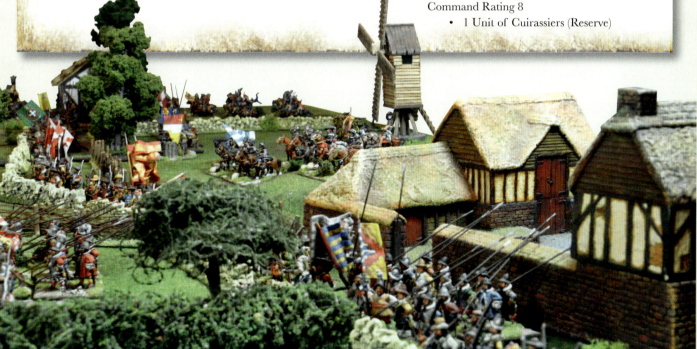

1636 - The Spanish besiege Corbie, France.

> 'Nowadayes all captain are accustomed to arraying their troops in more than one line, a tactic which the Germans call treyfach. This is what the Imperials did at Lutzen, Soultz, Nordlingen Wittstock, Freburg and everywhere except for Tilly in the battle of Breitenfeld-Leipzig. The latter placed his whole army along a single front and found himself in a bad way as a result'.

Raimondo Montecuccoli describing the 'German doctrine' in 1642

The Imperial force of Maximilian has had time to set up some rudimentary defences in front of the town, with an artillery battery to the fore. The war chest is placed in one of three locations by the Imperial player; the farmhouse, the old windmill or the manor house. The Swedish player will have no idea in which of the three locations the gold is hidden at the start of the game.

The Swedish march has taken much of the day to catch up with Maximilian, so time is of the essence. After eight game turns night will fall and the war chest can be removed safely under cover of darkness by the Imperial side.

If the Swedish capture and hold unopposed for one turn the building in which the war chest is hidden they will capture it and win the game. The Imperial side will win if they still hold the treasure at the end of the eighth turn.

How It Played

The Catholic League's artillery battery was set up in a hastily prepared defensive position on the small hill in front of the main Imperial lines in the centre of the battlefield. The war chest was placed – somewhat controversially – in the farmhouse, seemingly as that was the least obvious place it would be. This was done before the Swedish force began to move onto the field. The Swedish army spent its first turn marching into position; fortunately for them all the battalias successfully moved onto the battlefield and advanced toward the town.

With so many Swedish and Saxon troops suddenly looming into view, the Imperial gunners on the hill to the fore of their army were spoilt for choice for available targets. They opted – rather wisely – to concentrate their fire on the Yellow Guards battalia; although inflicting little damage they did succeed in slowing their progress by causing disorder in the pike block. Much of the remainder of the first Imperial turn was spent consolidating defensive positions, the left flank being anchored on the well-fortified manor house.

The Swedish army wasted no time in ordering a general advance, and although some Saxon regiments seemed less keen to join the fray, Winkel's and von der Porte's battalias closed rapidly on the Imperial artillery which was also coming under pressure from the cavalry of Axelsson. On the Swedish right, the Saxon troops of Carl Bose fairly sprinted across the open ground in front of them, determined to take the manor.

The threat of being overrun seemed to galvanise the Imperial gunners. A devastating hail of grapeshot tore a Swedish 'Blue' pike unit apart before the artillery was driven from the hill. The Imperial centre, held by Comargo, moved forward to counter and poured more fire into the beleaguered Swedes and suddenly the command of Oberst Winkel was on the verge of breaking. Emboldened by such gains the Imperial right moved forward too, Reinach ordering his men forward – a risky move given they were guarding the all-important farmhouse – to confront Nils Brahe and the Swedish Guards.

Swedish Cavalry

1637 - 'Tulip Mania' in Holland, the first recorded financial speculative bubble bursts.

Despite being outnumbered, the elite Swedish battalia showed its mettle and soon gained the upper hand in the fight, gaining valuable support from the cavalry to their left. The Imperialists were less fortunate in their support as Blankart's cavalry had 'blundered' off to their left and were heading for the windmill. The disparity in the horse was to prove crucial as Imperial troops engaged in combat to their front were caught in the flank by Axelsson's marauding Finnish cavalry with predictable results – Imperial troops cut down or streaming back toward the farmhouse.

At the manor house the advancing Saxon infantry of Bose dashed themselves to pieces against the walls of the manor house and were in desperate need of support, this arrived in the form of fresh units from the regiment of Vitzhum-Eckstadt. Given the desperate situation on the Imperial right, Cronberg's cavalry and Wahl's commanded shot regiments headed toward the centre of the battlefield effectively abandoning the Imperial troops holed up in the manor to their fate. Indeed, the manor was captured by the combined Saxon battalias, but only after the command of Carl Bose was annihilated. The remaining Saxon victors turned their attentions to looting the manor and searching for the elusive war chest.

Abandoning the manor had freed up valuable Imperial troops, and the combined infantry battalias of Wahl, Comargo and the rallied remains of Reinach's command combined to pour fire on Winkel's men and finally broke the Swedish Blue battalia.

As darkness began to fall the Swedish commanders had one last push to attack both remaining objectives, the farmhouse and the windmill. With two infantry battalias broken, and one Saxon battalia effectively out of the battle at the manor house, it was up to the Swedish Guards and von der Porte's Saxons along with the intact cavalry to get things done. Both cavalry wings attempted to converge in the centre to assault the windmill, while the infantry readied themselves to assault the farm.

Ready to abandon the windmill, the last Imperial troops ignored the Swedish cavalry and converged on the farm, all

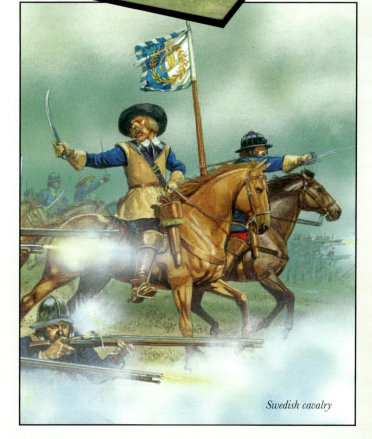

Swedish cavalry

except Reinach's survivors who decided to retire at speed. Wahl's commanded shot and Comargo's musket combined to provide one more crucial volley which was accurate enough to disorder most of the advancing enemy. This was to prove decisive as the Swedes ran out of time just as they captured the windmill, but fell tantalisingly short of the farm which contained their objective. Despite gaining much of the field it was to prove a painful defeat for the Swedish and Saxon forces.

Under cover of darkness the Imperial survivors withdrew with their valuable cargo and Maximilian was able to get the war chest back to the main Imperialist army in Ingolstadt and use the cash to raise more men to continue the fight.

THE ENGLISH CIVIL WARS

The English Civil War is the commonly used term for a series of three distinct conflicts from 1642 to 1651. These conflicts covered all of the British Isles, not just England, and rather than being a 'civil' affair was actually the first true modern revolution, resulting in the execution of the ruling monarch, Charles I.

This period saw extraordinary social, economic and religious turmoil against a backdrop of simmering tension between the King, appointed by God, and Parliament, appointed (nominally) by the people.

Although much of Europe was in the midst of the savage Thirty Years War, the British Isles had been spared the ravages of war on home soil. Therefore at the outbreak of war, aside from some officers who had served in foreign armies abroad, the fighting was done by inexperienced men led by enthusiastic amateurs. Many regiments were raised by local gentry or Members of Parliament (MP's) rallying local support. One such MP, Oliver Cromwell, went on to rule the Commonwealth.

The terms and images surrounding the traditional words Cavalier and Roundhead (Royalist and Parliamentarian respectively) are misleading. Initially terms of insult thrown at the other side, they were taken on board as caricatures which survive to this day. In fact, there was little or no difference between the appearances and demographic of the opposing armies, both drawing equally on all parts of society. In broad geographic terms the North and West came out for the king, the South and East for Parliament.

Scotland played a key role in the war. Charles I being a Stuart was of Scottish descent, but this did not stop the Scottish Covenanters declaring against him at the start of the wars, although they sided with him later when he agreed to their concessions. There was also a Royalist force active in Scotland under the dynamic figure of the Earl of Montrose.

Although huge areas of the country tried their best to remain neutral, and groups of men (commonly called Clubmen) formed together to protect their communities against any aggressor, avoiding the conflict was often difficult. In fact many communities were torn apart as even family loyalties were divided.

The Bishops' Wars 1639 & 1640

Although not officially a part of the English Civil Wars, the Bishops' Wars were a prelude to what was to come. King Charles I had effectively used his powers to rule the country without a parliament from 1629-1640, a period known as the 'Eleven Years Tyranny'. He had disbanded parliament following a number of disputes that had increasingly frustrated him; instead he turned to a few trusted advisors.

Unfortunately one of these advisors, the Archbishop of Canterbury, William Laud, pushed Charles down the path of a single unified prayer book across both England and Scotland. The Scots had other ideas, and an alliance of nobles and Presbyterians united in opposition against this act and signed the National Covenant. Soon after the General Assembly of

Regiment of the New Model Army displaying Colonel and 1st Captain colours.

1639 - The Battle of the Downs: A Dutch fleet decisively defeats a Spanish flotilla in English waters.

Oliver Cromwell 1599-1658

The man who grew up to be one of the most controversial figures in British history was born into a 'middle' gentry family in Huntingdon, Cambridgeshire. After the death of his father, young Oliver took over the family estate and was married in 1620. In 1628 he was elected as Member of Parliament for Huntingdon, and around this time suffered serious bouts of depression and illness. One of the repercussions of this depression was a spiritual awakening that left Cromwell with the unshakeable Puritan beliefs that were to shape the rest of his life.

At the outbreak of the Civil War, Cromwell sided with parliament and raised a troop of horse with which he soon secured all of Cambridgeshire for the parliamentarian cause. The early dominance of the Royalist horse in the war was noted by Cromwell who began to design ways to combat this. A recruitment drive of only "Godly, honest men" to his banner and a regimen of strict discipline soon paid dividends and as a cavalry commander Cromwell took control of most of East Anglia.

Rising rapidly to Lt. General of Horse in the Eastern Association, Oliver played a major role in the victory at Marston Moor where his disciplined troops won the day against their impetuous Royalist counterparts. It is rumoured that Prince Rupert himself coined the phrase 'Ironsides' to describe the stoic roundhead cavalry. The name stuck.

When the New Model Army was founded Cromwell managed to dodge the Self Denying Ordinance and took up the role of Lt. General of Horse for the army, and was a key figure at the decisive battle of Naseby. Once again the superior discipline of the Ironsides was a deciding factor. Despite no formal military training Cromwell was hailed as the "Greatest Soldier in Britain".

With the capture of the king, attention turned to destroying the last vestiges of resistance. In 1648 he put down revolts in South Wales before defeating the Scots at Preston. Always a more proficient politician than his commander, Sir Thomas Fairfax, Cromwell soon rose to prominence and was the driving force behind the trial and execution of King Charles and the forming of the republic in early 1649.

Ireland was next on the agenda, and a campaign that included the massacres at Drogheda and Wexford remain a stain on Cromwell's name. The Scottish once more raised troops against Cromwell as they declared for Charles II, but they were soundly beaten at Dunbar in 1650. With the support of the army, Cromwell's rise to power was complete. In 1653 he was made Lord Protector for life, given the right to dispense knighthoods and be called 'Your Highness'.

Oliver Cromwell died on 3rd September 1658; it is rumoured that a great storm gripped the country (some say it was a sign of the devil taking his soul). His eldest son, Richard succeeded him as Lord Protector but Richard never had the support of the army and within 12 months the protectorate was at an end. The restoration of Charles II soon followed.

A suitably miffed new king, still sore at the execution of his father, had Cromwell's body exhumed from its resting place in Westminster Abbey and beheaded. The body was hung in chains and the head placed on a spike outside Westminster Hall until 1685. Now that's holding a grudge.

Oliver Cromwell, hero of liberty or genocidal oppressor? This is a question that still resonates in the British Isles to this day.

Oliver Cromwell. Commander of Horse, or General. Command Rating 9

Special Rule: Will of Iron. Cromwell was renowned for the discipline he instilled into his men. When fielded as part of a New Model Army force, any unit that Cromwell joins will gain +1 to their Morale value while he accompanies them, and he also adds +2 to the combat resolution of any combat he joins.

the Church of Glasgow expelled the Episcopalian Bishops and Scotland became a Presbyterian nation.

Charles was livid at this rebuttal and a collision course was set. Without a parliament to raise money for the coming war, Charles had to resort to ill-trained militias to confront the Covenanter army, and these were not able to offer any meaningful resistance. Charles was forced into a humiliating step down, and a compromise was reached at the Treaty of Berwick in June 1639.

This compromise was not to last as neither side achieved what they wanted, and was only to prove a short term respite. The Covenanters stoked the fires of discontent by claiming that Charles' actions were not only unlawful but against the will of God.

Charles chose to turn to another of his advisors, Thomas Wentworth, who persuaded the king to recall parliament in order to raise the money needed to march on the rebellious Scots. Once again parliament, now led by John Pym, took the opportunity to air their grievances against Charles. His reaction was to disband this 'Short Parliament' (as it became known) within a month of reinstating it.

Without financial aid, Charles once again had to confront the Scots with an ill-trained and badly equipped army. Once again he was unsuccessful, although this time the Scots advanced as far south as Northallerton and – more seriously – captured Newcastle-upon-Tyne. Charles found himself once more having to bow to Scottish demands, and the Bishops' Wars were finished with hardly a blow struck in anger.

Sir Thomas Fairfax 1612-71

Thomas Faifax, eldest son of Ferdinand, 2nd Lord Fairfax, was born on the 17th January 1612 at Denton Hall in Yorkshire. After studying at Cambridge University young Fairfax got his first taste of war by joining Sir Horace Vere's English force helping the Protestant cause in the Netherlands. He must have made some in impression as he was married to Sir Horace's daughter, Anne in 1637. When King Charles raised troops for the Bishops' Wars against the Scots, Thomas went as commander of a dragoon regiment, but was sent packing by the Scots along with the rest of the English Army. Despite this setback, he was knighted for his troubles when back in London.

At the outbreak of the Civil War Sir Thomas and his father sided for Parliament, which certainly put them in the minority in Yorkshire. Despite defeat by a larger Royalist force at Adwalton Moor in 1643, Sir Thomas proved himself a very able and popular leader. Nicknamed 'Black Tom', by virtue of his dashing and dark countenance, he gradually gained the upper hand in Yorkshire by constant campaigning and canny generalship.

At the key battle of Marston Moor in 1644, despite being severely wounded, Sir Thomas managed to join up with Oliver Cromwell's cavalry on the opposite flank for a crucial attack that sealed victory for the joint Parliament/Covenanter army. This act guaranteed national notoriety as a valiant leader of men.

In 1645 his renown was such that he avoided the Self Denying Ordinance and became the Commander-in-Chief of the New Model Army. Managing to instill belief and discipline in this fledgling force, the victory against King Charles at Naseby signaled the beginning of the end for the Royalists. Indeed, under Sir Thomas's leadership the New Model Army did not lose a single battle, siege or storm. By 1647 he was the Commander-in-Chief of all Parliament's forces.

Fairfax was always wary of celebrity and was a far better soldier than politician, and as victory became assured he began to take a more withdrawn role as Cromwell and Ireton pushed to the fore.

In 1648 he became 3rd Lord Fairfax upon the death of his father, and went on to put down the revolt in Colchester. It was here that he was to gain the one black mark on his name, by controversially ordering the execution of Sir Charles Lucas and Sir George Lisle for reneging on their parole. His final act as head of the army was to put down the Leveller Revolt.

Sir Thomas played no active part in 'Pride's Purges' in the Commons, and distanced himself totally from the trial and execution of Charles I - his wife being an outspoken supporter of the king. The Commonwealth years were spent in quiet anonymity, and he was privy to the negotiations to restore the monarchy in the form of Charles II. In fact, Sir Thomas supplied the new king's horse at his coronation. After the restoration he went back to Yorkshire to live out his days in peace, a fitting end to a noble man.

Sir Thomas Fairfax. General. Command Rating 9

Inspiring leader: Will automatically rally any unit he joins (no need to roll) and will rally D3 Stamina points. Note: he may never rally a unit's last casualty marker.

More seriously for him, he had to recall Parliament (the Long Parliament) at the end of 1640; this time it was clear to MP's that they had leverage over the king. They used this power to put Archbishop Laud and Thomas Wentworth on trial for their lives and had them executed. Charles also agreed that he could no longer disband parliament without their consent. Where he drew the line was with the creation of the 'Grand Remonstrance' in which Parliament had laid out both the positives of his reign, but also his failings. This was an insult too far, and he made the rash move of marching to the House of Commons with an armed escort to arrest Pym and other senior politicians. However, Pym and his colleagues had fled after being tipped off, and the king raged impotently.

When parliament demanded that the country's military should fall under their control and not the king's, Charles realised that London was no longer a safe place for himself and his family. He marched north to raise the Royal Standard in Nottingham in August 1642, and so the Civil Wars began.

The First English Civil War 1642-1647

As soon as the Royal Standard was raised in Nottingham on that fateful summer day in 1642 there was a rush to gain recruits for the cause. As already mentioned, the king could call on much of the north and west of England, while Parliament recruited broadly from the south and east; however the real picture was far more confused than that. Local landowners were wooed by both sides to raise regiments (many Members of Parliament were also to raise regiments of their own), and these landowners could tip the balance of power in the shires.

Troops were also recruited from Scotland, Ireland and from those soldiers who had been fighting on the continent in the Thirty Years War. Local 'Trained Bands' were also dragged en masse into the fray; although it is the London Trained Bands that have received most of the popular attention, such forces were to be found throughout the country. With such a diverse supply of soldiery it is understandable that the quality of the troops varied considerably, as did the quality of command as many of the noblemen raising regiments were just enthusiastic amateurs.

1640 - The Battle of Newburn: the Scots Covenanters defeat the Royal army.

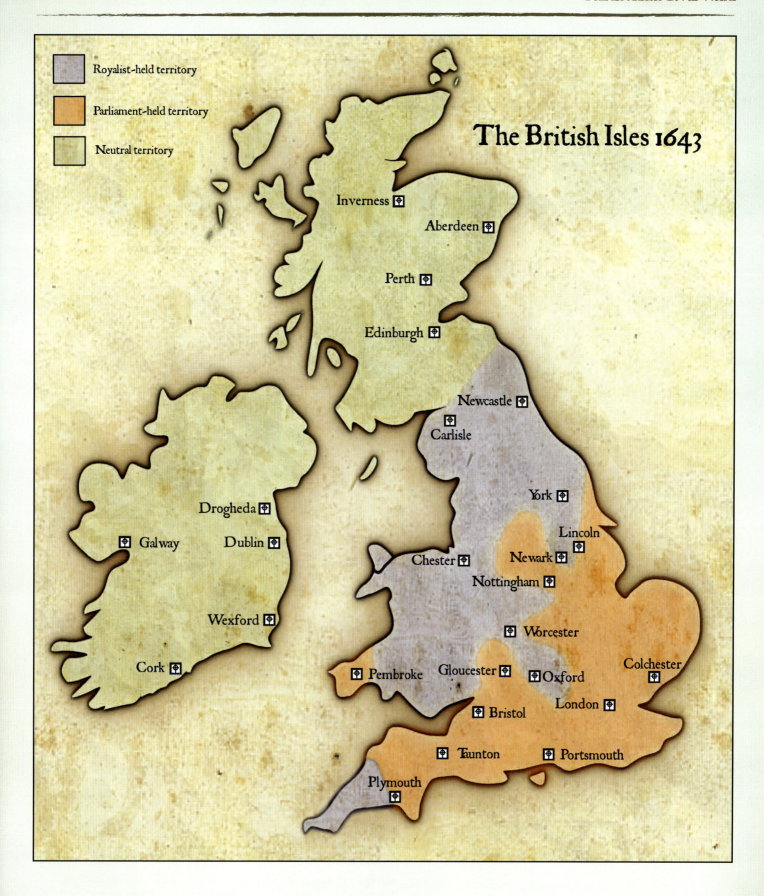

The British Isles 1643

Royalist-held territory

Parliament-held territory

Neutral territory

Inverness

Aberdeen

Perth

Edinburgh

Newcastle

Carlisle

Drogheda

Galway

Dublin

York

Lincoln

Wexford

Chester

Newark

Nottingham

Cork

Worcester

Pembroke

Gloucester

Oxford

Colchester

Bristol

London

Taunton

Portsmouth

Plymouth

"I detest this war without an enemy."

William Waller to Sir Ralph Hopton, 1643

Parliament was marginally more prepared for war, and commanded London and the main trade ports such as Bristol, Plymouth and Hull. The Navy had also come out in support of parliament, which allowed their armies to be better supplied. A counter to this was the fact that many parliamentarians were wary of committing to a total war, as defeat would mean execution for treason.

The Midlands was to be "where England's sorrows began" with parliament forces under the Earl of Essex sparring with Prince Rupert's royalists. On the 23rd September 1642 the cavalry of both armies stumbled across each other at Powick Bridge, just outside Worcester. In the ensuing skirmish Rupert led his men to victory from the front, gaining the reputation of a dashing and brilliant leader. Although only a skirmish in real terms the psychological effect was immense and the spectre of Rupert's unbeatable cavalry was to haunt the parliament forces.

A month later the first major battle of the war took place at Edgehill in Warwickshire. This battle was inconclusive, with many troops on both sides proving unreliable and neither side gaining any particular advantage. The road to London had been left open for Charles to make an advance on the capital. However when he finally made his move he was forced to turn back at Turnham Green when confronted by a much larger parliamentary force.

This was the closest Charles made it back to London, before he was taken there as a prisoner years later. With London closed to him the Royalist cause set up a new capital in Oxford and both sides settled in for a long winter, knowing that this certainly would not be over before Christmas.

The War Drags on

The year 1643 began so well for the Royalist cause, and the campaign season seemed to have turned the tide of the war inexorably in their favour. In fact by August of that year a whole series of Royalist victories had led to the term 'Royalist Summer' being used.

Bristol had been laid siege to and captured by forces under Prince Rupert, and victories in the south west for Lord Hopton had secured that region. Even up north things were looking a little less grim, with the defeat of Lord Fairfax's parliament army at Adwalton Moor.

These victories were not enough to gain complete dominance, and parliament started to fight back. Gloucester successfully held out against repeated Royalist efforts to capture it, with great loss of life. Another major though inconclusive battle was fought, this time at Newbury. (This venue was to prove popular so today this battle is known as First Newbury.)

As another year dragged to an end, the end of the war was no nearer to hand, and so both camps withdrew into winter quarters once more. By this time parliament had no fewer than five armies to feed and equip; those of the Earl of Essex, the Earl of Manchester, Sir William Waller, Lord

Alexander Leslie, 1st Earl of Leven

Alexander Leslie was born in 1580, the son of Captain George Leslie of Balgonie. Very little is known of his early years, and there is much speculation until he began his military career as a soldier in Dutch service in 1605. For the next two years he served with distinction as a captain in Horatio de Vere's regiment.

In 1608, like many other Scotsmen, he joined the Swedish army. He received a commission as ensign and over the years advanced through the ranks. He became a favourite of Gustavus Adolphus, and gained valuable experience in the Thirty Years War. Knighted and promoted to Lt.Colonel in 1626, Leslie began to actively recruit and train Scottish volunteers for the Swedish army. By 1636 he commanded much of Sweden's land forces as Field Marshall, his son Gustav rising to Colonel in the same army.

With the signing of the Covenant in Scotland, and the impending crisis developing, Leslie was called back to Scotland where he took command of the Covenanter forces, strengthened by veterans returning with him. The first test for Leslie's Covenanter force was the 2nd Bishops' War of 1640 where they easily dealt with the English army at Newburn and went on to capture Newcastle and much of the north of England. This forced King Charles to negotiate and in 1641 he attempted to win Leslie over by granting him the title 1st Earl of Leven and Lord Balgonie.

1642 saw the Covenanter force in Ireland and under the newly appointed Earl of Leven turn the tide in favour of the Protestants. He quickly returned to Scotland, leaving Ulster in the hands of Robert Munro. With the signing of the Solemn League and Covenant in 1644, the Covenanters were allied with the Parliament cause and Leslie led them on campaign in the north of England, culminating in the victory at Marston Moor where he was in overall command. His campaign in England was cut short as he hears of Montrose's Royalist successes in Scotland, and marched north to crush this uprising at the Battle of Philliphaugh.

By 1646 Leslie was back in England, first at Newark, then moving to occupy Newcastle. It was to the Scots that Charles I surrendered, and he remained under the Earl's care until handed over to parliament in 1647.

His last campaign was against his former allies, as he was Captain-General of the Scottish forces that opposed Cromwell at the defeat of Dunbar in 1650. Although nominally in command, Leslie was too old for active campaigning, and battle command decisions were out of his hands. After spending the years 1651-54 under arrest in England, the old Earl was released into retirement where he spendt his remaining years in Fifeshire at Balgonie Castle.

Lord Leven. General - Command Rating 9
65 Points

Tough as Old Boots: All units with 12" of Leven gain the 'Tough Fighter' ability.

Prince Rupert of the Rhine

Born in Prague in 1619 the son of Frederick V, Elector Palatine, Prince Rupert was the nephew of King Charles I.

Rupert first campaigned in the Thirty Years' War at the age of 14, and was held hostage in Austria for three years until released with Charles' aid. He came to England with his brother, Maurice, in 1642.

Very gifted in languages, the arts and mathematics, Rupert was a firm favourite and charismatic leader in the Royalist cause. He went on to become a feared and renowned cavalry commander, sweeping all before him in ferocious charges. Nicknamed 'Robert the Devil' by Parliament, it is clear the fear he instilled. Even his pet dog, Boye, was accused of being demonically possessed!

Headstrong and impetuous, the success of these charges was sometimes diminished by an inability to rein in after initial contact, and this cost the Royalist cause key victories.

Rupert's Blewcoat Regiment of Foote was one of the most renowned regiments in the war, fighting in most of the major battles and always with distinction. Starting the war as Lunsford's Regiment of Foote, in which capacity they fought at Edgehill, Rupert took over command in 1643, having been impressed with their fighting ability. They were easy to recognise in the heat of battle

due in no small part to the unique standards the regiment bore - standards designed by the Prince himself.

The regiment was eventually destroyed fighting a brave rearguard at Naseby in 1645, although the remnants did hold Bristol briefly. Rupert was exiled, along with Prince Maurice, in 1646 by Parliament, but came back to England after the restoration. In his later years he became an artist, inventor, naval commander and first governor of the Hudson Bay Company. He died in England in 1682 at the age of 62.

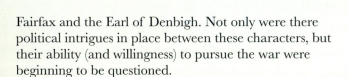

Prince Rupert of the Rhine.
General or Cavalry Commander.
Command Rating 9

Special Rule: Headstrong.
All the Cavalry units in the battalia Rupert commands gain Ferocious Charge at no points cost. All cavalry units in the army must take the Galloper ability (not Cuirassiers).

Fairfax and the Earl of Denbigh. Not only were there political intrigues in place between these characters, but their ability (and willingness) to pursue the war were beginning to be questioned.

The Tide Turns

The year 1644 saw the Scots Covenanter forces stepping in to aid parliament; this could only mean trouble for the king. A large force of Scots moved south to help with the siege of York and so Charles sent Rupert north to combat the threat.

Rupert did manage to raise the siege of York, but the following day (July 2nd) his army was smashed by the combined forces of the northern parliamentarians and Scots Covenanters at the Battle of Marston Moor. The north was now firmly in parliament's hands and they weren't to let it go.

Meanwhile, the armies under the Earl of Essex and Sir William Waller had moved on the Royalist capital of Oxford, in an attempt to bring the king to battle and defeat his army. Charles expertly slipped out of Oxford with his army while the noose was closing, and in the end, Essex's and Waller's forces split. Essex marched south to relieve the port town of Lyme (currently besieged by Prince Maurice), and Waller was ordered to follow Charles, which eventually led to the defeat of Waller's army at the Battle of Cropredy Bridge.

Charles then headed south with an army to put a stop to the Earl of Essex's attempts to take Cornwall; this was achieved

in great style at the Battle of Lostwithiel. Essex was caught between the West Country royalists and the king's own army and lost all his infantry in the fight, effectively destroying one of the main parliament armies. Although the king had defeated two of parliament's armies in the Midlands and south, it was not enough to counter the loss of the north.

Attempting to capitalize on their success at Marston Moor, the northern parliament army moved south to join Sir William Waller and a new army put in the field by the Earl of Essex. (Persistent he certainly was!) The aim was to combine and break the Royalist cause once and for all. Luckily for Charles, the Scots had moved back north to deal with the Royalist army of Montrose that was making a nuisance back home, and so could not add their numbers to another inconclusive battle at Newbury (unimaginatively called Second Newbury), and the king could retreat once more to Oxford for the winter.

Checkmate

In April 1645 Parliament passed the 'Self Denying Ordinance', a law that meant that Members of Parliament could no longer take command of the armies. There were to be two exceptions to this law: Sir Thomas Fairfax and Oliver Cromwell. The rationale of the law was to pave the way for a more professionally raised and commanded army, a 'new modelled army'.

The Marquis of Montrose

*"Let me be judged by the laws of God,
the laws of nations and nature, and the laws of this land."*

So spoke James Graham, 1st Marquis of Montrose at his trial in Edinburgh in 1650, a plea that inevitably would fall on deaf ears...

Handsome, aristocratic and highly principled, Montrose inspired great tales of derring-do and even poetry from the likes of Sir Walter Scott, but did the legend that the romantics paint of him really fit this tragic individual?

Montrose could have lived a settled life in his castle home at Kincardine, married happily to Magdalen who bore him five children. Instead he chose to fight arduous and savage campaigns that stretched him physically and mentally. He did this not once, but twice when he came back to Scotland from exile to once again raise an army for a Stuart King.

His forces were meagre at best, his resources even less. Yet he ran rings around even experienced Covenant armies that chased him all over Scotland, avoiding combat where he could, then turning to savage his foe with short sharp actions that inevitably led to rout and bloody pursuit.

Keeping an alliance together of the wild Irish men and the atavistic Highland clans must have been an incredible feat and, though he was ultimately defeated, it is all the more wonder that he achieved so much for so long with so little.

Montrose had a sense of theatre about himself and his role. He carried the Royal standard hidden, wrapped up and sewn into his saddle before passing it to his ensign, Hay of Dalgetty, and sounded a trumpet to signal his prescence on the battlefield, a sound his foes soon came to fear. In his daring game of cat and mouse against his Covenant foe he also adopted a code name, 'Venture Fair' and wore a bunch of oats in his bonnet as a popularist field sign.

He was far from being a 'fop' however, being a superb archer himself and capable of devising strategies that would confound and suprise his enemies. At Kilsyth, on a baking hot day, he had his men strip down to their bare shirts instantly easing their movements and adding to their ferocious appearance. His Highland troops were also savage, when roused, as at Alford where the veteran Nat Gordon ordered his wild Scots to gut and hamstring the Covenant cavalry with their long dirks, a process he calls 'houghing' - not a pretty sight.

Montrose was a gentleman of honour who died serving a cause he loved, but he also emerges as arguably the greatest of the Civil War generals.

James Graham, Marquis of Montrose.
General. Command Rating 10.

Special Rule: Master Tactician.
Montrose was renowned for picking his ground and defeating much larger enemy forces. He can redeploy one battalia after both armies have set up.

The New Model Army was initially formed by combining the forces of Essex, Waller and the Earl of Manchester, now forbidden to command. Parliament at last had the beginnings of an army that could bring the war to an end. Despite these three armies being drawn together, due to heavy losses the previous year there were still shortages in manpower. Recruitment once more went into overdrive, particularly in London and South-East England to fill the ranks, so the New Model Army was by no means yet the finished article.

Contrary to popular belief not all of Parliament's eggs were in one basket as there were a number of armies still in the field unaffected by the Self Denying Ordinance, although over time these were amalgamated into the New Model Army. Led by Fairfax, with Cromwell as deputy commander (and Commander of Horse), this army was to prove crucial.

Fairfax led his newly formed army to the Battle of Naseby where the Royalist Oxford army, led by King Charles himself, was routed in June 1645. From this point the First Civil War was a series of small scale battles and sieges leading to complete victory for Parliament. In March 1646 the last pitched battle was fought at Stow-on-the-Wold which was another in a long line of New Model Army successes.

King Charles surrendered to the Scots at Southwell, near Newark on 5th May 1646. He believed that the Scots could be bargained with, as he had at the end of the Bishops'

Wars. This was not to be, and he was handed over to Parliament, which effectively ended the war. The last Royalist garrison, that at Harlech Castle in Wales, finally surrendered on March 13th, 1647.

The Second English Civil War 1648

King Charles was imprisoned on the Isle of Wight, although he was extended the courtesy of living a comfortable life. In fact, he was handled so leniently that he was able to arrange a new treaty with the Scots. In return for royal enforcement of the Presbyterian faith north of the border the Scots would supply Charles with an army of 30,000 men.

This army promptly marched south, and was just as promptly routed by Cromwell at the Battle of Preston on the 28th August. That action saw the end of the Second Civil War, but now gave Parliament a dilemma of what to do with a king they could not trust and who could throw the country into another war at any time. The New Model Army (but not their leader, Fairfax) wanted Charles to stand trial for his life, but there were many moderates in Parliament who thought this was a step too far. In a not so democratic move 'Pride's Purge' ensured that only supporters of the New Model Army took their seats. With all opposition removed the 'Rump' Parliament gave itself power to pass laws without the consent of the King or the House of Lords.

It was this 'Rump Parliament' that put King Charles on trial and executed him for treason on the 30th January 1649. With the royal family, including the heir Prince Charles in exile, the monarchy itself was abolished. The House of Lords was disbanded and England became a republican 'Commonwealth and Free State'. Cromwell had by this time manoeuvred himself into a position of great power and he was selected to execute a campaign in Ireland. This he did with great savagery and put down the Irish threat by commanding the massacres of Drogheda and Wexford.

The Third English Civil War 1649-1651

The execution of Charles I did not sit well with the Scottish parliament and, in a direct snub to the newly formed Commonwealth south of the border, they declared the exiled Charles II King of Great Britain and Ireland. There was a condition, however, and this was that he agreed to Presbyterian Church rule across Britain before being allowed to land in Scotland.

Charles tried to improve his bargaining position by encouraging the Royalist champion, the Earl of Montrose, to come out of exile and raise a force once more. This Montrose did, but rather than a 'threatening' force he invaded Scotland with a small army and tried to recruit once more amongst the Highland clans. This plan never really got off the ground and his outnumbered army was destroyed at Carbisdale in April 1650. Charles abandoned Montrose to his fate, and the brave Earl was summarily executed in Edinburgh.

Shortly after this sad act had played out Charles signed the Solemn League and Covenant and gained the support of the Scottish parliament and their covenanter armies. Cromwell now rightly saw Charles II as the major threat to the new Commonwealth and left Ireland in the hands of his subordinates to lead an army north to confront the Scottish. The armies met at the Battle of Dunbar in September 1650 where the outnumbered Parliamentarian forces were victorious and Cromwell went on to occupy much of southern Scotland.

Early the following year Charles was officially crowned King of Scotland, but by this time was frustrated by the lack of unity in the Scottish Parliament and so looked south for more Royalist support. After another defeat at the hands of Cromwell's New Model Army at Inverkeithing in July 1651, Charles marched south across the border at the head of a small Scottish force and headed to the west of England. This was a traditionally Royalist area and the hope was that many English troops would flock to his banner. The support failed to materialise in the numbers needed and Cromwell defeated Charles at the Battle of Worcester in September 1651.

Charles was forced once more into exile, spending the weeks after Worcester evading capture in disguise. Moving through different safe houses and famously hiding out in an oak tree Charles finally made it to the coast and escaped to France. This effectively ended the English Civil Wars.

Protectorate and Restoration

Oliver Cromwell consolidated his power base after the threat from Charles was dealt with, and once again turned his attention to Ireland. In 1653 the last Confederate and Royalist forces in Ireland surrendered. By this time the country had been ravaged, and much of the Catholic land was handed over to Parliament backers and supporters.

Cromwell took on the role of Lord Protector of England, Scotland and Ireland later that year and effectively ruled the country until his death in 1658. He was succeeded by his son, Richard, but he had no authority with the army and so abdicated in 1659. George Monck, who had been made Governor of Scotland by Cromwell during the Third Civil War, led the movement for Charles to be invited back to England and proclaimed king.

Charles II arrived back in London on the 29th May 1660, the day of his 30th birthday. The restoration of the monarchy complete, a move was made to reconcile old adversaries with the Act of Indemnity and Oblivion – Charles was not going to make the same mistakes as his father – and concessions were made to parliament. There were notable people excluded from the act; namely the regicides who had signed the death warrant of Charles' father. Nine were executed, others were driven into exile or removed from positions of power. Even death was not going to get in the way of the new king's revenge; the bodies of Cromwell, Henry Ireton and John Bradshaw were exhumed and the corpses decapitated.

This stunning diorama, based on our Marksman miniature is the handiwork of Bennett Blalock-Doane. Now, if that pesky butterfly would just get out of the way...

English Civil War Colours

Foot regiments in the English Civil War were organised into anything from 6 to 12 companies and each of the companies went into battle with its own colour (flag). The colours were carried by the Junior Company Officer, the Ensign, and they were made of silk or taffeta measuring 6 feet square.

Ordinarily the Colonel's company colour was plain, literally a flag of one colour without devices. The cross of St.George would appear as a canton (a box in the corner) in all the other colours of English regiments. The Lt.Colonel's colour would display the St.George cross only, while the Major's colour was the same with the addition of a 'stream blazant' (wavy line) from the lower corner of the canton.

The various Captains' colours contained additional devices, generally at the Colonel's discretion. Usually the 1st Captain had one device, the 2nd Captain had two, etc. Devices commonly used include stars, discs, diamonds, and heraldic beasts.

There were alternative systems used amongst the regiments, such as dividing the colours geometrically (such as Prince Rupert's) or omitting the stream blazant for the Major meaning his colour would be distinguished by one device instead of that of the 1st Captain.

Scottish regiment standards were often based on the saltire of St Andrew in various colours, with the companies denoted by symbols or numerals in the centre. Colonel's colours, in contrast to their plain English counterparts, usually carried a heraldic device.

Foot colours are shown below at 50%, other standards at 100%.

Royalists

Royal Standard

Colonel Richard Bagot's Regiment
Major or 1st Captain

Colonel Sir Henry Bard's Regiment
Major

Earl of Northampton's Regiment
2nd Captain

Sir Ralph Hopton's Regiment
4th Captain

King's Lifeguard - Major

Sir Marmaduke Rawdon's Regiment
1st Captain

Marquis of Newcastle's Regiment -
3rd Captain

John Talbot's Regiment - Major

Prince Rupert's Blewcoats -
4th Captain

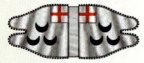

Washington's Dragoons

Gerard's horse cornet

The Queen's Lifeguards'
horse cornet

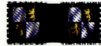

Prince Rupert's horse cornet

Major Wormsley's horse cornet

Parliament

Commonwealth flag

Sir Phillip Skippon's Regiment
Major

Blew Trained Bands of the City of
London - 4th Captain

Sir Thomas Fairfax's Regiment
Lieutenant Colonel

Colonel John Hutchinson's Regiment
1st Captain

Colonel Samuel Jones' Regiment
3rd Captain

Lord Brooke's Regiment - 7th Captain

Earl of Manchester's Regiment
3rd Captain

Lord Saye & Sele's Regiment
3rd Captain

Earl of Essex Regiment of Foote
2nd Captain

Charles Fairfax's regiment of foote,
Colonel's colour (New Model Army)

Skippon's regiment of foote,
5th Captain's colour (New Model Army)

Generic 3rd Captain's colour
(New Model Army)

Generic 4th Captain's colour
(New Model Army)

Generic 3rd Captain's colour
(New Model Army)

Colonel Sir William Balfour's
Cuirassiers regiment

Nathaniel Fiennes' horse cornet

Sir William Waller's horse cornet

Henry Ireton's horse cornet

The Earl of Essex's horse cornet

Scots Covenanter and Montrose's Army

Sir Mungo Campbell of Lawers' Regt

Aberdeen Militia

Conjectural Scots Lancers cornet

Conjectural Scots Lancers cornet

Conjectural Scots Lancers cornet

Scottish Royal Banner

Montrose Irish regiment

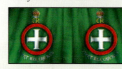

Montrose Irish regiment

Conjectural Scots Lancers cornet

1646 - The Battle of Great Torrington is the last major engagement of the First English Civil War.

English Civil Wars uniforms

The fighting men of the English Civil War had more uniformity than their counterparts on the continent in the Thirty Years War, but such uniforms were at the discretion of the Colonel who raised the regiment. The officers seemed to have worn their own civilian dress in a variety of styles and colour and it was only the ordinary fighting men who were issued with coats, breeches, stockings and headwear.

The uniform colours of the vast majority of regiments, both foot and horse, are unknown today, but we have listed some of the notable exceptions within this section. Some regiments have become known by colour, notably the Trained Bands of London, but this colour refers to the unit standards not the uniforms – although you can assume they are the same if you wish, with no fear of contradiction.

Red and blue were common on both sides, as were white or grey coats. This can be attributed to the availability of dyes rather than any grand desire to create army uniformity. The Scots Covenanter force was generally all in 'hodden grey' coats as they were a centrally raised standing army, although even here there were notable exceptions. The good news in all this is that your painted regiments can be used in both Royalist and Parliamentarian armies with the judicious swapping over of regimental flags; the King's Guard of today's battle can transform into Denzil Holles roundheads tomorrow.

King's Lifeguard (Royalist)

One of the first regiments raised, in 1642, from Lord Willoughby's estates in Lincolnshire. Also drew heavily from Derbyshire, Nottinghamshire and from Irish campaign veterans when the king set up headquarters in Shrewsbury. Accompanied the king in the major battles at which he was present.

Marquis of Newcastle's (Royalist)

Raised in the north of England, particularly Northumberland. Newcastle's Whitecoats (or Lambs) were vital in holding the north for the king, and in the victory at Adwalton Moor. Made a heroic last stand at Marston Moor for which they are best known.

Earl of Northampton's (Royalist)

Raised in Warwickshire and Oxfordshire and commanded by the Earl's son, William. Garrisoned Banbury and fought at Leicester and Middleton Cheney.

Henry Bard's (Royalist)

Originally Pinchbeck's regiment was part of Newcastle's Northern army. When Pinchbeck was killed at Newbury in 1643, Bard took over and the regiment was renamed. Originally raised in Yorkshire, the numbers were supplemented by recruits from Ireland. Fought at Cheriton Wood and Naseby.

Sir Gilbert Talbot's (Royalist)

Raised predominantly from North Wales and from veterans from Ireland, Talbot's regiment was part of the Oxford Army muster in 1644 and was sent to join the Cornish campaign. Fought at the battle of Crediton.

Sir Ralph Hopton's (Royalist)

Raised in the West Country. Played a major role at Braddock Down, Stratton and Lansdown. After the battle of Cheriton Wood the regiment was absorbed into the main Royalist army.

Richard Bagot's (Royalist)

Raised in Lichfield and responsible for holding that city for the king. Fought at Naseby, where they held the line against superior numbers.

Samuel Jones' (Parliament)

Raised in Hampshire as part of the Western Association. The regiment became known as the 'Farnham Greencoats' as they formed the garrison there in 1643, and held that key strategic position for Parliament.

Earl of Manchester's (Parliament)

Raised in the North West of England in 1643 by one of the most influential Parliamentarian MP's. The regiment fought at Edgehill, and later amalgamated into the northern Parliament army.

John Hutchinson's (Parliament)

Raised in Nottinghamshire and Derbyshire. Hutchinson's regiment held Nottingham castle for Parliament in the struggle for England's heartland, and was a thorn in Royalist plans to secure the East Midlands.

Blue Regiment of the London Trained Bands (Parliament)

One of the six newly re-organised London Trained Bands of 1642. They were militia rather than regular troops and were named after their flag colour. Fought at 1st Newbury, where they performed well. Held London for Parliament before being amalgamated into the New Model Army.

Lord Saye & Sele's (Parliament)

Raised in northern Oxfordshire around Broughton Castle. Fought at Edgehill before joining the campaign in the west where the regiment fought at Lostwithiel. In 1644 it was re-equipped at Portsmouth and later subsumed into the New Model Army.

Phillip Skippon's (Parliament)

Raised in London as part of Essex's army. Fought at 1st Newbury, Lostwithiel and 2nd Newbury. Later formed one of the founding regiments of the New Model Army and took part in the battle of Naseby at the centre of the Parliament line.

Lord Brookes' (Parliament)

Raised in London from amongst the traders and apprentices. Fought at the Battle of Edgehill as part of Ballard's brigade. Later took part in the siege of Lichfield where Lord Brooke was killed by the Royalist sniper, 'Dumb' Dyott.

Sir Thomas Fairfax's (Parliament)

Raised from the wool workers of Leeds, Halifax and Bradford by one of Parliament's most able commanders. The regiment was key in the war effort in the north fighting at Adwalton Moor, Bradford and Marston Moor. Fairfax was given overall command of the New Model Army.

1647 - Harlech castle, the last Royalist stronghold, falls.

ENGLISH CIVIL WAR ROYALIST ARMY

There are many reasons that draw gamers to a Royalist army. They had reliable infantry, dashing cavalry and fought for a noble but doomed cause. Uniform colours were many and varied, as were the standards the men fought under – a Royalist army is a real joy to paint. Early in the war many men had no uniforms at all, marching off to battle in their civilian clothes. When the first uniforms were introduced red and blue were the most popular colours, though colonels had free rein to choose their troops' coat colour. Reds, blues, greys, greens were all common, with an off-white issued to Newcastle's northern foot.

Your army may not be as well-equipped or as numerous as your opponent's, but it will be colourful and have some fantastic personalities, such as King Charles, Prince Rupert and the Marquis of Newcastle, amongst others, to lead it.

Command Ratings

Overall Commander: Random Command Rating (see page 35) .... 40 Points

Roll D6 for rating: 1: Command Rating 7, 2-5: Command Rating 8, 6: Command Rating 9

Infantry/Artillery Commander: Command Rating 8.. 40 Points

Cavalry Commander: Command Rating 8 .... 40 Points

The Horse

Unit	Unit Type	Weapon	Hand-to-Hand Value	Shooting Value	Morale Value	Stamina	Special	Points
Lifeguard Cuirassiers	Heavy Horse	Sword, Pistols	8	1	3+	4	Caracole, Heavy Cavalry +1	53

- Maximum of one Lifeguard Cuirassier unit per army

Unit	Unit Type	Weapon	Hand-to-Hand Value	Shooting Value	Morale Value	Stamina	Special	Points
Cavalry	Horse	Sword, Pistols	8	1	4+	3		41

- Any unit can be give the Galloper rule -2 points
- Up to two Units can be armed with a Carbine as traditional Harquebusiers @ 1 point each

Unit	Unit Type	Weapon	Hand-to-Hand Value	Shooting Value	Morale Value	Stamina	Special	Points
Dragoons	Horse Skirmishers/ Foot Skirmishers	Firelocks	3	2	5+	3	Fire & Evade, Marauder	35

The Foot

Unit	Unit Type	Weapon	Hand-to-Hand Value	Shooting Value	Morale Value	Stamina	Special	Points
Pikemen	Foot Pike Block	Pike	6	-	4+	4	Hedgehog	34

- Up to three Pike units can be upgraded to 'Large' @ 6 points each
- Any unit can be downgraded to Small @ -6 points each
- Up to one Pike unit can be 'Elite 4+' for 6 points

Unit	Unit Type	Weapon	Hand-to-Hand Value	Shooting Value	Morale Value	Stamina	Special	Points
Musketeers	Foot Battle Line	Matchlock Muskets	3	2	5+	3		27

- Maximum of two Musketeer units for every Pike unit
- Any unit can be downgraded to Small @ -8 points each

Unit	Unit Type	Weapon	Hand-to-Hand Value	Shooting Value	Morale Value	Stamina	Special	Points
Commanded Shotte	Foot Battle Line	Matchlock Muskets	3	3	4+	3	First Fire	34

- Maximum of two Commanded Musket units in the army
- Arm any units with Firelocks @ 1 point each
- Up to one unit can be upgraded to Large @ 8 points

1648 - The Battle of Preston - the New Model Army defeats the Scots.

Unit	Unit Type	Weapon	Hand-to-Hand Value	Shooting Value	Morale Value	Stamina	Special	Points
Storming Party	Foot	Firelocks, Assorted Assault Weapons	4	2	4+	3	First Fire	34

- Maximum of one Storming Party per Army
- Make unit Elite 4+ for 6 points
- Equip unit with a Petard for 20 points
- Equip unit with Grenades for 1 point

Unit	Unit Type	Weapon	Hand-to-Hand Value	Shooting Value	Morale Value	Stamina	Special	Points
Clubmen	Foot Warband	Mixed	2	1	6+	2	Rabble, Militia	7

- Shooting value of 1 represents thrown weapons

Firelock storming party

The Ordnance

- Maximum of on artillery piece per battalia

Unit	Unit Type	Weapon	Hand-to-Hand Value	Shooting Value	Morale Value	Stamina	Special	Points
Artillery	Ordnance	Various Cannon	1	3-2-1	5+	2		Varies

- Light Guns 17 points
- Medium Guns 21 points
- Heavy Guns 25 points

Unit	Unit Type	Weapon	Hand-to-Hand Value	Shooting Value	Morale Value	Stamina	Special	Points
Siege Artillery	Ordnance	Mortar	1	2	5+	2		25

- Maximum of one mortar

'There was one entire regiment of foot belonging to Newcastle, called the lambs, because they were all clothed in white woolen cloth'.

Marston Moor, 1644

Dramatis Personae

King Charles I. General, Command Rating 8 .... 58 Points
Lifeguard Cuirassiers and one Pike unit (the King's Guard) gain Elite and Valiant at no points cost

Prince Rupert of the Rhine. General or Cavalry Commander. Command Rating 9... 70 Points
  Special Rule: Headstrong

Lord Hopton. General, Command Rating 9 .... 60 Points
One Battalia are Cornish Foot: Pike units in this battalia gain Tough Fighters and Stubborn @ 6 points per unit
Cornish Foot can have a maximum of one Musketeer unit per Pike unit

1648 - The Peace of Westphalia ends the Thirty Years' War.

ENGLISH CIVIL WAR EARLY PARLIAMENT ARMY

An early Parliamentarian army offers much – they were better equipped than their Royalist counterparts, being able to count on the wealth of London and the south-east. Although they struggled against superior enemy cavalry at the start of the war, they quickly adapted and could often bring more men to bear.

Uniforms were of a wide variety of colours; and the flags they fought under were as varied as their Royalist counterparts. The choice of 'themed' armies is excellent with the London Trained Bands, the different regional Associations or local forces.

There were some great characters too: sly Waller with his reputation for picking the best ground; 'Old Robin', the Earl of Essex with his rather morbid habit of taking his coffin on campaign; and the indomitable Fairfaxes of the North.

Maybe not as dashing as the cavaliers or as effective as the New Model Army that replaced them, the early Parliamentarian armies were the brave rebels who allowed Parliament to carry on the war against King Charles I.

Command Ratings

Overall Commander: Random Command Rating (see page 35) .... 40 Points

Roll D6 for rating: 1-2: Command Rating 7, 3-5: Command Rating 8, 6: Command Rating 9

Infantry/Artillery Commander: Command Rating 8.. 40 Points

Cavalry Commander: Command Rating 7 .... 20 Points

The Horse

Unit	Unit Type	Weapon	Hand-to-Hand Value	Shooting Value	Morale Value	Stamina	Special	Points
Cuirassiers	Heavy Horse	Sword, Pistols	8	1	3+	4	Caracole, Heavy Cavalry +1	53

- Maximum of two Cuirassier units per army

Unit	Unit Type	Weapon	Hand-to-Hand Value	Shooting Value	Morale Value	Stamina	Special	Points
Cavalry	Horse	Sword, Pistols	8	1	4+	3	Caracole	41

- Up to two units can be equipped with Carbines as traditional Harquesbusiers @ 1 point per unit

Unit	Unit Type	Weapon	Hand-to-Hand Value	Shooting Value	Morale Value	Stamina	Special	Points
Dragoons	Horse Skirmishers/ Foot Skirmishers	Firelocks	3	2	5+	3	Fire & Evade, Marauder	35

- Maximum of two units per unit of Irish Cavalry

The Foot

Unit	Unit Type	Weapon	Hand-to-Hand Value	Shooting Value	Morale Value	Stamina	Special	Points
Pikemen	Foot Pike Block	Pike	6	-	4+	4	Hedgehog	34

- Up to three Pike units can be upgraded to 'Large' for 6 points
- Any unit can be downgraded to Small for -6 points each

Unit	Unit Type	Weapon	Hand-to-Hand Value	Shooting Value	Morale Value	Stamina	Special	Points
Musketeers	Foot Battle Line	Matchlock Muskets	3	2	5+	3		27

- Maximum of two Musketeer units for every Pike unit
- Any unit can be downgraded to Small @ – 8 points each

Unit	Unit Type	Weapon	Hand-to-Hand Value	Shooting Value	Morale Value	Stamina	Special	Points
Commanded Shotte	Foot Battle Line	Matchlock Muskets	3	3	4+	3	First Fire	34

- Maximum of two Commanded Musket units in the army
- Arm any units with Firelocks for 1 point each
- Up to one unit can be upgraded to Large for 8 points

1648 - The Peace of Munster ends the Dutch-Spanish Eighty Years' War.

Unit	Unit Type	Weapon	Hand-to-Hand Value	Shooting Value	Morale Value	Stamina	Special	Points
Storming Party	Foot	Firelocks, Assorted Assault Weapons	4	2	4+	3	First Fire	34

- Maximum of one Storming Party per Army
- Make unit Elite 4+ for 6 points
- Equip unit with a Petard for 20 points
- Equip unit with Grenades for 1 point

Unit	Unit Type	Weapon	Hand-to-Hand Value	Shooting Value	Morale Value	Stamina	Special	Points
Clubmen	Foot Warband	Mixed	2	1	6+	2	Rabble, Militia	7

- Shooting Value of 1 represents thrown weapons

Ironsides sally forth!

The Ordnance

- Maximum of two artillery pieces per battalia

Unit	Unit Type	Weapon	Hand-to-Hand Value	Shooting Value	Morale Value	Stamina	Special	Points
Artillery	Ordnance	Various Cannon	1	3-2-1	5+	2		Varies

- Light Guns 17 points
- Medium Guns 21 points
- Heavy Guns 25 points

Unit	Unit Type	Weapon	Hand-to-Hand Value	Shooting Value	Morale Value	Stamina	Special	Points
Siege Artillery	Ordnance	Mortar	1	2	5+	2		25

- Maximum of one mortar per army

Dramatis Personae

Earl of Essex. General, Command Rating 8 .... 45 Points
One Cuirassier unit can be upgraded to Essex's Lifeguard and gain Elite ability at no points cost

William Waller. General, Command Rating 8 .... 45 Points
After both armies have completed deployment, the Parliament player can redeploy up to three units.

Oliver Cromwell. Cavalry Commander, Command Rating 9 .... 60 Points
Two units of 'Ironside' cavalry can be fielded @ 60 points per unit

Unit	Unit Type	Weapon	Hand-to-Hand Value	Shooting Value	Morale Value	Stamina	Special	Points
Ironsides	Horse	Sword, Pistols	8	1	3+	4	Elite, Stubborn	60

1649 - Charles I is executed at Whitehall by Parliament.

ENGLISH CIVIL WAR NEW MODEL ARMY

The 'New Modelled Army' of Parliament was a reaction to the indecisiveness of Parliamentary commanders during the early war. The Self Denying Ordinance (3rd April 1645) overhauled the old guard of officers and allowed radical changes to be made in organisation, recruitment and training of the parliamentary forces. This was certainly not a superhuman army however; the men were pulled together from existing regiments, Royalist deserters and raw recruits.

They were highly motivated, and quickly well equipped and trained. They proved to be more than a match for their Royalist and later Scots Covenanter opponents. From 1646 they were issued with their red uniforms across all the regiments in the army. The New Model Army was the precursor of the legendary British Redcoat.

Those who want an army to look co-ordinated, have superior cavalry and solid infantry, and have access to a lot of firepower should look no further than the New Model Army. The addition of Oliver Cromwell or Thomas Fairfax makes this a formidable force indeed.

Command Ratings

Overall Commander: Random Command Rating (see page 35)...................................... 40 Points

      Roll D6 for rating: 1-4: Command Rating 8, 5-6: Command Rating 9

Infantry/Artillery Commander: Command Rating 8 .... 40 Points

Cavalry Commander: Command Rating 8 .... 40 Points

The Horse

Unit	Unit Type	Weapon	Hand-to-Hand Value	Shooting Value	Morale Value	Stamina	Special	Points
Ironsides	Horse	Sword, Pistols	8	1	3+	4	Elite 4+, Stubborn	60

• Maximum of four Ironsides units per army

Unit	Unit Type	Weapon	Hand-to-Hand Value	Shooting Value	Morale Value	Stamina	Special	Points
Cavalry	Horse	Sword, Pistols	8	1	4+	3		41

Unit	Unit Type	Weapon	Hand-to-Hand Value	Shooting Value	Morale Value	Stamina	Special	Points
Dragoons	Horse Skirmishers/ Foot Skirmishers	Firelocks	3	2	5+	3	Fire & Evade, Marauder	35

New Model Army

1650 - John Churchill, the future Duke of Marlborough, is born.

The Foot

Unit	Unit Type	Weapon	Hand-to-Hand Value	Shooting Value	Morale Value	Stamina	Special	Points
Pikemen	Foot Pike Block	Pike	6	-	4+	4	Hedgehog	34

- One Pike unit can be upgraded to 'Large' for 6 points
- Up to half the pike units can be 'Reliable' at 4 pts each

Unit	Unit Type	Weapon	Hand-to-Hand Value	Shooting Value	Morale Value	Stamina	Special	Points
Musketeers	Foot Battle Line	Matchlock Muskets	3	2	5+	3	First Fire	28

- Maximum of three Musketeer units for every Pike unit
- Up to half the musket units can be 'Reliable' at 4 pts each

Unit	Unit Type	Weapon	Hand-to-Hand Value	Shooting Value	Morale Value	Stamina	Special	Points
Commanded Shotte	Foot Battle Line	Matchlock Muskets	3	3	4+	3	First Fire	34

- Maximum of three Commanded Musket units in the army
- Arm any units with Firelocks at 1 point each
- Up to one unit can be upgraded to Large for 8 points
- Units can be armed with Grenades at 1 point each

Unit	Unit Type	Weapon	Hand-to-Hand Value	Shooting Value	Morale Value	Stamina	Special	Points
Storming Party	Foot	Firelocks, Assorted Assault Weapons	4	2	4+	3	First Fire	34

- Maximum of two Storming Parties per Army
- Make units Elite 4+ at 6 points each
- Equip units with a Petard for 20 points each

The Ordnance

- Maximum of three artillery pieces per battalia

Unit	Unit Type	Weapon	Hand-to-Hand Value	Shooting Value	Morale Value	Stamina	Special	Points
Artillery	Ordnance	Various Cannon	1	3-2-1	5+	2		Varies

- Light Guns 17 points
- Medium Guns 21 points
- Heavy Guns 25 points

Unit	Unit Type	Weapon	Hand-to-Hand Value	Shooting Value	Morale Value	Stamina	Special	Points
Siege Artillery	Ordnance	Mortar	1	2	5+	2		25

- Maximum of one mortar per army

Dramatis Personae

Sir Thomas Fairfax . General - Command Rating 9 .... 75 Points
   Special Rule: Inspiring leader

Oliver Cromwell . Commander of Horse or General – Command Rating 9........................ 85 Points
   Special Rule: Will of Iron.

Philip Skippon. Infantry Commander - Command Rating 8 .... 55 Points
   Special Rule: Skippon's Brave Boys.
   All Foot Units within 12" of Skippon receive the 'Brave' special ability.

1651 - The Battle of Worcester - The New Model Army defeats the Scots.

ENGLISH CIVIL WAR COVENANTER ARMY

The Scottish Covenanter armies fought in so many battles and fought on so many sides that you will never be short of an opponent. Massed ranks of hodden-grey foot are indeed an impressive sight on any gaming table, and it's that infantry that gives the Covenanters their backbone. Dour, sturdy types, these tough soldiers will rarely let you down. The Scots artillery park is usually full too; you will not be outgunned by those south of the border softies! Cavalry are a different matter, but best save the troopers for mopping up after the foot have done the damage.

This army is best suited to gamers who like to think big; big blocks of pike and big batteries of guns. It also helps if you like painting your troops the same colour and are happy to brighten things up with amazing flags.

Command Ratings

Overall Commander: Random Command Rating (see page 35) .... 40 Points

Roll D6 for rating: 1: Command Rating 7, 2-5: Command Rating 8, 6: Command Rating 9

Infantry/Artillery Commander: Command Rating 8 .... 40 Points

Cavalry Commander: Command Rating 7 .... 20 Points

The Horse

Unit	Unit Type	Weapon	Hand-to-Hand Value	Shooting Value	Morale Value	Stamina	Special	Points
Scots Lancers	Horse	Lance, Sword, Pistols	6	1	5+	3		38
Cavalry	Horse	Sword, Pistols	7	1	5+	3	Caracole	35
Dragoons	Horse Skirmishers/ Foot Skirmishers	Firelocks	3	2	5+	3	Fire & Evade, Marauder	35

Scots Lancers

1652 - The First Anglo-Dutch War begins.

The Foot

Unit	Unit Type	Weapon	Hand-to-Hand Value	Shooting Value	Morale Value	Stamina	Special	Points
Covenanter Pikemen	Foot Pike Block	Pike	6	-	4+	4	Hedgehog	34

- Any Pike unit can be upgraded to 'Large' for 6 points per unit

Unit	Unit Type	Weapon	Hand-to-Hand Value	Shooting Value	Morale Value	Stamina	Special	Points
Covenanter Musketeers	Foot Battle Line	Matchlock Muskets	3	2	5+	3		27

- Maximum of two Musketeer units for every Pike unit

Unit	Unit Type	Weapon	Hand-to-Hand Value	Shooting Value	Morale Value	Stamina	Special	Points
Commanded Shotte	Foot Battle Line	Matchlock Muskets	3	3	4+	3	First Fire	34

- Maximum of one Commanded Musket units in the army
- Arm unit with Firelocks @ 1 point each
- Unit can be upgraded to Large for 8 points

Unit	Unit Type	Weapon	Hand-to-Hand Value	Shooting Value	Morale Value	Stamina	Special	Points
Storming Party	Foot	Firelocks, Assorted Assault Weapons	4	2	4+	3	First Fire	34

- Maximum of one Storming Party per Army
- Arm unit with Firelocks for 1 point
- Equip unit with a Petard for 20 points
- Equip unit with Grenades for 1 point

Unit	Unit Type	Weapon	Hand-to-Hand Value	Shooting Value	Morale Value	Stamina	Special	Points
Highlanders	Foot Warband	Mixed Hand Weapons & Muskets	6	1	6+	3	Militia, Clansmen, Swordsmen	24

- Maximum of two units of Highlanders in the army

The Ordnance

- Maximum of three artillery pieces per battalia
- At least 50% the artillery must be 'Light' guns

Unit	Unit Type	Weapon	Hand-to-Hand Value	Shooting Value	Morale Value	Stamina	Special	Points
Artillery	Ordnance	Various Cannon	1	3-2-1	5+	2		Varies

- Light Guns: 17 points
- Medium Guns: 21 points
- Heavy Guns: 25 points

Unit	Unit Type	Weapon	Hand-to-Hand Value	Shooting Value	Morale Value	Stamina	Special	Points
Siege Artillery	Ordnance	Mortar	1	2	5+	2		25

- Maximum of one mortar per army

Dramatis Personae

Lord Leven. General. Command Rating 9 .... 65 Points
Special Rule: Tough as Old Boots.

ENGLISH CIVIL WAR ARMY OF MONTROSE

The Royalist Scots army of Montrose has always been a favourite with wargamers. A small force dependent almost entirely on its infantry, this force will usually be outnumbered on the battlefield. The Irish Brigade and access to those fiery Highlander regiments more than makes up for this, although the lack of good cavalry and artillery can cause problems.

This is an army that lends itself to getting to grips with the enemy as soon as possible. A good old fashioned Highland charge to rough things up a bit is always a solid battle plan. The ever-reliable Irish troops can be used to fall back on should that tactic fail. If cavalry contribute anything notable during the battle then that is an added bonus.

This is truly a force with a unique and unorthodox feel, and all the better for it.

Command Ratings

Overall Commander: Random Command Rating (see page 35) .... 40 Points
   Roll D6 for rating: 1-5: Command Rating 8, 6: Command Rating 9

Infantry/Artillery Commander: Command Rating 8 .... 40 Points
Cavalry Commander: Command Rating 7 .... 20 Points

The Horse

Unit	Unit Type	Weapon	Hand-to-Hand Value	Shooting Value	Morale Value	Stamina	Special	Points
Gordon Horse	Horse	Sword, Pistols	8	1	4+	3	Gallopers	39

- Maximum of two units in the army
- Each unit can add Lances @ 5 points per unit

Cavalry	Horse	Sword, Pistols	7	1	5+	3	Caracole	35

- Maximum of two units in the army
- One Cavalry unit can be armed with carbines for 1 point

The Foot

Unit	Unit Type	Weapon	Hand-to-Hand Value	Shooting Value	Morale Value	Stamina	Special	Points
Scottish Pikemen	Foot Pike Block	Pike	6	-	5+	4	Hedgehog	30

- Any Pike unit can be downgraded to Small @ -6 points each

Scottish Musketeers	Foot Battle Line	Matchlock Muskets	3	2	5+	3		27

- Maximum of two Musketeer units for every Pike unit

Irish Brigade Pikemen	Foot Pike Block	Pike, Assorted Melee Weapons	7	-	4+	4	Hedgehog, Stubborn, Elite 4+	46

- Maximum of three units in the army, all Irish Foot units must be in the same battalia
- Any unit can be downgraded to Small at -6 points per unit

Irish Brigade Musketeers	Foot Battle Line	Matchlock Muskets	4	2	4+	3	Stubborn, Elite 4+	43

- Maximum of six units in the army, all Irish Foot units must be in the same battalia
- Any unit can be downgraded to Small at -8 points per unit

1654 - Louis XIV is crowned at Rheims, beginning a 61 year reign.

Unit	Unit Type	Weapon	Hand-to-Hand Value	Shooting Value	Morale Value	Stamina	Special	Points
Commanded Musket	Foot Battle Line	Matchlock Muskets	3	3	4+	3	First Fire	38

- Maximum of one Commanded Musket unit in the army

Unit	Unit Type	Weapon	Hand-to-Hand Value	Shooting Value	Morale Value	Stamina	Special	Points
Storming Party	Foot	Muskets, Assorted Assault Weapons	4	2	4+	3	First Fire	34

- Maximum of one Storming Party per Army
- Equip unit with a Petard for 20 points
- Equip unit with grenades for 1 point

Unit	Unit Type	Weapon	Hand-to-Hand Value	Shooting Value	Morale Value	Stamina	Special	Points
Highlanders	Foot Warband	Mixed	7	1	5+	3	Ferocious Charge, Eager, Clansmen, Swordsmen	XX

Unit	Unit Type	Weapon	Hand-to-Hand Value	Shooting Value	Morale Value	Stamina	Special	Points
Kilpont's Archers	Foot Battle Line	Longbows, Swords	4	2	5+	3		28

- Maximum of one unit of Kilpont's Archers in the army

The Ordnance

- Maximum of two artillery pieces in the army

Unit	Unit Type	Weapon	Hand-to-Hand Value	Shooting Value	Morale Value	Stamina	Special	Points
Artillery	Ordnance	Various Cannon	1	3-2-1	5+	2		Varies

- Light Guns 17 points
- Medium Guns 21 points
- Heavy Guns 25 points

Unit	Unit Type	Weapon	Hand-to-Hand Value	Shooting Value	Morale Value	Stamina	Special	Points
Siege Artillery	Ordnance	Mortar	1	2	5+	2		25

- Maximum of one mortar per army

"I'll make thee famous by my pen,

And glorious by my sword"

James Graham, Marquis of Montrose

Dramatis Personae

James Graham, Marquis of Montrose. General. Command Rating 10 .... 85 Points
   Special Rule: Master Tactician

Alasdair MacColla, The Devastator . Commander of Irish Foot, Command Rating 9 .... 90 Points
   Special Rule: Bodyguard. Points include one unit of MacColla's Bodyguard

Unit	Unit Type	Weapon	Hand-to-Hand Value	Shooting Value	Morale Value	Stamina	Special	Points
MacColla's Bodyguard	Foot Battle Line	Two Handed Swords, Muskets	5	1	3+	2	Small Unit, Stubborn, Double Handed Infantry Weapons, Elite 4+, Valiant	N/A

- One unit only per army. Can only be fielded if Alasdair MacColla is Commander of the Irish Foot

1657 - The first (drinking) chocolate house opens in London.

THE SIEGE OF WORCESTER

It was at the Salute show in London that we first saw the gaming table featured here, and it made rather an impression. The terrain boards and figures were spectacular, and the idea of an alternative history scenario in this book was suddenly hugely appealing. The English Civil War is a terrifically versatile period to play as regiments can be used for a number of armies simply by swapping the colours and this game shows that, with a little imagination, whole new gaming opportunities are open to players.

After a brief chat the men responsible, Neil Tew, Andy Fox and David Marshall of the Nantwich Wargames Club, kindly agreed to bring the whole display up to Nottingham one sunny Sunday to play out the scenario in full in John Stallard's gaming room. The addition of Rick Priestley to the list of commanders and Dan Faulconbridge of *Wargames Illustrated* to capture the whole thing on camera meant we had quite a crowd gathered with the (mostly) impartial Steve Morgan taking on umpiring duties. Amazingly, this was to be the first time the scenario had been played to completion as all previous attempts at shows had been (unsurprisingly) disrupted by people stopping by the table to admire it.

Neil, Dave and Rick took on the roles of the Royalist Commanders, with Neil also assuming the added responsibility of adopting the persona of King Charles himself for the day. Andy and John were to command the Scots Covenanters and plot their defence of the Worcester city walls against attack, Andy donning the bonnet of Alexander Leslie in overall command.

Covenanter commander Stallard surveys the damage...

1658 - The Battle of the Dunes. Fought between France and Spain, with English troops on both sides.

Ye Alternative History — the Battel of Worcester 1651

Prince Rupert

An 'English' Civil War Battle

It has been a turbulent 12 years in 'English' history since the first Bishops' war in 1639.

After the humiliation of the Bishops' Wars King Charles I was forced to recall Parliament and ask for further money to fund war against the Scots. Parliament and the King after much bitter argument and disagreement find themselves at war in 1642.

The initial stages of the resulting war are something of a stalemate: the major battle at Edgehill is claimed by both sides as a victory. With the end of 1642 the King's forces are in the ascendancy; even with the pull back from London after Turnham Green. In 1643, the Royalists slowly gain the upper hand, with the storming of Bristol being a noted bloody high point.

1644 starts badly for the King with the Scots entering the war on Parliament's side with the Solemn League and Covenant, plus the crushing defeat at Nantwich. By mid 1644 Prince Rupert is sent north to raise the siege of York and defeat the Parliamentary-Scots forces.

At Marston Moor outside York Rupert commits to battle. The day is almost lost with the late arrival of the Marquis of Newcastle and his 'Whitecoats'. With much of the surprise gone it is a hard fought slogging match with the Royalists coming out victorious. The Scots army is especially harshly

treated by the Royalists; it retreats north and out of the war. A second major blow to Parliament was the death of Sir Thomas Fairfax.

With the Scots quietly withdrawing from the Covenant following Parliament's refusal to fund arrears of pay, the north of England is totally in Royalist hands.

By the start of 1645, the situation is looking poor for Parliament. Sir Ralph Hopton has completed his conquest of the south-west, the Marquis of Newcastle has control of the north and Prince Rupert is raising fresh troops in the north midlands.

In one last throw of the dice Cromwell, now in charge of the last major Parliamentary army, stands to give battle at Naseby. Again it is Newcastle's 'Whitecoats' who swing the battle in favour of the Royalist cause.

Cromwell, attempting to retrieve the situation, leads a desperate cavalry charge, but is cut down in the ensuing melee. Some say his horse threw him, having become stuck in a rabbit warren.

By late 1645 Parliament, without the decisive leadership of Oliver Cromwell and the military skills of Sir Thomas Fairfax, sues for peace.

The civil war in England ends in 1646. However, the war in Ireland continues and occupies the King's armies for the next four years. In what becomes an increasingly merciless and atrocity-ridden conflict the Royalist forces are ground down, resulting in stalemate.

As well as brutally pursuing the pacification of Ireland, Charles I pursues his religious reforms, which arguably started the whole series of wars. After a series of half-baked compromises and humiliations, the Scottish Kirk again raise an army and invade England in 1651, in what some term 'The Third Bishops' War'. The Scottish army led by the Duke of Hamilton pushes south along the Welsh borderlands hoping for local English parliamentary volunteers; none are forthcoming. King Charles I rushes forces from Ireland and the south-east of England to meet the invaders at the recently occupied city of Worcester.

Dispositions

All of the defending Scots infantry were deployed on or behind the besieged city walls. Two units of dragoons formed a forlorn hope in front of the city gates, while the flanks were held by wings of cavalry to offer an offensive element to bother the Royalist baggage and artillery.

The attacking Royalists had a somewhat more complicated set up, but one which would allow a three pronged attack. The central assault would consist of the combined strength of Rupert's, the King's and Talbot's battalias under Neil's watchful eye. The left flank was held by Lord Percy's battalia, ably controlled by Dave, while the right flank, under Rick, was comprised of Hopton's battalia and Prince Rupert's Horse. The Royal Artillery Train was placed centrally and the baggage train on the right flank, both at the rear of the army and hopefully out of harm's way.

Objectives

The Royalist forces would gain victory by having three unshaken units within the city walls at the end of any turn, and also have to keep their baggage train intact.

The Scots simply have to hold on for 10 turns without allowing the Royalists to break through.

Should the Royalists meet their victory conditions, but lose the baggage train or have King Charles or Prince Rupert captured then the result would be a draw.

With the figures in place the taunting could commence in earnest and we were ready to go.

> "Had he been victualled as well as fortified, he might have endured a siege of seven years."
>
> *Charles I relating to the Parliamentarian cuirassier commander Arthur Haselrigge*

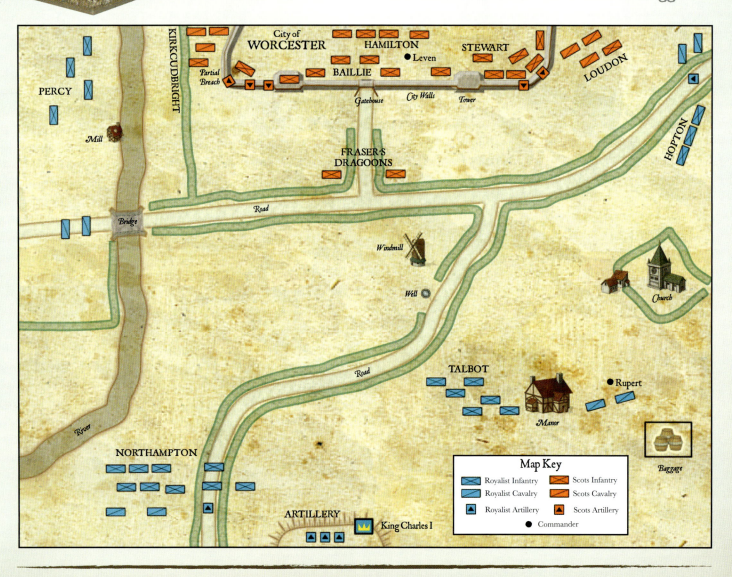

1659 - The French and Spanish sign the Peace of the Pyrenees.

The Royalist Army

KING CHARLES I
Army Commander, Command Rating 9

PRINCE RUPERT'S BATTALIA OF HORSE:
Prince Rupert, Command Rating 9
- Prince Rupert's Lifeguard of Horse
  (1 unit of Cuirassiers – Elite, Ferocious Charge, Galloper)
- Prince Rupert's Regiment of Horse
  (1 unit of Cavalry – Elite, Ferocious Charge, Galloper)

LORD HOPTON'S BATTALIA
Lord Hopton, Command Rating 8
- Lord Hopton's Regiment of Foot (2 musket units, 1 pike unit)
- Prince of Wales' Horse (2 cavalry units)
- 1 Light Gun

LORD PERCY'S BATTALIA
Lord Percy, Command Rating 8
- Lord Percy's Regiment of Foot (2 musket units, 1 pike unit)
- Storming Party (1 storming party unit) - Petard
- Lord Wilmot's Horse (1 cavalry unit)
- Thomas Howard's Horse (1 cavalry unit)

PRINCE RUPERT'S BATTALIA
Earl of Northampton, Command Rating 8
- Prince Rupert's Regiment of Foot
  (2 musket units, 1 pike unit)
- Earl of Northampton's Regiment of Foot
  (2 musket units, 1 pike unit)
- Sir Thomas Blackwell's Regiment of Foot
  (2 musket units, 1 pike unit)
- Richard Bagot's Regiment of Horse (1 unit of Cavalry)
- Charles Gerrard's Regiment of Horse (1 unit of Cavalry)
- 1 Light Gun

THE KING'S BATTALIA OF FOOT
Sir Gilbert Talbot: Command Rating 8
- The King's Guard Regiment of Foot
  (2 musket units, 1 pike unit – Elite, Valiant)
- Sir Gilbert Talbot's Regiment of Foot
  (2 musket units, 1 pike unit – Elite)

ROYAL ARTILLERY TRAIN
- 1 Siege/Heavy Gun
- 1 Medium Gun
- 1 Siege Mortar

The Scots Covenanter Army

ALEXANDER LESLIE, EARL OF LEVEN
Army Commander, Command Rating 9

SIR WILLIAM STEWART'S BATTALIA OF FOOT
Sir William Stewart, Command Rating 8
- Fraser's Firelocks (1 unit Commanded Shot)
- John Innes' Regiment of Foot (1 musket unit, 1 pike unit)
- Sir William Stewart's Regiment of Foot
  (2 musket units, 1 pike unit)
- Argyll's Highlanders (1 Highlander unit)
- 1 Medium Gun
- 1 Light Gun

WILLIAM BAILLIE'S BATTALIA OF FOOT
William Baillie, Command Rating 8
- Baillie's Regiment of Foot (2 musket units, 1 pike unit)
- Sir William Balfour's Regiment of Foot
  (1 musket unit, 1 pike unit)
- Lord Home of Wedderburn's Regiment (1 musket unit)
- 1 Medium Gun
- 1 Light Gun
- 1 Frame Gun

EARL OF LOUDOUN'S BATTALIA OF HORSE
John Campbell, Earl of Loudoun, Command Rating 7
- Earl of Leven's Regiment of Horse (1 cavalry unit)
- Sir Charles Arnott's Regiment of Horse (1 Scots Lancer unit)
- Lord Mauchline's Regiment of Horse (1 Scots Lancer unit)
- Lord Mauchline's Commanded Shot
  (1 Commanded Shot unit – Small)

LORD KIRKCUDBRIGHT'S BATTALIA OF HORSE
Lord Kirkcudbright, Command Rating 7
- Lord Hamilton's Regiment of Horse (1 Cavalry unit)
- Sir John Browne's Regiment of Horse (1 Cavalry unit)
- Lord Kirkcudbright's Regiment of Horse (1 Cavalry unit)
- Browne's Commanded Shot (1 Commanded Shot unit – Small)

LORD HAMILTON'S BATTALIA
Lord Hamilton, Command Rating 8
- Lord Hamilton's Regiment of Foot (2 musket units, 1 pike unit)
- General of Artillery's Foot Regiment (1 double handed infantry
  weapon unit)
- Fraser's Dragoons (2 units)

How It Was Played

A crash of arms and the thunder of hooves signalled the general Royalist advance that marked the beginning of the battle. The Cavalier commanders urged their troops forward with a few choice words and refreshment in hand. The plan seemed simple; assault from three sides at once, stretch the defenders to breaking point and then hammer at the weak points. Key to this strategy was getting the storming party with its lethal petard to the walls double quick to create a breach on the flank, while the artillery would pound away at a section of wall near the main gates to create a second breach. Although most regiments responded enthusiastically to their commands, the storming party along with most of Lord Percy's left flank command seemed more intent on finishing their breakfast than fighting and steadfastly refused to budge.

Undaunted by a lack of movement on their left, the centre pushed on, with Blackwell's foot taking the lead and began to exchange fire with the Scots' forlorn hope at long range. Talbot's foot led the King's Guard past the windmill towards the city walls, while Hopton's brave West Country lads surged forward on the right flank to threaten a weaker part of the defences. The Scots were content to sit tight behind their defences and look smug. This smugness soon came to an abrupt end: the only attacking move they attempted resulted in a blunder and Lord Kirkcudbight's entire battalia of horse disappeared the way they came – off the table! Suddenly the Scottish right flank looked rather vulnerable. Some smart shooting from the dragoons at least

Northampton's, Blackwell's and the King's Guard advance on Worcester town walls.

Snipers

Snipers played an important role in the English Civil War. 'Dumb' Dyott managed to dispatch the Parliamentarian Commander Lord Brooke at the siege of Lichfield with a fowling piece from the cathedral spire.

Rather than adding snipers to army lists we felt it was more appropriate to add a special rule for games where they are appropriate and fit a given scenario.

Snipers always hit on a 4+ and have a range of 24" and can target command stands. Any battalia command stand successfully hit by a sniper will be at -1 command for its next turn. This is to reflect the general panic that musket balls whizzing around the commander's ears will cause rather than such commanders being killed outright.

disordered some of the forward Royalist units in the centre, which would slow them down.

The second turn began with Rupert's Horse galloping forward at full speed to threaten the Scots' left flank; the Prince apparently deciding that guarding the baggage was well beneath him when glory was at had. This aside, the Royalist turn was one of frustratingly slow advances. The storming party was getting a bad reputation and their honour called into question; once again they seemed to show little inclination to storm anything. The Scots were having similar problems getting their men to show any urgency; Kirkcubright's Horse had obviously found a tavern just off table and refused to come back. Even the reserve behind the city walls seemed content with sitting down for a game of dice rather than reinforcing the walls. On the Scots' left flank Arnott's Lancers charged a unit of the Prince of Wales' Horse, who promptly counter charged. The lancers were routed and fled to the hills. Filled with confidence the Royalists performed a sweeping advance into the Earl of Leven's own cavalry regiment who were made of much sterner stuff, and were promptly destroyed themselves!

This cavalry exchange caught the eye of Prince Rupert, and digging in his spurs he led his cavalry into a charge against Lord Mauchline's Horse. The ferocious charge that Rupert gives to all the cavalry in his battalia was devastating and the Scottish regiment was swept aside; once again Leven's regiment was to feel the force of a sweeping advance, but this time they too were broken and the Royalists suddenly had complete cavalry superiority on their right flank. It was not all positive for Rupert's men however; in true fashion the uncontrolled pursuit had moved them into danger. They strayed too close to the city walls and came under fire from a wide array of cannons and musket shot, causing a hasty tactical withdrawal (with much cheering from the Scottish

A storming party with a surprise package for some unlucky soul...

side). Even more encouraging for our intrepid Scottish commanders was the return of Kirkcudbright's Horse battalia on their right flank who finally (and somewhat sheepishly) re-joined the fight.

With the preliminary skirmishes out of the way, turn 4 began with an assault on various parts of the wall as Royalist regiments charged forward with ladders to scale the defences. The pike elements of Northampton's and Hopton's regiments co-ordinated their assaults and the defenders were under pressure. Unfortunately the storming party would only amble forward one move and were stranded in front of the freshly emerged Scots cavalry of Lord Kirkcudbright.

On the Royalist right Hopton's pike were shattered on the walls and broke. Northampton's on the left managed to draw their combat and gained a precarious position at the top of their ladders (the defenders of a fortified position getting a morale bonus and a combat formation modifier meant that Worcester was going to be one tough nut to crack). Despite a constant barrage of artillery fire, the section of wall targeted to provide the central breach was not looking any weaker. Rupert's pike formation had managed to come to grips with the enemy forlorn hope in front of the city gates and sent them packing, while the King's Guard managed to blunder their command – luckily they staggered forward in roughly the right direction.

The Covenanter commanders seemed very eager for their turn to come around, and with good reason. The enemy storming party, struggling with their explosive cargo, was not only in front of Kirkudbright's Horse but also happened to be within 6" of the lead unit, Lord Hamilton's regiment. As this was within initiative command range no successful command roll was needed and they charged home. The outcome was never in doubt and the Storming Party

Walls & Breaches

One of the aspects we introduced for this scenario was the ability to cause a breach in a wall by cannon fire (as well as the usual petard rules).

We gave the walls 'structure points'. Once the number of hits from cannons (of any calibre) matches the structure points of a wall section then a 3" breach is formed. Each hit equals one structure point of damage.

City/Castle Walls	10+D6 Structure points
Stone Buildings	5+D6 Structure Points
Barricades	D6 Structure Points

For this battle the umpire kept the structure points of the Worcester walls hidden from both players.

disappeared in a flurry of mud, hooves and limbs. With equal glee they turned to the city walls as the Scottish cannons began blasting holes in Northampton's pikemen as they struggled to gain a foothold; but the green coated Royalists held firm.

The Royalists began turn 5 with both Rupert's and the King's Guard Foot regiments reaching the foot of their respective section of wall to assault. Northampton's pike were trapped on their ladders and going nowhere, but a breakthrough was made over near the right tower by Talbot's pike unit. They had spotted a weak point, a section of wall defended by a unit of Stewart's musketeers. With the help of some laudable dice rolling in combat Talbot's men drove the Scots back and formed a bridgehead. The unmistakable colours of this regiment were the first over the wall to Neal's obvious joy – they are his favourite regiment and always seem to perform well.

Andy and John were quick to spot the danger to their defences and frantically started plugging the gaps. Balfour's pike were sent to finally push Northampton's pikemen back; it was too much for the beleaguered Royalist unit and they finally broke, but the supporting musket units held firm. Over on the other side of the walls Talbot's pike were a different proposition. Still fresh, they remained atop the walls after fighting a draw against Stewart's pike unit that was eager to avenge their musket armed comrades. Meanwhile the Argyll Highlanders and Baillie's regiment were moved to cover the impending assault from the King's Guard and Rupert's Foot and the General of Artillery

regiment was moved to cover any breakthrough. The remaining Scottish Horse, buoyed by their success against the storming party celebrated by refusing to move any further. Expletives abounded!

We were half way through the maximum amount of turns and it seemed a good idea to take stock and raid John's larder. The Scottish defence was proving stubborn. Their initial deployment had made a frontal assault on the gate house impractical and so new breaches were needed. Despite strong Royalist advances and complete cavalry superiority on their right flank, the Scots still looked to be secure, although the pressure was starting to tell on some of the front line units. It was universally agreed that attacking a fortified city was every bit as hard as it sounds, and the relentless cannon fire from the Royalist artillery train didn't seem to be having the desired impact.

The game restarted with real intent on the part of the attackers. Now that many units were within 6" of the enemy, commands were given under initiative all along the walls. Rupert's pike unit charged up the ladders only to be pushed back by the waiting pikemen of Baillie's Foot. The King's Guard were greeted by the alarming sight of Highlanders atop their ladders and looked to be in serious trouble. Neal was thankful this unit had been given the 'Valiant' special rule because King Charles was in the field, without the re-roll they would have been off right there and then. They were given heart by the sight of their King and fought on. Talbot's and Stewart's pike blocks were embroiled in a savage combat just inside the city walls which ended in a

The King's Guard follow Talbot's into the fray.

1662 - Charles II sells Dunkirk to the French for £40,000.

Scots rush to plug gaps in the defences.

stalemate. Nearly all the Royalist infantry units were engaged in combat, offering support or pouring fire on the defenders. The notable exception being Lord Percy's Foot out on the left; they were still struggling to come to terms with the order "advance".

With the cavalry action on the Royalist right won, Prince Rupert found himself out on a limb and not in position to help out, and so began to move his men over to the other flank to assist there. Out on that left flank Lord Wilmot's cavaliers charged into the resting regiment of Lord Hamilton, finally seeing them off the table. They were followed by the rest of Kirkcudbright's command, much to the relief of everyone concerned – a muttered "good riddance" was to be heard from behind the walls. More shots from the Royal artillery rained down on the walls and cracks began to appear; cue nervous glances from our Scottish commanders!

There were now melees everywhere; Scottish reinforcements ran to the walls and pushed both Rupert's and Talbot's regiments back to their ladders. The remaining Royalist foot not already engaged surged forward, Blackwell's regiment headed for the section of wall that had been attracting the attention of so much artillery fire only to come under heavy fire from Baillie's musketeers who were manning that area. Even Percy's regiment were pushing forward, moving to attack a new part of the wall to ensure the Scottish defences were thinly spread. Attention now turned to the King's Guard, who had been close to breaking last turn. This time there were no such doubts amongst the king's men and they scattered Argyll's Highlanders in a brutal display of combat dice rolling. A counter-attack in the Covenanter turn by the General of Artillery's regiment was turned back by the Guard, and they broke that unit too. The Royalists were in the streets of the city!

However, the city walls were doing their job as wave upon wave of attacks were turned back. The Royalist

commanders were facing a crisis as many regiments were close to breaking and they took stock and rallied their men all across the battle field before a final push. Although the King's Guard were in the city, without support they would be cut off and massacred. The Scots were facing their own difficulties: gaps were appearing in their defences and it was proving difficult to manoeuvre the reinforcements in time.

The brave Scottish forlorn hope finally broke and fled which seemed to give heart to Rupert's entire battalia; Blackwell's regiment moved into position in front of the section of wall that had been subject to constant artillery fire. For some attackers the assault was taking its toll as units began retiring from the wall, Hopton's battalia was broken on the Royalist right flank, the survivors melting away into the Worcestershire countryside.

The battle was still in the balance moving into turn 9; then disaster for the Scots. The artillery fire finally brought a section of the city walls crashing down taking many brave Stewarts with it, crushed under tons of masonry. As the dust settled it was the black coats of Blackwell's who stood proud in the breach. Elsewhere a Scottish blunder proved decisive; an order to Balfour's regiment to reinforce the wall was somehow misinterpreted to 'Sally Forth'; the Royalist left under Lord Percy watched in amazement as Scottish troops left the protection of the wall to advance on their guns. They died in droves and the entire flank ceased to exist. Percy's own foot regiment took advantage and marched up to the unprotected section of the city walls. They were unopposed as they topped their ladders.

With three enemy units within the city and large sections of undefended walls, the Scottish commanders' thoughts turned to the safety of their remaining men and the civilians within Worcester. Terms were sought and surrender offered. King Charles had crushed one of the last remaining rebel armies and he could now turn his attention north.

"Smart Battaile"
The Battle of Gropredy Bridge, 29 June 1644

"All the ends I had were but to bring things to a fair and peaceable issue...
That God might have had his fear; the King his honor;
the Houses of Parliament their liberties and properties;
and nothing might have remained upon the score between us, but... love."

- Sir William Waller's Memoirs

This battle was one of the Royalist highlights in the Civil War in 1644, fought only three days before the shattering northern defeat of the hitherto invincible Prince Rupert at the Battle of Marston Moor (2 July 1644), by which it has been overshadowed.

Background

A meeting between the Earl of Essex and Sir William Waller took place on 6 June 1644. Essex decided the armies of these two Parliamentarian generals had two immediate goals to achieve. First, to crush the King's Army as and when it slipped out of the Royalist capital at Oxford (as the two armies of Essex and Waller closed in on Oxford). Second, to relieve the town of Lyme Regis in Dorset currently besieged by King Charles' younger nephew, Prince Maurice and his Army of the West.

With superior enemy numbers approaching and not wanting a siege of the Royalist capital Oxford, the King was compelled to make his famous 'night march', thus dispersing the forces of his chief asset, his Oxford Army. The Reading garrison was also withdrawn, along with more outlying garrisons around Oxfordshire, and the King slipped away to the northwest with nearly all of the cavalry and 2,500 selected musketeers, but no pikemen, colours or artillery.

Parliamentarian horse eventually intercepted the King, but after a skirmish the Royalists crossed over into Worcestershire and destroyed the bridge at Pershore. Realizing that the King was two days' march ahead, a Council of War was held. Essex decided he would proceed south to relieve Lyme Regis, ordering Waller (whose army had less baggage and lighter artillery) to pursue the King and attempt to bring him to battle. Waller objected strenuously, but was overruled. The generals in London, extremely displeased, commanded Essex to return – too late.

Advantage was with the King, as Essex's departure enabled him to concentrate his forces once more and, like a good strategist, had not delayed to bring his whole army together at Witney. The King then confidently sought out Waller, as the Royalist newspaper *Mercurius Aulicus* stated: "His Majesty being resolved that if Waller came to seeke him, he should find him ready, and if the hungry Rebell had a stomack unto lead and Iron, they should have their belly full."

Both Waller and Sir Arthur Heselrige wrote to the Committee of Both Kingdoms on 7 June, stating "We resolve to follow the King wherever an army can march."

The importance of this letter was such that Heselrige himself was sent by Waller to convey it to London (therefore he did not lead his horse regiment at the battle). Waller received 370 musketeers and a company of dragoons from Gloucester and various garrisons, and later seven troops of horse, 600 more foot and eleven artillery pieces from Coventry and Warwick.

The King doubled back and returned to Worcester on 15 June; many of the Royalist foot were transported by boat down the River Severn to Worcester early that morning. Waller repaired Bewdley Bridge and sent a letter to Essex urging him to return with his army, but to no avail. Essex had relieved Lyme on the 15th and occupied Weymouth, and was preparing to proceed farther west. Waller had been left to do as best he could (though an even worse fate was soon to overtake the cautious Essex at Lostwithiel!).

The rest of the Royalist foot rendezvoused with the King at Witney on the 19th; the army now numbered about 5,000 foot and "ten brass guns of various calibres". Prince Charles met up with the King on the 24th, after recovering from measles. The King had planned to march to Daventry on the 28th, but on receiving information that Waller's Army was near Banbury, he changed his plans and decided to march to on that town to give battle.

At 10am, the King's Oxford Army mustered on Castle Hill, about one mile east of town. The morning rain and mist prevented any observation of the Parliamentarians. Later that day the weather cleared and Waller's Army was seen drawn up in Hanwell Warren on the western side of the River Cherwell, about a mile in front of the King's forces on the eastern side. Since both armies were anxious to secure a place of advantage on which to fight, both sides manoeuvred for possession of Crouch Hill (a 500-foot high hill about a mile south-west of Banbury). However, Waller's Army was on the same side of the river as the hill and so with the shorter distance to travel, they won the race.

The situation on the morning of 29 June was that the King's Oxford Army stood on the eastern side of the River Cherwell, near the town of Banbury. Waller's Army faced the Royalists at the foot of Crouch Hill on the western side, about a mile away. Waller was famous for always choosing a good defensive position, and this one was such, described in *Mercurius Aulicus* as "…having a hill at his backe, a great hedge with a deepe ditch for the front, and flanked also with divers hedges and ditches." The King was anxious to get Waller to "quit his strength", since there was also marshy ground just to the front of his position. Sensibly, the King realized that an attack on Waller's current position would be "more dangerous to attempt to force him thence". Therefore, after waiting in vain, he decided to continue the march once more towards Daventry in order to "observe Waller's motion and to expect a fitter opportunity and place

The Parliament right flank deploys after crossing the River Cherwell.

to give him battle." The King's move met with success, as Waller's Army drew off from its high ground and draw parallel with the Cavaliers on the other side of the river, by marching along the road from Banbury to Southam. As the Royalists marched towards Daventry, both armies were in full view of each other, being about one or two miles apart. The Royalists believed Waller would not attack them.

However, the King ordered the van of his Oxford Army to quicken their pace to cut off a large party of horse sighted about two to three miles away near Daventry, obviously attempting to join Waller. This caused a large gap to appear in the army column as the rest were unaware of the order. The gap has been estimated about a mile and a half between the centre (just over the River Cherwell at Hay's Bridge) and the lead of the rear guard (which was just at the crossroads past the village of Wardington). This gap was a major tactical error.

Waller quickly seized his chance to cut off the rear of the army and "bite the heel according to his custom."" He split his army; most of the force under Lt.-General John Middleton would attack over Cropredy Bridge to cut off the front of the rear guard from the rest of the Royalist army; the rest under Waller, crossed the ford at Slats Mill to hit the army's rear. However, the Parliamentarians had been misinformed about the progress of the Royalists along the road to Daventry, and instead of only cutting off the King's rear, they were to find themselves caught between his centre and rear.

The Battle

The action began about 1pm, as Middleton's force spread out after crossing Cropredy Bridge. Most of the horse turned northwards along the River Cherwell and Hay's bridge, where the Royalist van and centre appears to have crossed the bridge, with the artillery and baggage train crossing last. The rear guards at the back of the last Royalist division across the bridge (presumably Col. Thelwall's commanded musketeers) quickly turned over a wagon to block the bridge and held it with musketeers, forcing the horse to retire. Messengers were sent to recall the van, and the King quickly ordered Lord Bernard Stuart to lead the King's Lifeguard of Horse back across Hay's Bridge. The Lifeguard subsequently charged and routed four troops of Sir Arthur Haselrige's Regiment of Horse, who were forming up ready to charge the Earl of Cleveland's battalia of horse that had drawn up on rising ground facing them.

By this time the foot and artillery of Middleton's force had crossed Cropredy Bridge and drew up in the fields beyond, along with the rest of the horse. Cleveland charged with his battalia, undaunted into the fire from the Roundheads, routing and chasing them beyond their cannon. He captured about 100 foot, along with eleven pieces of artillery and two wooden 'barricadoes' mounted on wheels (each carrying seven small brass and leather guns) after killing most of the gunners. Middleton's force had been thrown back across Cropredy Bridge, but he used dragoons to cover the retreat. It was now that Lt.-Colonel John Birch of Haselrigge's Foot persuaded the Tower Hamlets Regiment of Foot – in the process of crossing – to defend the bridge, supported by the Kentish Regiment, the rest of the trained bands and two "drakes" (light artillery pieces).

While Middleton's forces were trying to cut off the Royalists from Hay's Bridge, Waller had led his forces across Slats Mill Ford about a mile below Cropredy. The Earl of Northampton's battalia of horse, bringing up the Royalist rear, turned and rapidly drove the enemy cavalry back over the ford. Waller immediately withdrew his entire army to the high ground near Great Bourton, but left infantry to guard the lower ford near the mill. The same seems to have been done with Middleton's force. After making an orderly withdrawal back across Cropredy Bridge, the Tower Hamlets, Kentish Regiments and other so far unengaged foot of the centre along with some dragoons and 'two drakes', then guarded the bridge and ford.

The battle was over by 2pm, and the "fair and very warm weather" had no doubt taken most of the fight out of the armies. However the King was determined to gain possession of Cropredy since he now had all of his forces drawn up a mile above it in the fields around Williamscote, and so he ordered an advance about 3pm. The Royalists could not gain the other side of the river as Waller kept sending forward reinforcements down to the riverbank to keep them at bay and prevented the Cavaliers from crossing. Eventually the Royalist attack across the ford at Slat Mill succeeded, but advanced no farther, probably due to the boggy ground near Great Bourton, as well as from reinforcements sent forward by Waller. The end result was that the Royalists occupied the Slat Ford and the adjacent mill, captured some prisoners, and harassed the Parliamentarians for the rest of the day.

In the evening, the Royalists withdrew most of their horse and foot nearer to the river, facing the Parliamentarians who were drawn up on top of the hill. The Parliamentarian horse formed into three large bodies about this time and advanced down the hill, but retired in disorder after being fired on by Royalist artillery (some of which were the captured cannon!). The King then sent a trumpeter to ask for safe conduct for Sir William Walker (the King's Secretary-at-War) to deliver an offer of royal pardon for Waller's Army, but this was refused, and as his reply Waller fired twenty cannon shot into the area where the King was with his royal standard.

After the Battle

Both armies continued to face each other the following day, 30 June, like "snarling dogs", waiting for the other to quit the field first. It would have been quite a battle if either side had decided to attack (and a great 'what if' scenario!), but with Waller's forces severely hurt and no doubt demoralised, and the King's forces low on provisions such as food and powder, neither army did anything.

That evening the King received intelligence of the approach of 4,000 foot and 500 horse from Buckingham under Sgt.-Maj.-General Richard Brown, advancing to join Waller. The King decided to quit the field, which was done in orderly fashion on 1 July, at 4pm. At the time, both armies were unaware of the impending battle of Marston Moor (2 July), but to the soldiers of Waller's Army it really did not matter, as it was so far away. In fact "the defeat of that day at Cropredy was much greater than it appeared to be" and "it even broke the heart of Waller's Army". Waller's Army sustained about 700 casualties (killed, wounded and captured); the Royalists reported about 80 in total. While Waller lost no key commanders, the Royalists lost two – Sir William Boteler and Sir William Clerke – both killed, while Lord Wilmot had received two slight wounds (in the arm and a bullet grazed his hand).

Waller's Army was exhausted, had lost all of its artillery except for a couple of pieces it had recaptured, and the London troops and other local contingents were in mutiny to return home, especially after Brown's force had arrived, who they considered as their "replacements". In fact, Waller remarked after Cropredy Bridge that the Trained Bands: "…come to their old cry of home, home… they are so mutinous and uncommandable that their is no hope of their stay. Yesterday they were like to have killed the Major General [Brown] and they hurt him in the face. Such men are only fit for a gallows here and hell hereafter."

Waller's army was crippled and literally destroyed as an effective independent fighting force for the rest of the war. Yet in the long term, this success was to have disastrous consequences for the Royalist cause. Waller's letter to the Committee of Both Kingdoms stated that, "Till you have an army merely your own that you may command it is in a manner impossible to do anything of importance." Parliament found an answer within twelve months, with the creation of the New Model Army.

Following up the victory against Waller, the King marched into Cornwall, and after a series of events (and battles) eventually hemmed in Essex's Army at Lostwithiel, compelling it to surrender in the open field unconditionally.

The Set Up

This encounter is a non-standard and unique battle for the English Civil War period, in that one army (Parliamentarian) – split in two using a pincer movement – attempts to unexpectedly rush upon and cut off part of the other army (Royalist) and quickly destroy it before the rest of

1668 - Henry Morgan sacks Panama City yielding masses of treasure.

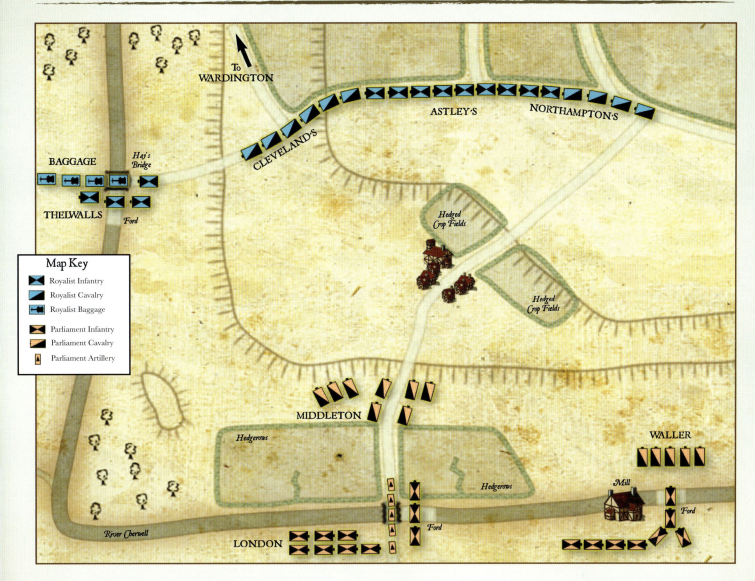

the army can regroup and come to bear. The Parliamentarians must press the attack with their horse early on, advancing and engaging as far away as possible from the river, gaining as much ground before the Royalist horse deploys, plus getting the rest of their forces across and pushing forward quickly to engage and bring the battle into full action. It seems that historically the Parliamentarians were not quick enough with all of their forces, probably due to the fact that a large number of units had to traverse over two points along the river, and possibly the ford and boggy ground slowed them down enough so that the Royalists could deal with the situation and eventually win the day.

While not noted on the map, it is important, regardless of deployments noted below, that opposing units are at least 24" away from each other.

Royalist Deployment & Victory Conditions: The van and front of the centre (body) of the army are considered off tabletop to the north beyond Hay's Bridge (only one commander and unit will return as reinforcements; see below). The artillery has just crossed Hay's Bridge (and is off the tabletop), with the baggage in the process of crossing, along with some infantry (Thelwall's Commanded Musketeers) crossing at the adjacent ford.

The rear of the centre of the army, comprised of Cleveland's Battalia is in column on the road near the crossroad leading to Wardington (dragoons deployed mounted three moves away on the eastern side of Cropredy Bridge, after having been chased away from the bridge itself by the advancing Parliamentarians); Astley's Battalia follows in column thereafter (the Wardington Ash should be just off the road and about even with the end of Cleveland's Battalia). The rear of the army, comprised of Northampton's Battalia is in column on the road following Astley's Battalia.

All the Royalist units start in disorder (except for the dragoons). This reflects the surprise and shock that occurred initially to the Cavaliers due to the Roundheads' sudden advance. Second and subsequent turns proceed as normal. Note that commanders are allowed to give a command for the entire battalia to reorder (unlike in the rules); this is a special condition for this battle.

Parliamentarian Deployment & Victory Conditions: Middleton's force is to have the horse in the van (all in column) deployed as desired two movements (18") across Cropredy Bridge since the Royalist dragoons have mounted and retired. Infantry in the van are to be deployed on road in column after the horse, with artillery following crossing the bridge, and foot of the rear part of the van thereafter (on the road and crossing the ford next to the bridge) on the western side of the river. Waller's force is in column at Slat Mill, with horse and dragoons within one movement (9") on eastern side of the ford, and foot in the process of crossing the ford, while on the western side they are waiting to cross.

The Parliamentarians automatically have the initiative on the first turn, with all of the Royalist units being in disorder (except for the dragoons at Cropredy Bridge). This reflects the surprise and shock that occurred initially to the Cavaliers due to the Roundheads' sudden advance. Second and subsequent turns proceed as normal.

The Terrain

The modern day features of the landscape are essentially the same as they were in 1644, though the bridge at Cropredy is a successor of the one during the Civil Wars. During that time it was stone, being two-spanned, but the upper part had a wooden railing rather than stone. Hays Bridge was entirely a wooden bridge. Something typical of bridges in this period was a ford being adjacent to the crossing. Troops crossing the river would make use of both the bridge and adjacent ford (most likely cavalry would use the fords) to make the crossing quicker. Therefore, next to each bridge on the downriver side (i.e., west for Hay's, south for Cropredy) there is an area wide enough to allow a column width section considered fordable.

The ford at Slat Mill crosses at a marshy area, so terrain should reflect this. Likewise, the area west of the ford is also marshy, extending north and south of the crossing. This crossing actually goes over two smaller branches of the River Cherwell, which are east of the river. Slat Mill should be placed just on the Parliamentarian side of the closest of these smaller branches, a couple of inches from the ford as the mill was supposedly "70 yards above the ford". Note that there are other areas marked as marsh, especially below Cropredy, since contemporary accounts state that "bogs" flanked Waller's position. The outskirts of the town of Cropredy are not needed, though a few buildings are needed to represent the village of Williamscote on the eastern side of the river.

Therefore the terrain was made up of various large, relatively open crop fields and pastures – perfect for cavalry – edged with hedgerows, with at least one or two openings (gates, etc.) Do not place hedgerows along road edges, unless it borders a pasture; given the various horse charges that occurred, this hints that not all fields were enclosed. It seems most enclosures were nearer to Cropredy Bridge, as Parliamentarian infantry were noted as lining hedges when they formed up. To a lesser extent there should be fields beyond the crossing at Slat Mill, but since Waller's cavalry did not seem impeded by these (no accounts mention this), they should be few and open. All hedgerows and stonewalls should hinder movement and cause disorder.

If possible (or to achieve entirely historically accurate terrain) most of the eastern (Royalist) side of Cropredy should gently rise from the river to the edge of the tabletop – the steepest incline rising from Slat Mill itself.

King Charles surveys his artillery train.

Special Rule - Wood Blinds

Waller's Army had two of these, each comprised of "seven leather and brass guns". The theory we have adopted is that this was a medieval-style mantlet to protect the crew, possibly mounted on two wheels, with a battery of seven gun barrels much like an organ or volley gun. For game purposes only one of these will be used, with the following suggested rules for its use.

Crew: 3

Movement: As light artillery

Fire Factors/Range: Each of the seven barrels is considered Very Light Artillery (i.e., a 1- or 2-pdr in size), but only able to fire hailshot at maximum 6" range; each barrel gives 1D6 to hit.

Firing Procedure: Each time it fires, roll 2D6 first and consult below to see how many barrels fire, and then roll a number of dice equal to that number of barrels to see if any hits are achieved.

    2 = Explosion *; no barrels fired
    3 = 1 barrel fires
    4 = 2 barrels fire
    5 = 3 barrels fire
    6-7 = 4 barrels fire
    8-9 = 5 barrels fire
    10 = 6 barrels fire
    11 = 7 barrels fire
    12 = Explosion *, but some barrels fire
        normally; roll 1D6 for number of barrels firing
        normally and roll to hit normally

* Explosion: Roll 1D3+1 for number of barrels to be permanently out of action due to explosion (this includes barrel that exploded), also killing one crew. In addition, wood blind is out of action for one turn for each barrel lost.

There should be a movement penalty (costs 2" per 1") for any units ascending the two levels of the hill from Slat Mill (on the southern side of Williamscote), which will slow the Parliamentarian cavalry's advance, as happened historically. Otherwise, no penalty should be given to movement for any other slopes on the tabletop. Again, this is not mandatory, and many gamers will ignore this, as it adds quite a bit of terrain to achieve (but is a proper historical representation of the battle, and looks smashing on the tabletop!).

With regard to dimensions of the 2-level hill itself – based on using a 6' x 12' tabletop (for which the map was designed) – the lower level of hill is 10' long by 4' wide; the upper level of hill is 8' long by 3' wide until the village then 2' wide thereafter towards Hay's Bridge. The centre of road that runs north/south along the hill is about 6" from the eastern tabletop edge. The centre of the village is about 4' from southern table edge. All roads should be about 3" wide. The river (4" wide) is about 8" from northern tabletop edge at Hay's Bridge, and about 4" from the western tabletop edge around Cropredy Bridge until near Slat Mill Ford, where it should be about 8" from the edge.

All roads should be wide enough for at least 2-3 figures, and it is most important that 4-figures wide should be used for columns, as that allows sufficient space to ensure the units fit on the tabletop at the points noted on the map.

As there are no sizeable woods known to be in the area, it is suggested that a few individual trees be used and scattered about, especially in the hedgerows, to give the tabletop a proper look. It is important that the single largest and tallest tree on the tabletop be used to represent the Wardington Ash (modern visitors to the area of the battle may find a particular pleasure in being able to visit the descendant of the actual Wardington Ash, under which King Charles I was "invited to dine" about a half hour prior to the battle). The Wardington Ash should be placed just off road to the west, about even with the end of Cleveland's Battalia.

Having a visually appealing tabletop is an aspect of wargaming that should never be overlooked, so go to it!

The Armies - Orders of Battle

For this scenario units that were considered 'raw' at this time in the Civil Wars are therefore 'Untested' for these rules. Units considered 'veteran' at this time in the Civil Wars are therefore 'Brave, Stubborn, Superbly Drilled, and Tough Fighters'.

When uniform coat colors and/or colours/cornets (flags) are known they are listed accordingly; where this is not 100% known, though probable, they are listed with a '?' (if any heraldic devices are known for a colour/cornet, these are listed as well; no devices listed means that they are unknown at this time). Important Note – do not feel compelled to match the unit coats, colours and/or cornets as listed – by all means, use which units you have available; the information is only presented for historical knowledge and purposes if you wish to build the exact units.

Parliamentarian - Army of the Southern Association
Field Word: "Victory Without Quarter"

Historically, about 6,200 foot, 2,520 horse, 360 dragoons, and 11 artillery pieces, as follows.

ARMY COMMANDER SIR WILLIAM WALLER
General of the Army of the Southern Association, Command Rating 8

SIR WILLIAM WALLER'S DIVISION
Comprised of two battalia, in column at Slat Ford, as follows.

SIR WILLIAM BALFOUR'S BATTALIA OF HORSE
Sir William Balfour, Command Rating 7
Five units in column and deployed within one movement (9") across Slat Ford.

- Sir William Balfour's & Sir William Waller's Lifeguards of Horse (1 unit of cuirassiers; Waller's Cornet: yellow field?) – Brave, Elite 4+, Heavy Cavalry, Marauder, Stubborn, Superbly Drilled, Tough Fighters
- Sir William Waller's Regt. of Horse (2 units of cavalry each) – Brave, Stubborn, Superbly Drilled, Tough Fighters, Marauder
- Col. William Purefoy's & Col. John Barker's Regts. of Horse (1 unit of cavalry) – Brave, Marauder
- Col. Richard Norton's Regt. of Dragoons (1 unit of dragoons) – Dragoons, Marauder

LT.-COL. JAMES GREY'S BATTALIA OF FOOT
Lt.-Col. James Grey of Bosseville's Foot, Command Rating 7.
Eight units in column, just starting to cross Slat Ford behind Balfour's Battalia, in the following order.

- Musketeers of Col. John Barker's Regt. of Foot (1 unit of matchlock muskets) – First Fire
- Musketeers of Col. Godfrey Bosseville's Regt. of Foot (1 unit of matchlock muskets; Coat: red) – First Fire, Untested
- Combined Pikemen of Sir Hardress Waller's and Colonels Godfrey Bosseville's & Alexander Popham's Regts. of Foot (1 unit of pike; Coats: mixed yellow, red & blue) – Hedgehog
- Musketeers of Col. Alexander Popham's Regt. of Foot (1 unit of matchlock muskets; Coat: blue?) – Brave, First Fire, Stubborn, Superbly Drilled, Tough Fighters
- Musketeers of Sir Hardress Waller's Regt. of Foot (1 unit of matchlock muskets; Coat: yellow?) – Brave, First Fire
- Commanded Muskets (3 units of commanded muskets each) – First Fire, Large Unit

LT.-GENERAL JOHN MIDDLETON'S DIVISION
Lt.-Gen. John Middleton, Command Rating 8.
Comprised of five battalias, in column advancing from Cropredy Bridge, as follows.

CAPT. JOHN BUTLER'S BATTALIA OF HORSE
Capt. John Butler, Adjutant-General, Command Rating 7
Three units in column deployed within two movements (18") on eastern side of Cropredy Bridge.
- Sir Arthur Haselrigge's Regt. of Horse (2 units of cavalry each; Coat: blue?) – Brave, Stubborn, Superbly Drilled, Tough Fighters, Marauder
- Col. Edward Cooke's Regt. of Horse (1 unit of cavalry) – Brave, Marauder

COL. JONAS VANDRUSKE'S BATTALIA OF HORSE
Col. Jonas Vandruske, Command Rating 7
Five units in column deployed within two movements (18") on eastern side of Cropredy Bridge.

- Col. Jonas Vandruske's Regt. of Horse (2 units of cavalry each) – Brave, Marauder
- Col. George Thompson's Regt. of Horse (2 units of cavalry each) – Brave, Stubborn, Superbly Drilled, Tough Fighters, Marauder
- Sir Michael Livesay's ("The Kentish Horse") Regt. of Horse (1 unit of cavalry; Coat: red?) – Brave, Marauder

LT.-COL. JEREMY BAINES' BATTALIA OF FOOT
Andrew Potley, Sgt.-Maj.-General of Foot, Command Rating 7
Lt.-Col. Jeremy Baines, Quartermaster-General of Foot, Command Rating 7
Note: Potley counts as a General for game purposes above Baines, and all rules apply for giving orders.
Three units in column crossing the ford next to Cropredy Bridge in the following order.

- Musketeers of Sir William Waller's & Col. Samuel Jones' Regts. of Foot (1 unit of matchlock muskets; Waller's Coat: yellow?; Waller's Colours: blue field; Jones' Coat: green lined white; Jones' Colours: white field) – Brave, First Fire, Stubborn, Superbly Drilled, Tough Fighters
- Combined Pikemen of Sir William Waller's, Col. Samuel Jones' Regt. of Foot ("The Farnham Garrison"), Sgt.-Maj.-General Andrew Potley's & Col. James Holborne's Regts. of Foot (1 unit of pike; Coats: mixed yellow?, red?, and green lined white, Jones' Colours: white field) – Brave, Hedgehog
- Musketeers of Sgt.-Maj.-General Andrew Potley's & Col. James Holborne's Regts. of Foot (1 unit of matchlock muskets; Coats: red?) – Brave, First Fire, Stubborn, Superbly Drilled, Tough Fighters

ARTILLERY & ARTILLERY GUARD
Col. James Wemyss, General of the Train of Artillery, Command Rating 7
Five artillery pieces and one unit crossing Cropredy Bridge in the following order; artillery limbered, foot in column.
- 2 Light guns, 1 Wooden Blinder (very light gun) & 2 Medium guns
- Sir William Waller's Firelocks,
- Col. James Wemyss' Regt. of Foot
- Sir Michael Livesey's Regt. of Dragoons (1 unit of firelocks; dragoons are dismounted for scenario; Waller's & Wemyss' Coats: blue?; Livesey's Coat: red?) – First Fire

THE CITY BATTALIA OF LONDON & RESERVE
Maj.-General, Sir James Harrington, Command Rating 7
Seven units in column on western side of Cropredy Bridge, waiting to cross at bridge and/or ford, in the following order.
- Musketeers of the Trained Bands of the Tower Hamlets (1 unit of matchlock muskets; Colours: red field with silver wreath & writing) – First Fire
- Combined Pikemen of the City of London Battalia (1 unit of pike) – Hedgehog, Large Unit
- Musketeers of the White Auxiliaries of Southwark (1 unit of matchlock muskets; Colours: white field) – First Fire, Untested
- Musketeers of the Yellow Auxiliaries of Westminster (1 unit of men matchlock muskets; Colours: yellow field) – First Fire, Untested
- Musketeers of Sir Arthur Haselrigge's Regt. of Foot (1 unit of matchlock musket; Coat: blue; Colours: yellow field since winter 1643/44, but possibly blue field with white stars as devices?) – Brave, First Fire, Stubborn, Superbly Drilled, Tough Fighters
- Combined Pikemen of Sir Arthur Haselrigge's & Col. Ralph

Weldon's Regts. of Foot (1 unit of pike; Haselrigge's Coat: blue, Colours: yellow field since winter 1643/44, but possibly blue field with white stars as devices?; Weldon's Coat: red, Colours: red field) – Hedgehog

- Musketeers of Col. Ralph Weldon's ("The Kentish Regiment") Regt. of Foot (1 unit of matchlock musketeers; Coat: red; Colours: red field) – First Fire

Notes: Number of figures in each regiment of foot is reduced to reflect those infantry regiments that 'commanded musketeers' for the rear guard were drawn off from. The three London Trained Bands would be in mixed coloured coats (i.e., no uniform), but with some buffcoats (seemingly a London Trained Band common item). Historically, the artillery consisted of "11 brasse pieces" (2 Large, 5 Medium & 4 Light guns, plus 2 Wooden Blinders), but naturally reduced for the scale of the rules/scenario (the large guns were left on the hill overlooking Cropredy, and thus were not a part of the early part of the battle – or for the scenario – but did play a part in the fight that continued when the Royalists tried to cross the river later that same day, so add one large gun if playing that action).

Optional Rules – Continuing the Fight

The following are two options for continuing the battle, depending on the outcome of the initial engagement. One is straightforward, while the other is a good 'what-if'.

Part 1 – Later that Day: The King then gave orders for his army to attempt to finish Waller's Army by forcing the crossings at Cropredy and Slat Mill. This requires the tabletop to be reset slightly, about 4' added on the western side of the river for extra terrain. This can be accomplished easily if a cloth is used for the ground cover, by having a few feet hanging off the western edge during the first battle. Then simply remove the terrain from the eastern side, carefully slide the cloth towards the east, and add terrain to the western side as needed.

Allow Parliamentarians to regroup and form a battle line stretching from a hill near Pewet Farm (just beyond Slat Mill) to Cropredy, as desired. If however, it looks as if the Parliamentarians are winning from the first phase of the battle, then the King orders a break-off to regroup for another try, and it's therefore a 'Minor Victory' for Parliament. A 'Major Victory' is awarded if Waller's Army manages to break or rout 50% or more of the Royalist units engaged.

If the outcome of previous battles resulted in a Parliamentarian defeat, then any broken/routed units are allowed to reform, but will be -1 stamina and +1 worse for morale (saving throw), to reflect casualties. Likewise, Royalist units are allowed to reform, with stamina and morale also as noted above, but only for those units that were broken during the early part of the battle; all others are to be as normal. Otherwise all other rules apply. In addition, if fight continues, then ammunition rules should be used for Royalist units (historically they were low on ammo; one reason the King decided to withdraw); each time a Royalist unit rolls a '1' on the dice, then that unit is -1 dice of shooting for the rest of the game, until there are no dice left for shooting (i.e., out of powder).

Part 2 – Second Day at Cropredy Bridge: Depending on the outcome of the first day, if it followed history, then both armies continued to face each other the following day, 30 June, like "snarling dogs", waiting for the other to quit the field first. It would have been quite a battle if either side had decided to attack, but with Waller's forces severely hurt and no doubt demoralized, and the King's forces low on provisions such as food and powder, neither army did anything.

A good 'what-if' would be to continue the fight, with a reduction in ammunition for the Royalists (all units have only one dice maximum for shooting), who would be formed-up at just outside Cropredy facing the Parliamentarians (use a few buildings to represent Cropredy itself). The Parliamentarians erected hasty earthworks atop the hill during the night, so these should be sufficient to protect the infantry and the artillery with minor defense (i.e. -1 to hit defenders due to being obscured behind cover, and defenders get +1 to morale if in cover).

The City of London Battalia of Foot are in a bad way should the fight be prolonged into a second day. Dissent in the ranks grows to a level bordering on mutiny.

At the beginning of every Parliament turn, roll a dice for each unit in this battalia not engaged in hand-to-hand combat. On a roll of a '1' the unit has mutinied and marches to the rear of the table crying "Home!, Home!"

Royalist – The King's Oxford Army
Field Word: "Hand and Sword"""

Historically about 5500 foot, 4400 horse and dragoons, and 18 artillery pieces were in the King's Oxford Army during this campaign. However, only about 3300 foot, and 3450 horse and dragoons participated in the battle. This means the Vanguard units (see Optional Armies section) were not really involved and are therefore left out of this scenario, with the exception of Thelwall's 'Commanded Musketeers' and the King's Lifeguard of Horse. Likewise since neither

King Charles I nor his Lord General (Lt.-General Patrick Ruthven, Earl of Forth & Brentford) were in command of the action that occurred, they have also been left out as 'Generals'. Subordinate generals are used instead, as they were the ones that actually commanded on the day. The following units and commanders are those that were known to have been in the battle and are therefore part of the scenario.

Col. Anthony Thelwall's Battalia of Commanded Muskets

Col. Anthony Thelwall, Command Rating 8

Four units in column just north across the river via the ford next to Hay's Bridge; one unit should still be in the ford. The wagon train (4 wagons) has almost crossed over the bridge (one or two should still be on the bridge), and is placed along the road accordingly.

- Col. Anthony Thelwall's Commanded Musketeers (4 units of matchlock muskets each; Coats: mixed) – Brave, First Fire, Large Unit, Stubborn, Superbly Drilled, Tough Fighters

Earl of Cleveland's Battalia of Horse

Earl of Cleveland, Command Rating 8

Six units in column at crossroads to village of Wardington, heading north towards Hay's Bridge in the following order; dragoons deployed three moves (27") away from Cropredy Bridge.

- Earl of Cleveland's Regt. of Horse (1 unit of cavalry; Coat: red?) – Brave, Gallopers, Marauder, Stubborn, Superbly Drilled, Tough Fighters
- Lord Wentworth's Regt. of Horse (1 unit of cavalry) – Brave, Gallopers, Marauder, Stubborn, Superbly Drilled, Tough Fighters
- Prince Charles' & Col. Richard Neville's Regts. of Horse (1 unit of cavalry) – Brave, Gallopers, Marauder, Stubborn, Superbly Drilled, Tough Fighters
- Sir William Boteler's & Sir Nicholas Crispe's Regts. of Horse (1 unit of cavalry) – Brave, Gallopers, Marauder, Stubborn, Superbly Drilled, Tough Fighters
- Col. James Hamilton's & Sir William Clerke's Regts. of Horse (1 unit of cavalry) – Brave, Gallopers, Large Unit, Marauder
- Col. John Innes' Regt. of Dragoons (1 unit of dragoons/matchlock muskets; Coat: red?) – Dragoons, Large Unit, Marauder

Earl of Northampton's Battalia of Horse

James Compton, 3rd Earl of Northampton, Command Rating 8
Four units in column behind Sir Bernard Astley's Battalia in the following order.

- Earl of Northampton's Regt. of Horse (1 unit of cavalry; Coats: red?) – Brave, Gallopers, Marauder, Stubborn, Superbly Drilled, Tough Fighters
- Lord Wilmot's Regt. of Horse (1 units of cavalry) – Brave, Gallopers, Marauder, Stubborn, Superbly Drilled, Tough Fighters
- Col. Thomas Weston's (ex. Lord Denbigh's), Col. George Gunter's & Sir Allen Apsley's Regts. of Horse (1 unit of cavalry) – Brave, Gallopers, Marauder
- Lord Percy's Regt. of Horse (1 unit of cavalry) – Brave, Gallopers, Large Unit, Marauder

Sir Bernard Astley's Battalia of Foot

Commander: Sir Jacob Astley, Sgt.-Maj.-General of Foot, Command Rating 9;
Adjutant-Commander: Sir Bernard Astley, Command Rating 8

Nine units in column behind the Earl of Cleveland's Battalia of Horse in the following order. [Note: Sir Jacob Astley counts as a General for game purposes above Sir Bernard Astley, and all rules apply for giving orders.]

- Musketeers of Lord Hopton's & Sir Allen Apsley's Regts. of Foot (1 unit of matchlock muskets; Hopton's Coat: blue, Colours: red field, with white stars as devices; Apsley's Coat: red, Colours: black & white gyronds) – Brave, First Fire, Stubborn, Superbly Drilled, Tough Fighters
- Pikemen of Lord Hopton's, Sir Allen Apsley's & Col. John Talbot's Regts. of Foot (1 unit of pike; Coat: mixed blue, red, yellow) – Brave, Hedgehog, Stubborn, Superbly Drilled, Tough Fighters
- Musketeers of Col. John Talbot's Regt. of Foot (1 unit of matchlock muskets; Coat: yellow; Colours: white field, black dog devices) – Brave, First Fire, Stubborn, Superbly Drilled, Tough Fighters
- Musketeers of Col. Francis Cooke's & Sir Bernard Astley's (ex. Lord Hertford's) Regts. of Foot (1 unit of matchlock muskets; Cooke's Coats: blue?; Colours: blue field with white balls as devices; Astley's Coat: blue) – First Fire
- Pikemen of Col. Francis Cooke's, Sir Bernard Astley's, Sir William Courteney's & Col. Henry Shelley's (1 unit of pike) – Hedgehog
- Musketeers of Col. Henry Shelley's & Sir William Courteney's Regts. of Foot (1 unit of matchlock muskets) – First Fire, Untested
- Musketeers of Col. Matthew Appleyard's (ex. Sir Charles Vavasour's) Regt. of Foot (1 unit of matchlock muskets; Coat: yellow) – Brave, First Fire, Stubborn, Superbly Drilled, Tough Fighters

1675 - The building of the present St. Paul's cathedral begins.

- Pikemen of Col. Matthew Appleyard's & Sir John Paulet's Regts. of Foot (1 unit of pike; Coats: yellow) – Brave, Hedgehog, Stubborn, Superbly Drilled, Tough Fighters
- Musketeers of Sir John Paulet's Regt. of Foot (1 unit of matchlock muskets; Coat: yellow) – Brave, First Fire, Stubborn, Superbly Drilled, Tough Fighters

Reinforcements

HENRY, LORD WILMOT,
Lt.-General of Horse, Command Rating 8
Each turn starting with turn 2, Lord Wilmot has a 50% chance of arriving on the road north of Hay's Bridge. He will act as a general with regard to command upon arrival.

THE KING'S LIFEGUARD OF HORSE
Commander: Lord Bernard Stewart, Command Rating 7

Historically once the King saw that Waller had launched a surprise attack on the rear of the army, he immediately sent his own Lifeguard of Horse under Lord Bernard Stewart with orders to assist. Therefore the King's Lifeguard of Horse will act as an independent unit with its own attached commander (i.e., it does not count towards any battalia with regard to making it become broken, and takes command from its own permanently attached commander for the scenario). The unit arrives on random turn; starting turn 3, 50% chance unit arrives in column on the road on the north side of Hay's Bridge each turn. Note that by having a commander attached, this unit can – at the minimum – use the "Follow Me" order each turn for one movement, rather than attempt a command roll to try for more than one movement per turn.

- The King's Lifeguard of Horse (1 unit of cavalry; Coat: red; Cornet: red field, gold 'CR') – Brave, Eager, Elite 4+, Gallopers, Marauder, Stubborn, Superbly Drilled, Tough Fighters, Valiant

Note: Historically the wagon train consisted of 30 wagons.

'by all these means together, the foot, (all but three or four hundred who marched without any weapons but a cudgel,) were armed with musket, and bags for their powder, and pikes; but in the whole there was not one pikeman had a corslet, and very few musketeers who had swords.'

Clarendon on the eve of Edgehill (Royalist forces)

Royalist foot with attached light gun.

How the Game Played

The Parliamentarians under Lt.-General Middleton managed to achieve outstanding command rolls (3 moves) for both Butler's and Vandruske's Battalias of horse on the first two turns, and thus quickly advanced up the hill towards the Royalists who, startled at the enemy's aggressiveness, could barely deploy in line at the edge of the upper plateau. The Parliamentarian artillery deployed along the edge of the lower plateau, Lt.-Colonel Baines' Battalia of Foot deployed near the outskirts of the village and the City of London Battalia eventually crossed Cropredy Bridge and began to deploy more to the north of the artillery to cut off any would-be Royalist reinforcements from over Hay's Bridge.

The Royalist horse of Cleveland's Battalia made a good fight of it, causing enough damage to Butler's Battalia of Horse to break it. However, eventually Cleveland's Battalia was likewise broken, leaving only Astley's Royalist infantry to deal with the remaining Parliamentarian cavalry under Vandruske. They inflicted some decent casualties on them from musket fire while the Parliamentarian artillery attempted to inflict casualties of its own on the Royalist pike in hedgehog on the edge of the upper plateau facing what was left of Vandruske's horse on the lower level. Astley seemed to have all well in hand, but things eventually turned worse on his left flank.

Waller's forces were slow to advance against the Royalist flank. (After the first turn, the commander missed both rolls, for both of his battalias for three turns in a row!). This allowed the Royalist horse of Northampton's Battalia to deploy and then eventually charge down the steep hill, sensing that the Parliamentarians were confused (rather than just a cunning ploy to get them to come down from their lofty commanding position!). The Royalist cavalry came off the worse for wear after two turns of combat, with Northampton's Battalia broken, though the Parliamentarian horse battalia facing them (Sir William Balfour's) was very cut up and almost done with as well. With Northampton's Battalia gone, this left the entire flank of Astley's infantry exposed to Grey's Battalia of Foot as Waller ordered them up the hill.

Even though Lord Wilmot, followed by the King's Lifeguard of Horse, had finally managed to get through the congestion at Hay's Bridge and arrive on the field, the delay of Thelwall's Battalia trying to cross back over from Hay's Bridge resulted in not enough reinforcements to allow the Royalists to win a decisive victory. In fact, it was determined that with no real cavalry left on the field, the Parliamentarians would win a marginal victory, forcing the Royalists to retreat. The game came down to both sides only needing one more battalia broken to cause the entire army to be likewise, and it was the Royalists that (due to some really poor die rolls) saw this happen first.

The scenario really hinged on the Parliamentarians getting successful (and plentiful) command rolls, as well as using initiative properly to keep up the pressure on the Royalists before they could bring their better forces to bear.

The Royalist centre pushes on towards Williamscote.

1678 - French buccaneer Michel de Grammont raids Spanish-held Venezuela.

Parliament battalia formed up to defend the village.

Bohemian soldier's dagger,
16th to 17th Century
(Stallard collection)

"I had rather have a plain russet-coated captain that knows what he fights for, and loves what he knows, than that which you call a gentleman and is nothing else."

Letter from Cromwell to Sir William Spring, Sept. 1643.

Scottish cavalry off to give someone a chibbin'...

WARS OF THE SUN KING

Europe in the second half of the 17th century was dominated both politically and, more interestingly for us, militarily, by the actions of Louis XIV of France, also known as The Sun King - or *Le Roi-Soleil* for the Francophiles amongst you. Louis ascended the throne at the

tender age of four in 1643 at a time when France was embroiled in the Thirty Years War. During his early years France was managed by Cardinal Mazarin, who negotiated the peace treaty which bought that conflict to an end, and also through the Fronde, the civil wars that threatened the young Louis' reign before it had really begun.

Mazarin died in 1661 at which point Louis took over the reins of a country still reeling from internal division and near bankruptcy. The young king wasted no time in setting out an agenda of expansionism through force of arms, a tone that was constant throughout his seventy two year reign. A true believer in the divine right of kings, Louis' aims were for his France to take and hold all the territory of Charlemagne.

With this in mind he set about enlarging his military capacity, both in numbers and training. The Marquis of Louvois and Viscount Turenne were tasked with the command of a new look army, one drilled to exacting

The Grand Alliance army of Dutch, English, Scots and Danish attend church.

1680 - The Great Comet of 1680 is the first comet discovered by telescope.

standards by Jean Martinet – the term 'martinet' is still used today to describe strict discipline.

Throughout the century France's main antagonist had been Spain, and in 1660 Louis married Maria Theresa, the daughter of King Philip IV of Spain. Although he had signed an accord which removed his queen from the succession of any Spanish territories, Louis was playing the long game and was banking on this marriage to provide a platform for a move on Spain. When Philip died in 1665, Louis used the non payment of his wife's dowry as a loophole in the succession agreement and promptly announced her as the true ruler of the Spanish Netherlands. Philip's son, Charles II of Spain was still an infant and a product of Philip's second marriage; as such Louis argued that according to the law of Brabant – in the Spanish Netherlands – children of a first marriage had priority of succession.

French forces poured north under two veterans of the Thirty Years War, Turenne and the Prince of Conde, and swept all before them. The French capture of Flanders had taken everyone by surprise; the Dutch and English immediately ceased their trading war and in 1668 entered into the Triple Alliance with Sweden against Louis. Spain too was concerned enough to make peace with the Portuguese and concentrate on her northerly neighbours. With such an array of opposition, Louis entered into a secret agreement with the Holy Roman Emperor Leopold I, which guaranteed French claims on the Spanish Netherlands on the death of the young Charles II. At this time it was widely considered the infant king Charles would not last long, afflicted as he was by many ailments probably due to a little too much in-breeding within the Hapsburg dynasty. With this agreement in his pocket, Louis 'graciously' entered into the Treaty of Aix-la-Chapelle by whoch he withdrew his forces from parts of the occupied lands but kept much of his gains in Flanders.

The Dutch War 1672-78

The Triple Alliance that had been formed to confront Louis' ambitions was not to last. As early as 1670 he had entered into the secret Treaty of Dover with Charles II of England, in which France bought English compliance in her plans against the Dutch. Further political moves to isolate the Dutch from their allies were made in Sweden and the German provinces. All this to ensure that any French move back into the Spanish Netherlands would go unhindered. The French army had been increased to nearly 120,000 men by this time; the Sun King meant business.

In 1672 France, England and a number of German provinces declared war on the Dutch United Provinces. A combined Anglo-French fleet was defeated by Dutch Admiral Michiel de Ruyter at the Battle of Sole Bay, which proved to be a temporary setback. On land, French forces

William of Orange, William III of England 1650-1702

William was born in The Hague, the son of Stadtholder William II and Mary, the daughter of Charles I of England. He was born at a time when the Dutch were in a continuous struggle for independence, threatened by French expansionist plans.

In 1677 he married Mary Stuart, the daughter of James, Duke of York (the future King James II of England) and this marriage put him firmly in line for the English throne as James' Catholic leanings were made apparent. In 1688 he was invited to take the English crown by leading English figures and the resulting 'Glorious Revolution' saw him being crowned King William III alongside Queen Mary. Scotland soon offered him full support, but rebellions in Ireland marked the first years of his rule despite winning a comprehensive victory at the Battle of the Boyne in 1690.

His constant struggle against the forces of Louis XIV were always the priority, the Jacobite uprisings being an inconvenience to be put down quickly to get back to serious business in The Netherlands. Louis would refer to William as 'my mortal enemy', so dogged was the English king even when on the receiving end of French victories.

From 1694 William ruled alone after the death of his wife. His reign still focused around the fighting season in the Low Countries where he would campaign from Spring until Autumn each year. William died in 1702 from pneumonia after a fall from his horse and was succeeded by his sister-in-law, Anne. His ability to end the conflict between crown and parliament, that had plagued England for decades, ensured that future Jacobite rebellions from James' descendants would always be opposed.

once more poured north and this time captured the entire province of Utrecht. The Dutch Grand Pensionary, John de Witt, was shortly afterwards lynched by an angry mob and William of Orange – later William III of England – became the Stadtholder of the Dutch Provinces.

The Dutch slowed the French advance by opening the sluices and flooding vast areas of their homeland. Meanwhile William successfully started to build an alliance once more against the French. England sought peace with the Dutch in 1674 with the Treaty of Westminster. Soon the Holy Roman Empire and Spain also moved against France. Sweden was soon France's lone ally, but she had her hands full as the Danes declared war on her (again). The Swedish victory at the Battle of Lund in 1676 put them back in their place.

Despite this mounting opposition, Louis' French forces gained more victories; during this period they gained a reputation of invincibility on the battlefield. Conde faced William of Orange's combined force of Austrians, Spaniards and Dutch at the Battle of Seneffe in August 1674. Despite being outnumbered the French emerged victorious. Turenne, also outnumbered, managed to defeat the Imperial forces of Raimondo Montecucculi at Turkheim and capture Alsace, and ravage the Palatinate. Unfortunately for the French, Turenne was killed by a cannonball at Salzbach in 1675, but not before he had helped France gain huge advantage in the war. With all the carnage being wrought on his new allies, Charles II of England wisely kept his forces out of the land war.

By 1678 the financial toll of the war was beginning to cause unrest in France, but Louis had managed make such gains that he entered negotiations at the Peace of Nijmegen in a very strong position. France had to return Maastricht to the Dutch, but Franche-Comté was now in French hands, along with other territory in the Spanish Netherlands. The Sun King was nearing the height of his powers and France was the dominant force in Europe; but Louis wanted more.

The League of Augsburg and the Glorious Revolution

The major advantage that Louis gained from the Peace of Nijmegen was that it split up the allies ranged against him. The Holy Roman Empire was threatened from the east by the Ottoman Turk expansion and England was happy to stay compliant with regular payments from the French treasury. Louis could pick on the rest individually, and started by annexing Strasbourg in 1681. The remainder of Alsace was next, followed by another invasion into the Spanish Netherlands and the capture of Luxembourg. As a warning to others he even had Genoa flattened for daring to support Spain; by 1684 France had bullied her opponents into submission.

Later in 1684 Louis revoked the Edict of Nantes, which had protected the rights of French Protestants – Huguenots – from persecution. Nearly 200,000 Huguenots left France and the surrounding Protestant countries once more had something to galvanise them into action. In addition to this the League of Augsburg was formed in 1686 which allied the Holy Roman Empire, Spain, Sweden, Bavaria, Saxony and The Palatinate against France. It wasn't just the

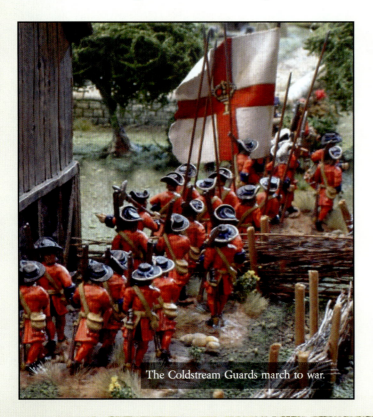
The Coldstream Guards march to war.

King Louis XIV of France – 1638-1715

Louis XIV, Le Roi Soleil (The Sun King) was one of the greatest European monarchs in history. Born in St. Germain-en-Laye in 1638, Louis became king at the age of four on the death of his father, Louis XIII. His mother, Anne of Austria, and Cardinal Mazarin ruled during his early years and these were troubled times for France, with civil unrest and rebellion rife.

With the death of Mazarin in 1661, Louis took control of the country and would reign with absolute power for a further 54 years. An advocate of the 'Divine Right of Kings', Louis set about dismantling feudalism and centralising power at his Versailles palace where he could control the nobility. He went on to become the 'ideal' of kingship, his rule conveying culture, greatness and glory. France was to become the number one power in Europe, its armies unbeaten for nearly 50 years. To this day his reign is the longest of any European king.

It wasn't until the turn of the 18th century that France's superiority was challenged, and Louis died shortly after the peace treaty of Utrecht ended the War of the Spanish Succession in 1715. He was succeeded by his great grandson, Louis XV, after surviving his own eldest son and grandson.

Protestants who were getting tired of Louis' bully-boy tactics. With the Imperial victory at the second Battle of Mohacs against the Ottoman Turks in 1687, the Empire was now in a better position to contribute fully to this alliance.

All of this Louis could probably have predicted and planned for; what he wasn't prepared for was the changing situation in England. Charles II had died in 1685 and was replaced by his even more compliant brother, James II. James was Catholic and committed to the peace with France. He had never been a popular king, having already put down one rebellion at the Battle of Sedgemoor. As he was over forty years old with no male heir, and with two Protestant daughters (Mary and Anne), the main political figures in England believed that a return to Protestant rule would be inevitable on his death. This made tolerable the pro-Catholic legislation he was determined to push through in the short term.

This situation changed completely with the birth of a son, James Francis Edward in 1688 as England was faced with a ruling Catholic dynasty. Leading noblemen turned to James' daughter Mary and her husband William of Orange to save England from 'popery and slavery'. The Glorious Revolution involved William landing in south-west England with 10,000 men, soon to be augmented as many of James' army went over to him. One of the leading army figures to offer his support to William was John Churchill, later the Duke of Marlborough.

James chose flight over fight, and was allowed to escape to France into the court of Louis XIV. Mary was crowned Queen of England with William as her King. William of Orange was now King William III and England had gone from a near vassal of Louis' France to a country ruled by his most implacable foe.

1682 - Louis XIV moves his court to Versailles.

War of the Grand Alliance 1688-1697

This conflict is also known as the Nine Years War, the War of Palatine Succession and the War of the League of Augsburg. William wasted no time in pulling together a new alliance to stop Louis' ambitions; this time Great Britain, Spain, the Holy Roman Empire, Savoy and a number of German states lined up against the French.

Louis' first aim was to keep William occupied away from the Continent, and for this reason he supplied the exiled James II with 6,000 men and transport to Ireland where he could meet up with the Duke of Tyrconnell. The idea was to raise the Catholic forces in Ireland to combine with James' loyalist troops and the French regiments to enable James to take back his kingdoms one at a time. In Scotland, James Graham of Claverhouse, Viscount Dundee raised the first Jacobite rising in support of James, and a combined Irish and Highlander force beat a Lowland Scots army at the Battle of Killiecrankie. Unfortunately for the Jacobites, Dundee was killed in the action and they suffered a number of defeats after this.

In Ireland William, supported by the Duke of Schomberg with a mix of English, Dutch, Danish and Huguenot troops, met James in battle for the first and only time at the Boyne in 1690. The outcome was victory for the Williamite forces over James' Jacobites. This effectively put an end to the rising in Scotland also. Having secured his throne, William made for the Continent once more.

There was a planned French invasion of England, but once again the English navy held strong and Louis had to be satisfied with the domination of his land forces. Dominate they certainly did, led by the brilliant Francois Henri de Montmorency-Bouteville, the Duke of Luxembourg. The war was characterised by a number of sieges with infrequent major battles; these usually went the way of the French who were living up to their invincible reputation. The battles of Fleurus and Steenkirk exemplified this pattern; however these were marginal victories and a major advantage could not be reached. Nice and Barcelona also

The Earl of Bath's regiment – not all English regiments were redcoats!

"I never can beat that cursed humpback," William of Orange said of him.

"How does he know I have a hump?" retorted Luxemburg, *"He has never seen my back."*

fell and Savoy was forced into a peace agreement, but new allies lined up against Louis, Sweden and Denmark even put aside their differences. In the background there was always William III working tirelessly against him.

The war spread to the New World as English and French colonists in North America entered the conflict in what is known there as King William's War.

After 1695, with the death of the Duke of Luxembourg, the French lost much of their impetus. By 1697 France had once more been run into the ground financially. At the Peace of Ryswick Louis had to return most of his gains and formally recognise William III as King of England. After nine years of war, with a standing army of over 300,000 men, he had gained almost nothing.

Once again Louis was looking to the future. With the imminent death – finally – of a childless Charles II of Spain, France used this peace to once more split up the allies. Very soon France and the Grand Alliance would be at war again, this time in the War of the Spanish Succession, but that is a story for another day.

Francois-Henri De Montmorency, Duc de Luxembourg - 1628-1695

Luxembourg was born to serve in the French army, and was widely regarded as The Great Conde's most able protégé. He gave over 50 years of his life in the service and made his name in the Dutch Wars of 1672-78. During the War of the Grand Alliance Luxembourg was given command of all French troops in the Spanish Netherlands where his instinctive leadership won spectacular victories over William of Orange at Steenkirk in 1692 and Neerwinden in 1693.

The deformity of his hunchback never slowed his advance in his military career nor in his private life which caused some scandal, his morals being constantly questioned. He was always a controversial figure whose friendships, lifestyle and cutting wit alienated many, including Louis XIV.

1683 - A massive Turkish army besieges Vienna until the siege is raised by the Poles and their German allies.

GRAND ALLIANCE ARMY 1690

This is an army much overlooked by wargamers, certainly in Britain, possibly due to the French armies being so dominant at the time. This is a shame as it is a fantastic army to collect and game with, full of colour and variety as you can represent regiments from England, Scotland, The Netherlands and Denmark amongst others.

They actually performed well and the army is full of reliable troops all round, with a few elite Guard regiments who really pack a punch. The Grand Alliance army has since fallen in the shadow of the slightly later Marlburian armies which receive far more press, notably due to the successes of the Duke of Marlborough who managed to end France's domination at the beginning of the 18th century. Hopefully this book will go some way to redress the balance a little.

Command Ratings

Overall Commander: Random Command Rating (see page 35) .... 40 Points

    Roll D6 for rating: 1: Command Rating 7, 2-5: Command Rating 8, 6: Command Rating 9

Infantry/Artillery Commander: Command Rating 8 .... 40 Points

Cavalry Commander: Command Rating 8 .... 40 Points

The Horse

Unit	Unit Type	Weapon	Hand-to-Hand Value	Shooting Value	Morale Value	Stamina	Special	Points
Heavy Cavalry & Guard Cavalry	Heavy Horse	Sword, Pistols	7	1	3+	3	Heavy Cavalry +1	51
Cavalry	Horse	Sword, Pistols	6	1	4+	3		37
Dragoons	Horse/ Battle Line Foot	Firelock	4	2	4+	3	Fire & Evade, Marauders	40

Scottish infantry dominate the allied centre.

1684 - Pope Innocent XI forms the Holy League with Venice, Poland and the Empire to drive the Ottoman Turks from Europe.

The Foot

Unit	Unit Type	Weapon	Hand-to-Hand Value	Shooting Value	Morale Value	Stamina	Special	Points
Foot Guards	Foot Battle Line	Musket	4 (6)	3	3+	4	Plug Bayonet, First Fire, Crack.	49

- Any unit can upgrade to Flintlocks @ 1 point per unit
- Add a company of Grenadiers. Unit gains 'Grenades' rule @ 1 points per unit
- Up to two units can be Dutch Guards. Gain 'Elite' and' Stubborn' special rules @ 11 points per unit
- Any unit can include a Pike Company @ 5 points per unit
- Maximum of three units in the army

Unit	Unit Type	Weapon	Hand-to-Hand Value	Shooting Value	Morale Value	Stamina	Special	Points
Grenadiers	Foot Battle Line	Musket	5 (7)	3	3+	4	Plug Bayonet, First Fire, Elite, Grenades	53

- Maximum of two units per army

Unit	Unit Type	Weapon	Hand-to-Hand Value	Shooting Value	Morale Value	Stamina	Special	Points
Line Infantry	Foot Battle Line	Musket	4 (6)	3	4+	3	Plug Bayonet, First Fire	37

- Any unit can upgrade to Flintlocks @ 1 point per unit
- Add a company of Grenadiers. Unit gains 'Grenades' rule @ 1 points per unit
- Any unit can include a Pike Company at5 points per unit
- Any unit can be 'Untested' for free
- Up to two units can be Guard Dragoons. Gain 'Crack' special rule @ 3 pts per unit
- All units may skirmish

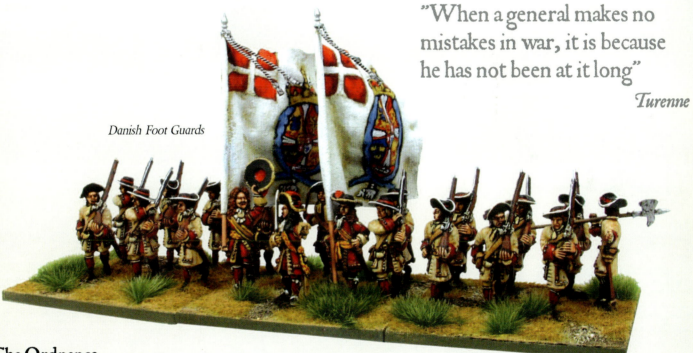

Danish Foot Guards

"When a general makes no mistakes in war, it is because he has not been at it long"

Turenne

The Ordnance

- Maximum of three artillery pieces per battalia

Unit	Unit Type	Weapon	Hand-to-Hand Value	Shooting Value	Morale Value	Stamina	Special	Points
Artillery	Ordnance	Various Cannon	1	3-2-1	4+	2		Varies

- Light Guns: 19 points
- Medium Guns: 23 points
- Heavy Guns: 27 points

Unit	Unit Type	Weapon	Hand-to-Hand Value	Shooting Value	Morale Value	Stamina	Special	Points
Siege Artillery	Ordnance	Mortar	1	2	5+	4		27

- Maximum of one mortar per army

1685 - In October, Louis XIV, the grandson of Henry IV, renounces the Edict of Nantes and declares Protestantism illegal.

FRENCH ARMY 1690

The French army of Louis XIV dominated the battlefields of Europe throughout the second half of the 17th century. Well equipped and comprehensively trained, all elements of this army can be relied upon to get the job done. The addition of foreign regiments, notably Irish and Swiss, along with the elite Guard units make this a very satisfying army to collect and game with.

An additional bonus for gamers is the fact that flag and uniform guides for the army are readily available. This is truly one of the most impressive looking armies on any tabletop.

Command Ratings

Overall Commander: Random Command Rating (see page 35) ....40 Points

Roll D6 for rating: 1: Command Rating 7, 2-5: Command Rating 8, 6: Command Rating 9

Infantry/Artillery Commander: Command Rating 9 ....60 Points

Cavalry Commander: Command Rating 8...40 Points

The Horse

Unit	Unit Type	Weapon	Hand-to-Hand Value	Shooting Value	Morale Value	Stamina	Special	Points
Maison du Roi Cavalry	Heavy Horse	Sword, Pistols	8	1	3+	3	Heavy Cavalry +D3	53

- Any unit can be downgraded to 'Small' @ -8 pts
- Maximum three units in the army

Unit	Unit Type	Weapon	Hand-to-Hand Value	Shooting Value	Morale Value	Stamina	Special	Points
Cavalry	Horse	Sword, Pistols	7	1	4+	3		39

Unit	Unit Type	Weapon	Hand-to-Hand Value	Shooting Value	Morale Value	Stamina	Special	Points
Dragoons	Horse/Foot	Firelock	4	2	4+	3	Fire & Evade, Marauders	40

- Up to two units can be Guard Dragoons. Gain 'Stubborn' special rule @ 5 pts each
- All units may skirmish

Here be dragoons! French cavalry drive off the Dutch.

1685 - The Monmouth Rebellion is crushed at Sedgemoor.

The Foot

Unit	Unit Type	Weapon	Hand-to-Hand Value	Shooting Value	Morale Value	Stamina	Special	Points
Foot Guards	Foot Battle Line	Musket	4 (6)	3	3+	4	Plug Bayonet, First Fire, Elite, Stubborn	56

- Any unit can upgrade to Flintlocks @ 1 point per unit
- Any unit can include a Pike Company @ 5 points per unit
- Maximum of three units in the army

Unit	Unit Type	Weapon	Hand-to-Hand Value	Shooting Value	Morale Value	Stamina	Special	Points
Grenadiers	Foot Battle Line	Musket	5 (7)	3	4+	4	Plug Bayonet, First Fire, Elite, Grenades	49

- Any unit can be downgraded to 'Small' @ -8 pts

Unit	Unit Type	Weapon	Hand-to-Hand Value	Shooting Value	Morale Value	Stamina	Special	Points
Line Infantry	Foot Battle Line	Musket	4 (6)	3	4+	3	Plug Bayonet, First Fire	37

- Any unit can upgrade to Flintlocks @ 1 point per unit
- Any unit can include a Pike Company @ 5 points per unit
- Add a company of Grenadiers. Unit gains 'Grenades' rule @ 1 point per unit
- Any unit can be 'Steady' @ 5 points per unit
- Any unit can be 'Untested' @ 0 points per unit

French infantry battalia deployed for battle.

The Ordnance

- Maximum of three artillery pieces per battalia

Unit	Unit Type	Weapon	Hand-to-Hand Value	Shooting Value	Morale Value	Stamina	Special	Points
Artillery	Ordnance	Various Cannon	1	3-2-1	4+	2		Varies

- Light Guns: 19 points
- Medium Guns: 23 points
- Heavy Guns: 27 points

Unit	Unit Type	Weapon	Hand-to-Hand Value	Shooting Value	Morale Value	Stamina	Special	Points
Siege Artillery	Ordnance	Mortar	1	2	5+	4		27

- Maximum of one mortar per army

1686 - The Dominion of New England is formed.

BATTLE OF WALCOURT
25TH AUGUST 1689

This scenario is based on the Battle of Walcourt, fought on 25th August 1689 in an area of Flanders now part of Belgium. Walcourt was one of the first large engagements of a conflict known variously as the War of the Grand Alliance, The War of the League of Augsburg and the Nine Years War. It lasted from 1688 to 1697. The war was an extension of previous wars between Louis XIV's France and other powerful nations in Europe. France and Louis had ideas of territorial expansion in various directions. Friction along the borders of his kingdom and within France's wider sphere of influence often resulted in war. In this particularly turbulent phase, William of Orange (now King William III of England) headed a powerful coalition which drew together forces from Holland, England, Scotland, Denmark, Brandenburg, Sweden, Spain, Portugal, Bavaria and the mighty Habsburg

Empire. This group, known as the League of Augsburg or Grand Alliance, was all about containing Louis XIV and his megalomaniacal ambitions to rule the world!

Walcourt is different in several ways from other battles of the period. It is an encounter engagement with both armies deploying from marching formations straight into combat. It opened with a series of smaller encounters in which advanced guard contingents from the French army bumped into forward units of the Alliance army. There were equal chances

1687 - Isaac Newton publishes Philosophiæ Naturalis Principia Mathematica.

for both sides to win, the forces were relatively modest by the standards of the period and some famous regiments took part in the action. Altogether, a nice attractive little package for wargaming!

This scenario is concerned more with a variation on a theme as opposed to a straight refight, but it is necessary to provide a very brief summary of the historical version of events before you begin to lay out the troops and decide how you want to handle it.

The Historical outcome of Walcourt

The French commander, Le Duc d'Humières, moved north into the Spanish Netherlands (now known as Belgium) with 24 battalions of Foot and 75 squadrons of

Horse (roughly 24,000 men). He camped to the south of Walcourt on 24th August. Walcourt is near Charleroi in southern Belgium and will be well known to those interested in Napoleon's 100 Days Campaign of 1815.

Overall command of the 35,000 Grand Alliance troops in Flanders was given to the 69-year-old Prince Georg Friedrich of Waldeck. They were positioned to the north of Walcourt as the French army approached. The British contingent in the army (roughly 8,000 men) was commanded by the Earl of Marlborough, a man not wholly trusted by his new Dutch overlords who suspected him of continuing loyalty to the deposed King James II.

The new Dutch King of England, William III was doubtful about the quality of the English soldiers in his army. When compared to his native Dutch, the English clearly lacked organisation, administrative discipline, and an established logistics tail to support their combat troops. Waldeck had some sympathy for his new boys and admired John Churchill's efforts at professionalisation, but did comment on their un soldierly manner, shabby clothing and poor footwear! This was no spit and polish Victorian parade ground army, but rather a sloppy, poorly dressed fledgling force which didn't even march in time. It did prove very shortly that it could fight!

On 25 August, foraging parties from Waldeck's army supported by 600 English infantry of Colonel Robert Hodges' Regiment (later 16th Foot) were sent into the area around Walcourt. The French discovered them and drove the foraging parties back on Hodges outposts about two miles south of the town. Hodges' men were able to hold the French vanguard at bay, gather in the foragers and fall back on a mill nearer the town. Just before midday, Marlborough had come up and was surveying the scene. Hodges, taking fire from enemy guns, was ordered to withdraw to high ground east of Walcourt where the main Allied force was forming up from its march from camp.

Battle rages around the church.

D'Humières now focused on Walcourt, which was held by a battalion-strength garrison. The ground was difficult, but the defences were in poor condition. Several attacks were made, but growing losses made it a desperate business for the French. Humières sent a detachment of the *Gardes Françaises* to try and burn down the gates. This did not work and the town was secured by Brigadier-General Thomas Tollemache, colonel of the Coldstream Guards who brought his regiment together with some German Foot into action in the early afternoon. The French commander broadened the front, throwing uncoordinated attacks against the enemy right beyond Walcourt. A counter-attack by Waldeck around 6pm launched the Dutch under Slangenburg against their left and Marlborough against their right. The English used a combination of Foot and Horse during this phase. The French buckled but did not break, and Villars launched a counter-attack with his own Horse which checked the pursuit. This is not surprising as during this period the French cavalry was generally considered superior to its opponents both in quality and tactics.

The disengagement was controlled, but the French had been thwarted in their opportunistic enterprise. No attempt was made to follow up by Waldeck. For a few days after the two armies glowered at each other with desultory artillery exchanges being the only activity.

So with the historical Walcourt in perspective let's turn to our game. Already there are possibilities. Walcourt can be fought in stages:

1. Hodges's foragers being discovered by the French advanced guard and a rear guard type scenario fought with small forces, perhaps even as a skirmish.

2. Attacks against a small garrison in Walcourt by French Foot, including a detachment of the legendary *Gardes Françaises* in their blue uniforms.

3. The developing army level action on both flanks, with Walcourt in the centre

4. The retreat and rearguard covering action by Villars' Horse against Dutch and English Horse and Foot.

Alternatively you could roll it into a large game incorporating all of the above. We chose to focus on the encounter battle, option 3.

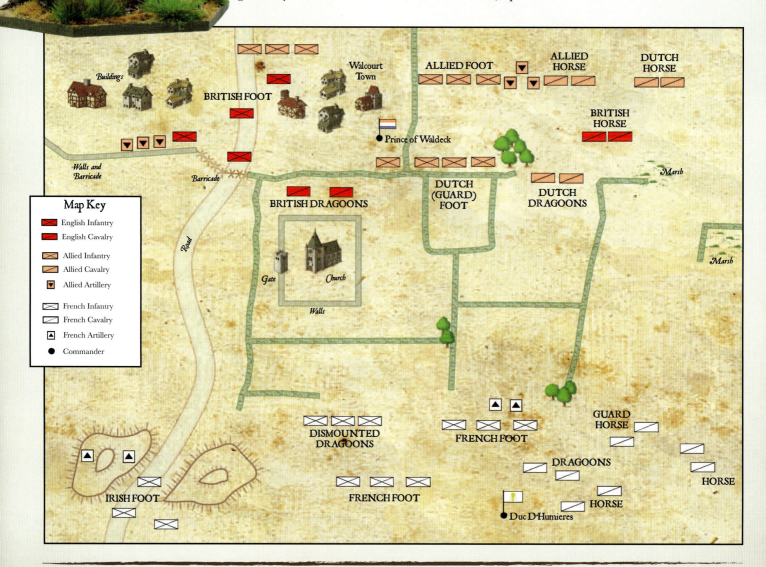

1689 - The Battle of Killiekrankie; MacKay's are overwhelmed by the Highland charge.

French Army

Duc d'Humières
Army Commander, Command Rating 7

1ST BRIGADE (PICE NO. 1)
Command Rating 9
- 3 battalions of French Foot (one may be Gardes Françaises)

2ND BRIGADE (PICE NO. 2)
Command Rating 8
- 3 battalions of French Foot

3RD BRIGADE (PICE NO. 3)
Command Rating 8
- 3 battalions of Irish Foot

4TH BRIGADE (PICE NO. 4)
Command Rating 8
- 3 battalions of dismounted dragoons

1ST HORSE BRIGADE (PICE NO. 5)
Command Rating 9
- 2 large regiments of Horse

2ND HORSE BRIGADE (PICE NO. 6)
Command Rating 9
- 2 regiments of Horse
  (one may be Maison du Roi)

3RD HORSE BRIGADE (PICE NO. 7)
Command Rating 9
- 2 regiments of Horse

4TH HORSE BRIGADE (PICE NO. 8)
Command Rating 8
- 2 regiments of Dragoons

ARTILLERY (PICE NO. 9)
Command Rating 8
- 4 field artillery pieces

Régiment Piedmont lead the French assault.

Grand Alliance Army

PRINCE OF WALDECK
Army Commander, Command rating 7

1ST BRIGADE (PICE NO. 1)
Command Rating 8
- 4 battalions of British Foot

2ND BRIGADE (PICE NO. 2)
Command Rating 9
- 4 battalions of Dutch (including 2 Guards)

3RD BRIGADE (PICE NO. 3)
Command Rating 8
- 3 battalions of Dutch or Subsidy Foot

1ST HORSE BRIGADE (PICE NO. 4)
Command Rating 8
- 2 regiments of British Horse

2ND HORSE BRIGADE (PICE NO. 5)
Command Rating 8
- 2 regiments of Dutch or Subsidy Horse

3RD HORSE BRIGADE (PICE NO. 6)
Command Rating 8
- 2 regiments of Dutch or Subsidy Horse

4TH HORSE BRIGADE (PICE NO. 7)
Command Rating 8
- 2 regiments of Dutch or Subsidy Dragoons

5TH HORSE BRIGADE (PICE NO. 8)
Command Rating 8
- 2 regiments of British Dragoons

ARTILLERY (PICE NO. 9)
Command Rating 8
- 3 field artillery pieces

ARTILLERY (PICE NO. 10)
Command Rating 8
- 3 light artillery pieces

The orange colours of the Dutch Gard te Voet, as usual, in the thick of the action.

1691 - The Battle of Aughrim, William III's troops defeat the Jacobites in Ireland.

Scenario Special Mechanisms

Arrival timing and location

As this was an encounter battle we used a few scenario specific mechanisms to provide unpredictability to our game. Firstly we numbered each brigade in both armies. Secondly, we divided the table baseline of both armies into six sections each two feet in length and labelled those A to F. We used dice (D10, discounting 10 for the French, and any previously rolled number) to determine who, when and where fresh brigades arrived. This can really change the whole shape of a game and actually makes the same scenario play differently every time.

From turn 1 each commander diced to determine which brigade was arriving and then used a D6 to determine on which two foot length of baseline it would turn up. This process continued each turn until all brigades and artillery had arrived.

Initial set up

In keeping with the historical battle the Alliance army was permitted one brigade in and around Walcourt as the game commenced.

Imbalance of forces

Eventually the French will be outnumbered, as the ratio in the historical battle was 1.45 to 1 in favour of the Allies. To counter this imbalance and make things a little more exciting, we staggered the arrival of the Alliance reinforcements by only allowing them to bring on brigades on alternate turns for the first six turns. This meant the French players had more troops earlier and so had to move fast. This helps simulate the element of surprise.

Troop nationalities

Apart from British regiments the army was composed of many nationalities. At least half of the rest of the regiments in the Army of the Grand Alliance should be Dutch. The remainder could also be Dutch or Subsidy troops. Subsidy troops were basically legitimised mercenaries. They were officially raised units from other countries who were hired out by their rulers to other nations at war. The Dutch did not have enough men of their own but had plenty of cash and so hired Swedes, Danes, Germans from small principalities, Brandenburgers (Prussians), Swiss, Scots (not in the pay of the Scottish Government) and many more. Take your pick if you have a favourite! In an era famous for unscrupulous and larger than life personalities such a practice was both common and lucrative.

The French army should in the main, be composed of native French regiments. For some colour, you may include a few Swiss, Italian, Walloon or German regiments. We chose to field a couple of Irish regiments, which is of course totally inaccurate at this early stage of the war. The Irish only appeared in numbers from mid-1690, and then in far larger numbers from 1691, but we love the Irish so they were in! We deliberately have not provided a full historical order of battle to allow gamers to use whatever units they have in their collections.

Troop ratings

We have seen in the historical account that the Dutch were not confident in the abilities of their English allies. Around 23% of the Alliance army was composed of British troops (either Scots or English as the concept of the United Kingdom was still 18 years in the future). The British should not be given quality ratings that are too high. Even their Guards units should not be rated better than +4 for morale. Some special rules can offset the British lack of experience and get them performing a little better and details of how to do this can be found in the Special rules section of this scenario. The entire army including the British should be treated as fairly standard regular troops. One unit in each brigade could be upgraded, and to add a little spice perhaps one unit in each of two Foot brigades and one Horse brigade could be downgraded to a 5+ morale rating. Alternatively the *Untested* rule could be applied.

French cavalry should be given an edge in close combat. Their tactics and showing during the period merits this adjustment. It is a picture that was somewhat reversed with the superiority passing to the Grand Alliance during the War of the Spanish Succession.

Guard quality units should be restricted to about 10% of each army.

Special Rules

There is an extensive special rules section in the book. I have chosen to highlight some which I believe will capture the flavour of the period and the context and nature of the battle at Walcourt.

Scots/English Regiments

The British approach appeared to excite and perplex their Allies in equal measure. Somewhat inexperienced and lacking in martial discipline, but aggressive, brave and keen to fight, they were every commander's nightmare… unpredictable!

Eager should apply to all British units. I personally would also apply the *Freshly Raised* rule to all units except British Guards and the senior line regiments such as Schomberg's. *Crack* should be given to the Guards and the senior line units of both Foot and Horse if present. *Pike Company* can be given to any Foot unit except Fuzileers or Dismounted Dragoons. *Plug Bayonet* should be given to up to half of the Foot, with priority to the older or more prestigious formations.

If you are feeling generous apply the *Valiant* special rule to half of the British regiments.

Other Grand Alliance regiments

The Dutch Guards should be *Stubborn*. All other units should have *Plug Bayonet* and one battalion per brigade can use the *Crack* special rule. Any Danish or French Huguenot battalions cannot use the *Pike Company* rule.

1692 - The Battle of Steenkirk, the French triumph over William's combined forces.

Guards

During this period the Guard units of every army were used differently from the Guards in later periods. We are used to the concept of Napoleon's Old Guard being kept as a precious battlefield reserve, but during the Nine Years War the Guards were often used in the forefront of the assault. Louis the XIV used his 10 battalions of Guards (6 French and 4 Swiss) as a hammer with which to smash down enemy defences and they were very good at it!

The Dutch Guards (Gard te Voet) were legendary and led the assault over the river Boyne on 1st July 1690. The English King's Footguards, Coldstream and Scotch Footguards were always in the front line, as were the

famous Garden til Fods (Danish Footguards). A Guard regiment can provide a centrepiece to your army. They were not however always spit and polish soldiers. The Dutch Guards were known for their battle worn and scruffy appearance!

One unit of Horse which is not British can use *Heavy Cavalry* representing either a Dutch or German Cuirassier regiment.

French Regiments

The French army was very large and generally professional and of good quality. French Guards (Gardes Francaises or Gardes Suisses) should be *Stubborn*. I would also apply the *Reliable* and *Superbly Drilled* rules. All French infantry should have *Plug Bayonet* and any or all can use *Pike Company* except Fuzileers if used. One battalion per brigade can use *Crack* to represent the senior unit.

The *Marauder* rule for dragoons should not apply to either army and the *First Fire* rule should apply to all Foot of both sides.

Battle Report

The battle pitted Adrian Howe as Prince Waldeck against Bob Talbot as Duc d'Humières. In keeping with history Ade chose to deploy his British brigade in the environs of Walcourt. This was the sole formation on the table at the commencement of turn 1. Two battalions took position in the town rather as Tollemache's men had done. The others stood back as support, north of Walcourt.

His first arrivals were two brigades of Horse which appeared on his left flank. He attempted to use these aggressively against an almost identical number of French Horse which had also appeared in the first couple of turns directly opposite. Both sides moved down into lower ground between the deploying armies. Despite the fact that two of the Dutch regiments were Guard units, The Black Dragoons of van Eppinger and William's Gardes du Corps no less, the French made headway in the initial impact. The Black Dragoons, a strong regiment of good quality were pushed back by the French Dragoon regiment of Artois, supported by that of La Reine. William's crack Lifeguard

was then committed to stem the flow and cut through the enemy dragoons, scattering them every which way. Alas, as is often the case with cavalry, they went too far! Their pursuit left them under the very muzzles of enormous guns of position which the French had just dragged into their centre to anchor the developing deployment. The guns spoke and the elite Horse were cut to shreds. We winced as we imagined the reaction of King William on hearing the despatches read out to him. We hoped the officer in command of the Gardes du Corps was fortunate enough to have died gloriously at the head of his regiment, as a fate worse than death would undoubtedly be his if he had survived! It must be said that all of this action was punctuated by an extremely high level of blundering. This was not, I would say, out of keeping with some of the military behaviour of the age, but Bob and Ade seemed to elevate blundering to an art form!

Whilst this ferocious cavalry scrap was occurring, newly arrived French dragoons deployed in the dismounted role, were engaged in an assault on the walled churchyard of Walcourt. The English would have to do something about that! Help was at hand. By now a brigade of the utmost quality had arrived to brace Waldeck's centre. To the east of Walcourt, two battalions of the legendary *Gard te Voet* (Dutch Footguards) had arrived, together with another two fine regiments; Brandenburg and Waldeck-Pyrmont. These seasoned units deployed quickly and confidently in order to repulse an assembling attack by six battalions of French and Irish Foot who stood south of the town.

The drums rolled and the grey and red ranks of the French and Irish advanced to meet the blue wall of the Dutch Guards. In the fields around Walcourt the infantry battle raged and in an effort to raise the stakes, Bob launched a battalion of converged grenadiers into an attack on the churchyard. Lobbing their grenades and charging forward they managed to throw back the Royal Fuzileers and make some headway into Walcourt. This was a major achievement for the French and the high watermark of their attack.

1692 - The Salem Witch trials begin in Massachusetts.

The cavalry melee to the east of the town continued sporadically, but with little advantage being gained and the butcher's bill rising relentlessly. It was all good fun, but no real breakthrough came for either side.

The final French push was to be in the centre against the powerful Dutch brigade containing the Footguards. Brigade Languedoc was given the honour to deliver the attack, supported by Brigade Piemont. Under intense pressure the Dutch held, despite mounting losses. D'Humières added a little extra to the attack, having moved a regiment of the Maison du Roi cavalry – the finest in Europe – into a position flanking the brave Dutch. Under fire from two battalions to their front, the 2nd battalion were not able to face left as the red-coated Maison Rouge thundered into their exposed flank and trampled them down. This charge rolled up the entire battalion, which was destroyed in the melee. The loss of such an iconic unit might have demoralised a lesser general, but recognising that now was the moment to demonstrate true fighting spirit, Waldeck pulled an ace from the hat. Walcourt was under direct threat and the Coldstream Guards coolly advanced through the streets to bayonet charge the French grenadiers who had been moving steadily through the town since turn 4. The Englishmen were true and steady and won the day. The town was Waldeck's once again and the battle was over as the French were too disorganised to recover, regroup and mount another attack before darkness.

Other rule systems

Some may find it a little odd that I was asked to contribute a scenario for this book bearing in mind I wrote *Beneath the Lily Banners* which is specifically for the period 1660-1721, a time frame into which this battle falls dead centre. It was in fact a great opportunity to compare mechanisms, gameplay and results, and I thoroughly enjoyed the experience. BLB's scope is focused on the 61 years between the end of the English Commonwealth and the end of the Great Northern

War and its mechanics specifically cater for the type of troop types and ratios so characteristic of this era. Having played the battle several times using BLB, I was curious to see whether the outcome would be similar. The players apart from myself, had little experience of BLB and so, using *Pike & Shotte*, they made the moves they thought best under the circumstances confronting them. Although in detail the mechanics are fundamentally different in several areas, the actual result of our game was close to that achieved with BLB and to the historical result. Strangely in our game, some of the historic incidents were performed on the tabletop by the historic units and at the right time! Considering the arrivals and positions were randomised, this was quite special! That the final charge went to the Coldstream Guards and within the environs of Walcourt provided a very fitting end to a great day's gaming.

Getting the flavour of this war

This battle occurred during a time of rapid and fundamental military change. The troop ratios used by the combatants were no accident and so to obtain the right feel in a wargame it is important to get the ratios as close as possible to real life. Much more cavalry was employed in proportion to infantry than in Napoleonic warfare. Try and obtain a ratio of one cavalry model to two infantry models. If you don't, battles in the period may look very pretty but are likely to degenerate into very predictable, linear fire fights where attrition governs the outcome. If you get the correct balance the cavalry will provide the fluidity and the surprises. It is important to recognise that the pike was being phased out but remained relatively common and numerous on the field of battle. Some countries had dropped it early such as Denmark and Bavaria, but the French, English and Dutch retained the pike for ten years or more following Walcourt. A debate rages on as to when the pike finally disappeared from British regiments, with some knowledgeable enthusiasts insisting it was still in active service beyond Blenheim. Infantry formations should be restricted to lines or march columns with no other formations being used. It is just not historically correct.

Credits

The terrain for Walcourt was custom built by Adrian Howe, who is well known for his dramatic battlescapes. The troops are painted by and in the collection of Barry Hilton with contributions by Bob Talbot. Barry created the scenario. Photographs are by Barry as is the text of the scenario.

Note

Although several new units were specifically painted for this scenario many of the regiments are part of a collection which has been seen on the UK wargames circuit since 1990. Some of these veteran regiments have over 100 battles under their belts and service records, performance and casualties stats have been meticulously maintained over 21 years of gaming. It's that kind of period, once it gets its hooks into you…

Dramatis Personae

This is truly an era of larger than life personalities. In charge of the English contingent at the battle of Walcourt was none other than John Churchill, at that time Earl, not Duke, of Marlborough. He will have some positive impact on the performance of units under his command. Colonel Hodges was also particularly cool and calm under pressure in the early stages of the battle. Waldeck, although victor at Walcourt was to be decisively beaten and humiliated less than a year later at Fleurus and so may be portrayed as a doddering old soldier well past his prime. He did remember, signally fail to follow up his victory by doing nothing after the French withdrawal. Villars, the French Horse General, was full of vim and so could have a positive effect on French cavalry. His rearguard action was well handled.

1693 - The Battle of Neerwinden/Landen, the French defeat the Williamite forces.

Points System & Army Lists

The more observant readers (or those who have been looking for such things) will have noticed that each army listed within this book has contained points for each troop type. Many wargames rules utilise the concept of 'points values' to select competing armies. This is especially common with rules intended for use in tournaments in which a large number of players bring their armies to battle against a variety of opponents over the course of a day or a weekend.

While these rules did not set out with such aims in mind, the play testing period and the feedback received made it clear that enough gamers wanted a system to ensure that competing armies start off on a more-or-less equal footing.

Hopefully this will not deter those worthy souls who simply want a game where no such system is needed. Sir Thomas Fairfax certainly never asked King Charles how many points he was bringing to Naseby!

All the lists included throughout the book have been put together using the following points system; this should give you a standard format should you wish to create lists of your own. I'm certainly not claiming that the lists are flawless, so feel free to make any amendments you wish to make your own games more enjoyable.

Commanders

The actual worth of commanders tends to vary depending on the size and nature of the battalias they are commanding. Having one extra or one fewer commander than your opponent can make a big difference. However, having too many commanders is futile as they will soon run out of troops to command.

COMMAND RATINGS	
Comand Rating	**Points**
6	10
7	20
8	40
9	60
10	80
Variable	40

The variable command rating is reserved for Army Generals in the lists whose command rating is determined by rolling a D6. Some armies are more likely to get better leaders for 40 points, but that's war.

Lord Percy's Royalist foot prepare to storm the breach as Howard's cavalry offer support.

1694 - A treasure fleet of 13 ships is lost off Gibraltar with the loss of approximately 1,200 lives.

Infantry

The base value for an English Civil War musketeer unit is 27 points, with the following fighting qualities and no special abilities.

Unit	Unit Type	Weapon	Hand-to-Hand Value	Shooting Value	Morale Value	Stamina	Special	Points
Musketeers	Foot Battle Line	Matchlock Muskets	3	2	5+	3		27

This points value is arrived at by adding the values of its fighting abilities using the list below:

Hand-to-Hand Combat: 1 point per pip

Shooting: 1 point per pip if range up to 12"
2 points per pip if range up to 18"
3 points per pip if range up to 24"

Morale: 4 points per pip

Stamina: 4 points per pip

Values for 'Large' and 'Small' variant units can be arrived at by totting up the values as appropriate and adjusting for any special rules as noted later.

Cavalry

The base value for an English Civil War cavalry unit is 41 points, with the following fighting qualities and no special abilities.

Unit	Unit Type	Weapon	Hand-to-Hand Value	Shooting Value	Morale Value	Stamina	Special	Points
Cavalry	Horse	Sword, Pistols	8	1	4+	3		41

This points value is arrived at by adding the values of its fighting abilities using the list below:

Hand-to-Hand Combat: 2 points per pip

Shooting: 1 point per pip if range up to 12"
2 points per pip if range up to 18"
3 points per pip if range up to 24"

Morale: 4 points per pip

Stamina: 4 points per pip

Values for 'Large' and 'Small' variant units can be arrived at by totting up the values as appropriate and adjusting for any special rules as noted later.

Artillery

The base value for standard medium cannon is 21 points

Unit	Unit Type	Weapon	Hand-to-Hand Value	Shooting Value	Morale Value	Stamina	Special	Points
Medium Artillery	Ordinance	Medium Cannon	1	3-2-1	5+	2		21

This points value is arrived at by adding the values of its fighting abilities using the list below:

Hand-to-Hand Combat: 1 point per pip

Shooting: 4 points per pip if range is up to 12"
8 points per pip if range is up to 24"
12 points per pip if range is up to 36"
16 points per pip if range is up to 48"
20 points per pip if range is over 48"

Morale: 2 points per pip

Stamina: 2 points per pip

SPECIAL RULES

The special rules column indicates which useful rules, if any, have been applied to that entry, apart from useful rules for weapons, which are included in the unit type description.

Rule	Summary of Rule	Points cost
Bad War	Re-roll missed Combat Attacks against Landsknechts	Free
Bows	+1 Morale Saves; Cannot offer closing fire	+2 points per pip Shortbow +1 point per pip
Brave	Shaken Units Rally without an Order	+5 points
Caracole	Cannot countercharge enemy cavalry	Free
Clansmen	Cannot offer support in combat	-1 point
Crack	Re-Roll one failed Morale Save if you currently have no Casualties	Morale 3+ − +4 points Morale 4+ − +3 points Morale 5+ − +2 points Morale 6+ − +1 point
Crossbows	Cannot offer Closing Fire	+2 points per pip
Double-Handed Infantry Weapons	-1 Morale Save	+2 points
Dragoons	Free mount or dismount move; Fire and evade; Count as skirmish cavalry when mounted, skirmish infantry when dismounted	Free
Eager	Free move on charge order	+3 points
Elite	Overcome Disorder Dice Roll	+2 points per pip, (Standard 4+ Elite:+6 points)
Fanatics	Morale Save +1 Until Shaken	+5 points
Ferocious Charge	Re-Roll missed Combat Attacks following a Charge	+3 points Infantry, +5 points Cavalry
Fire & Evade	Can give closing fire and then evade when charged	+2 points
Firelocks	Short range extended to 12"	+1 point
First Fire	+1 Dice on First Shot	+1 point
Freshly Raised	Variable effect – see page 105	-3 points
Galloper	Must countercharge if able to; standard move of 12" as if Light Cavalry; will always engage the enemy on a sweeping advance where able to.	- 2 points
Grenades	Enemy ignores all morale bonuses for cover when engaged in combat	+1 point
Heavy Cavalry +1	+1 Combat Result on a Charge	+4 points
Heavy Cavalry +D3	+D3 Combat Result on a Charge	+8 points
Hedgehog	No flanks or rear; combined formation of pike and shotte elements Immovable; all shooting units in the hedgehog have shooting value of 1	Free
Lancers	-1/-2 Morale Save on the Charge	+5 points
Large Unit	+1 Shooting Value (if the unit has ranged weapons); +2 Hand-to-Hand; +1 Stamina; May ignore disorder by taking one damage (unless this causes the unit to be shaken)	Shooting unit +8 points Non-shooting unit +6 points

1696 - Peter the Great becomes sole Czar of Russia.

Marauders	Ignore Distance Modifiers for Command	+5 points
Mercenary	Will quit the battle if a Rally test is failed when Shaken	-3 points
Militia	No Move on Equal Command Roll	-3 points
Pikes	Can form a hedgehog formation with non pike units of same battalia; Cavalry receive no combat bonuses when fighting an ordered pike unit; Pike unit gets double combat value when fighting charging cavalry	Free
Pike Company	Cavalry receive no combat bonuses when fighting a unit with a pike company that is ordered; the unit containing a pike company receives double combat value when fighting charging cavalry	+5 points
Plug Bayonet	+2 Hand-to-Hand value; +1 Combat result against enemy Warband infantry; once used, cannot fire for remainder of battle	+ 2 points
Rabble	Every unit must receive a separate command; Cannot act on a battalia or group order	-5 points
Reliable	+1 Command	+4 points
Sharp Shooters	Re-Roll one Missed Shot	+3 points
Small Unit	-1 Shooting Value (only if the unit has ranged weapons) -2 Hand-to-Hand; -1 Stamina	Shooting unit -8 points, Non-shooting unit -6 points
Steady	Passes First Break Test	+5 points
Stubborn	Re-Roll one Failed Morale Save	+5 points
Superbly Drilled	Free Move	+5 points
Swordsmen	+D3 Combat result against enemy infantry	+4 points
Terrifying Charge	Charged Enemy must take a Break Test	+5 points
Tough Fighters	Re-Roll one Combat Hit	Infantry +1 point Cavalry +2 points
Untested	Randomise Stamina	Free
Valiant	One Free Break Test Re-Roll	+3 points
Wavering	Break Test when you take a Casualty	Reduction equal to double the unit's Stamina value

Dutch infantry of the Grand Alliance.

1697 - The Treaty of Ryswick is signed to end both the Nine Years War and King William's War.

Using smaller and larger models

As we have made plain throughout our book, the *Pike & Shotte* game was created to allow us to use our own collections of 28mm size models. This is a nominal size for models based on an average height for a man of 28mm – although many models advertised as 28mm are actually larger. This means that not all models from different manufacturers can be used together, even though they might all be described as 28mm. Most wargamers have their favourite manufacturer and will choose to build their collections around that manufacturer's offerings.

28mm sized models may be our choice, but they are not the only choice by any means. It is possible to buy wargames models of various sizes or scales ranging from the very smallest 6mm sized or (1/300) through to traditional 54mm tall 'toy soldiers'. The most popular intermediate size is 15mm metal miniatures which have the advantage of being individually cheaper than larger models and allowing games to be fought over smaller tables. 20mm is the nominal size of 1/72 scale plastic models offered by companies such as HäT, Airfix, Revell and many others. At one time soft plastic figures were widely and gladly used by wargamers, which makes it rather strange that they are not more popular today. The variety of soft plastic models available to those willing to make use of them is far greater than in days of yore when Airfix models were eagerly bought by pioneer wargamers. 30mm is a size that was once popular in the early days of wargaming, and models tend to be far more slender than contemporary 28mm equivalents which are about the same height. However, they'll pass alongside 28mm models easily enough. 40mm is an old fashioned toy soldier size – the Britains' 'B' series size – a sort of economy version of the classic 54mm toy soldier, which is itself the largest practical size for wargames.

If you want to use Pike & Shotte to play games with smaller sized models – 5mm, 10mm, 15mm or 20mm being the most readily available – then we'd suggest either halving all ranges and distances or playing in centimetres rather than inches. In all cases it is the space occupied by the units that matters most – and the 'halve distances' rules assumes units will have a typical frontage of about half that of a standard 28mm sized unit – so about 120mm rather than 240mm. This does allow games to take place on smaller tables, which might be an important consideration for some players. We have tried this out with 10mm models using centimetres and can report very satisfactory results.

With 20mm models, you can pretty much play the rules as written if you prefer and this does give you some leeway for increasing the size of the units to fit the 28mm unit footprint. This is an option for all smaller sized models – you can always make your units bigger and play the rules as written. This actually brings the ranges and movement more closely in line with the figure scale. If you want to recreate an English Civil War battalia with 600 or so figures, then it is certainly possible with 6mm figures!

For models larger than 28mm, it is recommended that players reduce the number of models in each unit so that the units are about the same size as described in the game. All distances and measurements can then be made without any further

40mm English Elizabethan troops during the Irish campaign.

Mrs Miggins' pies – worth fighting for...

1698 - The London palace of Whitehall is destroyed by fire.

15mm Polish-Lithuanian Commonwealth army (Fire & Sword range).

15mm Ottoman Janissaries from Wargamer's Fire & Sword range.

The Polish charge a Cossack camp (15mm Fire & Sword range).

modifications. Although the authors have not attempted games with 54mm models we have pressed a few 40mm toy-style models into service without any trouble.

With large models such as this, units tend to look better when the number of ranks is reduced by about half that described in the game. This is because 40mm sized models are not much wider than 28mm models – but are very much longer. This is especially true of cavalry. As a result, deeper columns become very unwieldy, but this is easily overcome by halving ranks. This means that lines will be one rank deep, attack columns two or three ranks, and march columns as deep as possible.

With 40mm models of the toy soldier type, it seems rather odd to fasten the models to bases – it just doesn't seem to fit with the traditional style of the models somehow. Because the units

are built up of far fewer models, it is no great hardship to move the models individually, so we can do without bases altogether if we wish. Of course, it will be necessary to arrange the ranks so that units occupy roughly the same width, but the game easily accommodates a little variation in unit width so this need not cause any problems – apart from the models falling over. But if you enjoy the aesthetic of the 'old school' toy solder, the opportunity to line them all up again will doubtlessly appeal.

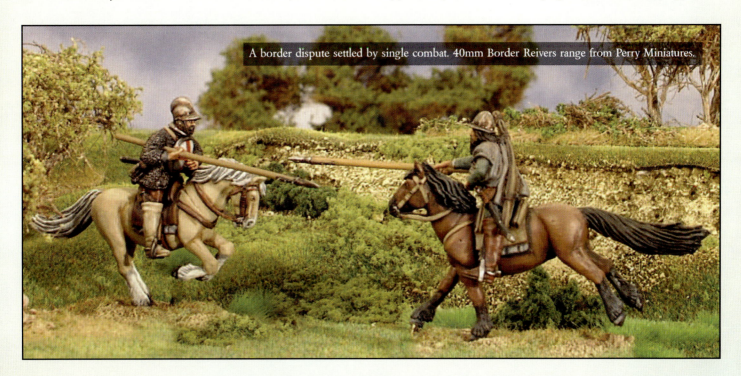

A border dispute settled by single combat. 40mm Border Reivers range from Perry Miniatures.

QUICK REFERENCE SHEET

SEQUENCE OF PLAY

In a full turn both sides take a player turn as follows:

Command
• Check Battalia Morale >half lost or shaken,
• Rally Elite
• Initiative moves (within 6" of enemy)
• Other moves (Proximity Rule 12"),
• Rally, "Follow-me!"

Shooting
• Shoot with units

Hand-to-hand
• Both sides resolve any
• hand-to-hand fighting
• **Remove**. Disorder Markers

COMMAND MODIFIERS

Modifier Situation

-1	For every full 12" between the Commander and the unit he is issuing an order to.
-1	There are one or more enemy units within 6" of the unit receiving order
+1	Unit receiving the order is in March Column (or is Limbered Artillery) not on a road or track
+2	Unit receiving the order is in March Column (or is Limbered Artillery) on a road or track

BLUNDER TABLE

D6	Result
1	**Rapid Retreat.** Make two full moves away from the closest visible enemy
2	**Retreat.** Make one move away from closest visible enemy
3	**Move left.** One full move left; may charge if possible
4	**Move right**. One full move right; may charge if possible
5	**Forward!** Move one full move forward; may charge if possible.
6	**Charge!** charge closest visible enemy. Roll a D6 for moves: 1-2: 1 move, 3-4: 2 moves, 5-6: 3 moves

MOVING UNITS TABLE

Heavy and Siege Artillery, . .Immovable	
Hedgehog Formation	
Manhandled med. artillery . . . . . . .3"	
Infantry, Light artillery, Wagons, ...6" Limbered Artillery, Baggage Train	
Cavalry & Dragoons . . . . .9"	
Light Cavalry . . . . .12"	
Commanders on Foot . . . . .18"	
Commanders on Horseback . . . . . .27"	

MOVEMENT MODIFIERS

Woods	Half pace. Skirmish & Command only
Rough	Maximum one move. Skirmish & Command normal
Linear Obstacle	Takes a full turn. Pike disordered on roll of a 6. Skirmish & Command move normally.
Buildings	One move segment to enter or leave

FREE MOVE: March Column, Baggage on road, & fail Command roll. Disordered & Shaken Units one move away.

SHOOTING RANGES

Pistols and thrown weapons	6"
Arquebus, Carbines & Shortbows	12"
Muskets, Firelocks, Bows & Crossbows	18"
Light Artillery	24"
Medium Artillery	36"
Heavy & Siege Artillery	48"

SHOOTING VALUE MODIFIERS

+1 Dice	Large Unit
-1 Dice	Small Unit
None	Column
1 Dice	Hedgehog
1/face	Units in Buildings.

'TO-HIT' MODIFIERS FOR SHOOTING

-1	Attackers shaken and/or disordered.
-1	The target is Not Clear, Skirmishing, or Artillery.
+1	Close Range/ Closing Fire.

HAND-TO-HAND VALUE MODIFIERS

1 Dice	Column
2 Dice per face	Unit in a building
Total combat values	Hedgehog
+2 Dice	Large Unit
1-2 Dice	Small Unit.

'TO-HIT' MODIFIERS FOR HAND-TO-HAND COMBAT

+1	Attackers charging or counter-charging
+1	Winning
-1	Shaken and/or Disordered
-1	Attackers in Skirmish order
-1/face	Engaged in flank or rear

MORALE SAVE MODIFIERS

+1	Cover
+2	Buildings and Fortifications
-1	Unit in column
-2	Hit by Light or Medium Artillery.
-3	Hit by Heavy or Siege Artillery.

'to serve specially for execution if the Enemy in Battle be overthrown...'

Late 16th century tactical use of the bill, or 'brown bill'

www.warlordgames.com

Permission given to photocopy for personal use only. © Copyright Warlord Games Ltd 2011. All Rights Reserved.

1699 - The pirate Captain Kidd is captured in Boston.

COMBAT RESULT BONUSES

Bonus	Modifiers
+1	Rear Support.
+1	Flank Support.
+2	Cavalry versus non-pike block infantry.
+2	Pike versus Cavalry.
+3	Hedgehog versus Cavalry.
+3 or +2	Occupied Buildings. units fighting from buildings count +3 if large or standard sized, +2 if small.

BREAK TEST MODIFIERS

-1	-1 per each excess casualty
-1	the unit is *disordered*.
-1	the unit has suffered at least one casualty from *artillery*

BREAK TESTS

Unit must take a Break Test if it: suffers *excess casualties* from shooting, is *shaken* by closing fire, *defeated* in hand-to-hand combat, *draws* hand-to-hand combat and is *shaken*, or a unit it is supporting *breaks*. Roll 2D6, add any break test modifiers, and consult the table below:

Break Test	Combat Type	Result
4 or less	Any	**Infantry, Cavalry and Artillery:** Unit *breaks* and is destroyed
5	Any	**Artillery:** Unit *breaks* and is destroyed
		Infantry and Cavalry: Unit retires one full move away from enemy. If unable to disengage, make another full move away from enemy. If still unable to disengage, unit *breaks* and is destroyed.
6	Any	**Artillery:** Unit *breaks* and is destroyed
	Shooting	**Infantry & Cavalry:** Unit *holds its ground*.
	Hand-to-Hand	**Infantry & Cavalry:** Unit retires one full move away from enemy. If unable to disengage, make another full move away from enemy. If still unable to disengage, unit *breaks* and is destroyed.
7 or more	Shooting	**Infantry, Cavalry and Artillery:** Unit *holds its ground*
	Hand-to-Hand	**Infantry:** Unit holds its ground
		Cavalry: Unit retires one full move away from enemy. If unable to disengage, make another full move away from enemy. If still unable to disengage, unit *breaks* and is destroyed.
		Artillery: Unit *holds its ground*

SPECIAL RULES

Bad War	Re-roll missed Combat Attacks Against Landsknechts	Galloper	Must counestcharge if able to; standard move of 12" as if Light Cavalry; will always engage the enemy on a sweeping advance where able.	Pike Company	Cavalry receive no combat bonuses when fighting a unit with a pike company that is ordered; the unit containing a pike company receives double combat value when fighting charging cavalry
Bows/shortbow	+1 Morale Saves; Cannot offer closing fire				
Brave	Shaken Units Rally without an Order	Grenades	Enemy ignores all morale bonuses for cover when engaged in combat		
Caracole	Cannot countercharge enemy cavalry			Plug Bayonet	+2 Hand-to-Hand value; +1 Combat result against enemy Warband infantry; once used, cannot fire for remainder of battle
Clansmen	Cannot offer support in combat	Heavy Cavalry +1/+D3	+1/+D3 Combat Result on a Charge		
Crack	Re-Roll one failed Morale Save if you currently have no Casualties	Hedgehog	No flanks or rear; combined formation of pike and shotte elements; Immovable; all shooting units in the hedgehog have shooting value of 1	Rabble	Every unit must receive a separate command; Cannot act on a battalia or group order
Crossbows	Cannot offer Closing Fire			Reliable	+1 Command
Double-Handed Infantry Weapons	-1 Morale Save	Lancers	-1/-2 Morale Save on the Charge	Sharp Shooters	Re-Roll one Missed Shot
Dragoons	Free mount or dismount move; Fire and evadez Count as skirmish cavalry when mounted, skirmish infantry when dismounted	Large Unit	+1 Shooting Value (if the unit has ranged weapons); +2 Hand-to-Hand; +1 Stamina; May ignore disorder by taking one damage (unless this causes the unit to be shaken)	Small Unit	-1 Shooting Value (only if the unit has ranged weapons)
				Steady	Passes First Break Test
				Stubborn	Re-Roll one Failed Morale Save
Eager	Free move on charge order			Superbly Drilled	Free Move
Elite	Overcome Disorder Dice Roll	Marauders	Ignore Distance Modifiers for Command	Swordsmen	+D3 Combat result against enemy infantry
Fanatics	Morale Save +1 Until Shaken	Mercenary	Will quit the battle if a rally test is failed when shaken		
Ferocious Charge	Re-Roll Missed Combat Attacks Following Charge			Terrifying Charge	Charged Enemy must take a Break Test
Fire & Evade	Can give closing fire and then evade when charged	Militia	No Move on Equal Command Roll	Tough Fighters	Re-Roll one Combat Hit
Firelocks	Short range extended to 12"	Pikes	Can form a hedgehog formation with non pike units of same battalia; Cavalry receive no combat bonuses when fighting an ordered pike unit; Pike unit gets double combat value when fighting charging cavalry	Untested	Randomise Stamina
First Fire	+1 Dice on First Shot			Valiant	One Free Break Test Re-Roll
Freshly Raised	Variable effect – see page 105			Wavering	Break Test when you take a Casualty

1700 - Louis XIV accepts the crown of Spain on behalf of his grandson. The War of Spanish Succession begins a year later.

THANKS TO...

Publishing this book would not have been possible without a host of enthusiastic, talented individuals:

Miniatures and terrain courtesy of the collections of: *Neil Bitten, Bennett Blalock-Doane, Paul Cubbin, Paul Daniels, Andy Fox, Barry Hilton, Ian Hinds, David Marshall, Paul's Modelling Workshop, Alan Perry, Michael Perry, Paul Sawyer, Konrad Sosinski, John Stallard, Neil Tew, Wargames Illustrated, Dale Yates.*

Playtesting: *Trevor Allen, Andrew Chesney, GCN clubs, Robert Giglio, Dave Lawrence, Daryl Nichols, Phoenix Wargaming Club, Questing Knight Games, Peter Rossetti, STAGS Wargaming Club, John Stallard, Triple Helix Wargames.*

Miniatures painted by: *Bruno Allanson, Andrés Amián Fernández, Bennett Blalock-Doane, Jim Bowen, Paul Cubbin, Darren Linington, Alan Mander, Matthew Perks, Alan Perry, Michael Perry, Paul Sawyer, Dale Yates.*

We hope you've enjoyed the photographs of our collections of painted armies. The models featured in Pike & Shotte come from a number of manufacturers and suppliers including the following:

Warlord Games
www.warlordgames.com
Unit T4/T10, The Technology Wing, The Howitt Building, Lenton Boulevard, Nottingham NG7 2BD, UK.
E-mail: *info@warlordgames.com*

Perry Miniatures
www.perry-miniatures.com
PO Box 6512, Nottingham, NG7 1UJ, UK.   E-mail: *perryminiatures@aol.com*

North Star Military Figures
www.northstarfigures.com
Unit 37, Lenton Business Centre, Lenton Boulevard, Nottingham NG7 2BY, UK.   E-mail: *mailorder@northstarfigures.com*

Grand Manner
www.grandmanner.co.uk
Unit B, Harolds Court, Saxon Business Park, Hanbury Road, Bromsgrove, Worcestershire, B60 4FL, UK.
E-mail: *grandmanner@live.co.uk*

Wargamer
www.wargamer.pl
Ul.mehoffera 26/10, 03-131 Warsaw, Poland.   E-mail: *kontakt@wargamer.pl*

Warfare Miniatures
www.leagueofaugsburg.com

Wargames Foundry
www.wargamesfoundry.com
24-34 St. Marks Street, Nottingham NG3 1DE, UK.
E-mail: *sales@wargamesfoundry.com*